VMware Horizon 6 Desktop Virtualization Solutions

Plan, design, and secure your virtual desktop environments with VMware Horizon 6 View

Ryan Cartwright

Chuck Mills

Jason Langone

Andre Leibovici

[PACKT] enterprise

PUBLISHING

professional expertise distilled

BIRMINGHAM - MUMBAI

VMware Horizon 6 Desktop Virtualization Solutions

First published: June 2012

Second edition: September 2014

Production reference: 1150914

Published by Packt Publishing Ltd.
Livery Place
35 Livery Street
Birmingham B3 2PB, UK.

ISBN 978-1-78217-070-9

www.packtpub.com

Cover image by Aniket Sawant (aniket_sawant_photography@hotmail.com)

Credits

Authors

Ryan Cartwright

Chuck Mills

Jason Langone

Andre Leibovici

Reviewers

Tim Arenz

Bruce Bookman

Jason Gaudreau

Raimundo Rodulfo

Puthiyavan Udayakumar

Acquisition Editors

Mary Nadar

Meeta Rajani

Content Development Editor

Sweny M. Sukumaran

Technical Editor

Manan Badani

Copy Editors

Roshni Banerjee

Gladson Monteiro

Sayanee Mukherjee

Alfida Paiva

Project Coordinator

Rashi Khivansara

Proofreaders

Simran Bhogal

Maria Gould

Ameesha Green

Indexers

Hemangini Bari

Mariammal Chettiyar

Tejal Soni

Priya Sane

Graphics

Ronak Dhruv

Production Coordinator

Nitesh Thakur

Cover Work

Nitesh Thakur

Foreword

The new release of Horizon 6 delivers many new features such as virtualized and remote desktops and applications through a single platform to end users. The virtual desktop and application services, which include RDS hosted apps, apps packaged with VMware ThinApp, SaaS apps, and even Citrix-based virtualized apps, are now accessed from one unified workspace.

Chuck and Ryan are technical evangelists who used VMware products for many years to provide solutions to several major companies. Chuck has spent the last few years focusing on developing end user computing solutions, and Ryan is working to provide solutions using vCenter Operations Manager, Site Recovery Manager, and many other vSphere products.

This book will give readers the knowledge and confidence to install, configure, and understand Horizon View 6. The book begins with the basic components of View and explains how the components work together to build a VDI solution. There will be a discussion regarding the importance of defining a solution methodology to be used when planning and designing the View solution. Find out possible combinations of end devices for your project and what options should be considered. The display protocol, PCoIP, is covered, and the book gives you advice on how to configure solutions to provide the best end user experience.

Any VDI solution success is a result of proper sizing, and all the items to consider, such as network, compute and know the maximums for the View environment. This book will review how to set up redundancy to provide high availability for your VDI infrastructure. Storage is always an important component of View and you need to consider what the decisions are. One of the compelling reasons for a VDI solution is the security it brings. Learn what you can do to make sure the solution provides the required security.

Most VDI projects include moving users from their physical endpoint to new virtual desktops. Review some of the options you have to accomplish this. After you have invested all the time to create a robust and solid solution, you need to protect it. The book will guide you through the components and how each one should be protected, along with reviewing some of the backup methods. The book closes by showcasing many of the new and exciting features in View 6, such as Cloud Pod Architecture, details on VSAN, and new application hosting solutions.

I feel this book will be very useful for the novice as well as an experienced reader. The authors have written this book based on real-life experiences in implementing View solutions. They are aware of the many challenges and issues around designing a successful VDI solution. The intent of this book is to give you knowledge along with confidence to provide the best VDI solution using Horizon View.

Skip Gumble
Director of Sales, End User Computing

About the Authors

Ryan Cartwright (@ryandcartwright) has been involved in virtualization technologies since 2005. His focus has been on enterprise systems engineering and architecture and operational support with many Fortune 500 customers. He is currently a senior consultant for the cloud management team within the Professional Services Organization for VMware. Prior to joining VMware, he was a senior consultant and sales engineer in GANTECH, focusing on end user computing and software-defined data center. Before his roles in the consulting field, Ryan worked for Stanley Black & Decker in a variety of roles, focused on enterprise architecture for global virtual infrastructure and integration through mergers and acquisition. He has been working with VMware View since v3.5 and has designed and implemented multiple VMware View environments for Fortune 500 companies for a variety of use cases. He currently holds VCP5-DCV and VCP5-DT certifications as well as a Nutanix Platform Professional (NPP) #55 certificate.

I'd like to mention my previous employers Stanley Black & Decker and GANTECH for helping and providing me the foundation of my virtualization knowledge through real-life experiences, and for always challenging me to accept and tackle the next key project or new role within their organizations.

I would like to thank Sam, my wife, who has supported my career moves and geek speak over the years, my parents who encouraged me to get into Information Technology when entering high school, Packt Publishing for providing me the opportunity to write my first book, and Chuck Mills for coauthoring the book with me and providing mentorship over the past 2 years.

Chuck Mills (@vchuckmills) has been involved in virtualization technologies for more than 10 years and has focused on using these technologies to create efficient and resilient solutions for data centers and desktops. He is currently the End User Computing Practice Director for GANTECH, Inc. Prior to joining GANTECH, he was a solutions architect for Allegis Group, and prior to that, he was the Director of Information Technology for Maryland Legal Aid and ESP of Maryland, where both companies achieved data centers that were 100 percent virtualized. He is one of the leading experts on VMware Mirage, having worked with it prior to the VMware acquisition. He has implemented Mirage in 5000 plus endpoint environments for PoCs, pilots, and Windows XP migrations. Chuck has designed and led teams on effective View solutions, including a successful worldwide PoC. He has given numerous presentations regarding virtualization and their benefits, including VMworld and VMware Partner Exchange. He is a former member of the VMware Customer Council (VCC), coleader of the Maryland VMUG, and has been a vExpert since 2011. He also maintains a blog dedicated to virtualization at www.vchuck.com.

I would like to thank my wonderful wife, Michelle, and my children, Bradley, Brooke, Corbin, and Chuck III, for all the support and encouragement to make this book possible.

I would also like to thank GANTECH for allowing me to live my EUC passion and Packt Publishing for the opportunity to be a part of this book. A special thanks to my VMware friends I have met over the years and especially Ryan Cartwright who continues to impress me with his ever growing VMware products knowledge.

About the Reviewers

Tim Arenz (@timarenz) has been involved in application and desktop virtualization solutions for over 8 years and has designed and implemented many solutions based on AppSense, Citrix, Microsoft, and VMware technologies with up to ten thousand users. He is currently working as a senior consultant in the Professional Services Organization at VMware in Germany. In his role, he specializes in end user computing, mainly focusing on ThinApp and Horizon Mirage, but also works with customers and partners on Horizon View and Workspace projects.

On his personal blog at http://horizonflux.com, Tim shares news and best practices about VMware's End User Computing product portfolio.

Bruce Bookman is a Silicon Valley software and hardware veteran who has held roles from frontline technical support to Director of Software Quality Assurance. Recently, he has been a VMware subject matter expert and Level 3 technical support escalation engineer for a solid state storage company, Fusion-io. In late August 2014, he joined Oracle as a senior quality analyst for Oracle Cloud. He is the author of technical articles covering virtualization on Developer.com, and he has created and delivered technical training modules on virtualization and other topics. He has received recognition for his customer advocacy and dedication to customer success.

Jason Gaudreau has over 23 years of industry experience and is currently a senior technical account manager at VMware, a leading information technology provider of enterprise application solutions.

His focus is on virtualization solutions and aligning infrastructure technologies to meet strategic business objectives. He has concentrated on data center virtualization, desktop virtualization, and building internal private clouds in a variety of technical roles over the past 10 years.

He has been an active blogger on virtualization since 2012 at `www.jasongaudreau.com` and can be reached at his Twitter handle `@JAGaudreau`. He is honored to be designated a vExpert by VMware in 2013-2014 and EMC Elect in 2014.

Before VMware, Jason was an IT architect for AdvizeX Technologies, and was involved in IT leadership at Unum Group, where he helped to develop the organization's IT strategy.

When not talking shop, he enjoys spending time with his wife, Christine, and two kids, Dylan and Tyler.

Raimundo Rodulfo has more than 20 years of working experience in engineering and technology, including technical leadership roles in the United States and Latin America, for private and public sector organizations such as Siemens, NCR, Bellsouth, and City of Coral Gables. He currently works as the Assistant Chief Information Officer for a local government municipality in South Florida. He performs technical and service operations management, project management, engineering, systems and business process analysis, software development, strategic planning, budget analysis and preparation, Business Intelligence and applied data analytics, management, planning, and operation and maintenance for the city's IT and telecommunications systems.

He is an electrical and electronics engineer with more than 20 years of working experience in Telecommunications and IT as systems and applications manager, network and telecommunications manager, project manager, electrical and electronics engineer, business analyst, R&D, O&M, NOC engineer, and assistant chief information officer (current position). His work experience includes City of Coral Gables, Florida; Bellsouth (Cellular MTSO/Switch, NOC, R&D); Siemens; NCR; Choice One Telecom/USA Telephone; and projects and training with Agilent, Motorola, Lucent Technologies, Alcatel, Microsoft, Cisco, CheckPoint, VMware, and other organizations. He has managed enterprise network infrastructure projects for City of Coral Gables and engineered hardware/software systems and automation projects for City of Coral Gables, Bellsouth, Siemens, NCR, and other organizations. He performed operations management, strategic planning, business process analysis, and optimization for City of Coral Gables, operations standardization and compliance, and worked in the implementation of ERP systems and applications.

He has worked as a revision team lead, balloting group members and actively participating in IEEE, ISO, and IEC engineering standards working groups, developing standards and guidelines for engineering and management systems, electronic appliances, software, websites, and services information.

He is a member of CIO/CISO Governing Body and other professional organizations.

He is a licensed electrical engineer (E.I.) by the Florida Board of Professional Engineers (FBPE) and the National Council of Examiners for Engineering and Surveying (NCEES).

He is an Information Technology Infrastructure Library (ITIL) certified professional. He is also a Certified Virtualization Expert (CVE®) and certified Project Management Professional (PMP®).

Thanks to the staff at Packt Publishing (project coordinators, editors, and everyone involved) for inviting me to participate in this project and guiding me through the process.

Puthiyavan Udayakumar has more than 7 years of IT experience with expertise in Citrix, VMware, Microsoft products, and Apache products. He has extensive experience in designing and implementing virtualization solutions using various Citrix, VMware, and Microsoft products. He is an IBM certified solution architect and Citrix certified enterprise engineer, with more than 15 certifications in infrastructure products. He is the author of the books *Getting Started with Citrix® CloudPortal™* and *Getting Started with Citrix® Provisioning Services 7.0*, both by Packt Publishing. He holds a Master's degree in Science, with a specialization in System Software from Birla Institute of Technology and Science, Pilani.

I would like to thank Packt Publishing for giving me the opportunity to review this book. This book is well written by the author, and the project is well coordinated by the project coordinator.

www.PacktPub.com

Support files, eBooks, discount offers, and more

You might want to visit www.PacktPub.com for support files and downloads related to your book.

Did you know that Packt offers eBook versions of every book published, with PDF and ePub files available? You can upgrade to the eBook version at www.PacktPub.com and as a print book customer, you are entitled to a discount on the eBook copy. Get in touch with us at service@packtpub.com for more details.

At www.PacktPub.com, you can also read a collection of free technical articles, sign up for a range of free newsletters and receive exclusive discounts and offers on Packt books and eBooks.

PACKT LIB ℗

http://PacktLib.PacktPub.com

Do you need instant solutions to your IT questions? PacktLib is Packt's online digital book library. Here, you can access, read and search across Packt's entire library of books.

Why subscribe?
- Fully searchable across every book published by Packt
- Copy and paste, print and bookmark content
- On demand and accessible via web browser

Free access for Packt account holders

If you have an account with Packt at www.PacktPub.com, you can use this to access PacktLib today and view nine entirely free books. Simply use your login credentials for immediate access.

Instant updates on new Packt books

Get notified! Find out when new books are published by following @PacktEnterprise on Twitter, or the *Packt Enterprise* Facebook page.

Table of Contents

Preface

VMware Horizon 6 Desktop Virtualization Solutions is a guide for architects, solution providers, consultants, engineers, and anyone planning to design and implement a solution based on Horizon View 6. This book is based on information taken from hands-on experience, real-world situations, and implementations, in order to capitalize on practical virtualization desktop learning. You will understand not only the settings and configurations needed to build a successful virtual desktop solution, but also learn the thought process behind making those decisions.

This book will not replace the official administration or installation guides for VMware View or ThinApp published by VMware, but should be used as a guide to supplement the hard work of the writers at VMware. This book is designed to be used during the design phase, which is before an implementation is started. All of the major components of Horizon 6 will be covered in this book.

The VDI solution

Virtual Desktop Infrastructure (VDI) is a powerful solution where the desktop operating system is hosted on a centralized server within a virtual machine. The VDI solution facilitates full personalization of the user's desktops and allows access to the virtual desktops anywhere, from any device at any time. The VMware Horizon View product provides the components needed to implement this solution. Companies are realizing the flexibility, efficiency, and other benefits that Horizon View can provide. View enables administrators to manage desktops from a central location and provide the end users with the ability to access their environments remotely from any location. View is maturing into a reliable way for IT to maintain security and manageability while still accommodating employees' desires to be mobile and connected.

Proper planning can mean the difference between a successful VDI deployment and an unhappy end user. Some of the popular reasons to provide a Horizon View solution include:

- **Workforce mobility**: Mobility and accessibility is a major driving force today; users everywhere are on the go, and providing them with convenience is the key. When you use View to separate the software (OS, applications, and data) from the PC hardware, the actual hardware device becomes the connection point and is capable of connecting that user to the software. This allows any device to access the information on your virtual desktops.

  There is a shift in technology where the user's desktop lives in a data center (or the cloud) instead of the device being used. The user desktop can appear on almost any device with connectivity to the Internet. Today, virtual desktops are accessible from iPads, smartphones, thin/zero clients, laptops, home computers, work computers, kiosks, and business centers… just about from anywhere.

- **Security**: There is no question that one of the top concerns is security for today's IT environments. Data can be the organization's lifeline, and if that information is lost, corrupted, or stolen, a company's existence can be in danger. With a VDI solution, the OS, applications, and data are separated from the physical device that is being used to access the environment and are on the servers in the data center. This also allows simplified management and better utilization to keep the virtual desktop up to date with security patches, and as mentioned, the actual data resides in protected rooms.

  With View, sensitive data is protected on a company's server rather than sitting on unprotected desktops or roaming around in public spaces such as the airport, a coffee shop, or a hotel room. This can be a powerful motivator for moving to VDI for the cost reduction benefits.

- **Centralized management**: View provides the end users with a complete virtual desktop that behaves just like a physical desktop. The virtual desktop also allows administrators to deploy new desktops in minutes rather than days or weeks, using automatic desktop-provisioning tools. This gives users their own personalized desktop environment without the need for sharing applications or retraining the end user. Administrators can also manage these deployed virtual desktops from any location and perform the necessary upgrades, patches, and desktop maintenance without requiring the device to be "brought in". This allows a quicker response to the ongoing need of keeping the desktops up to date based on business needs.

- **Windows 7/8 migrations**: Organizations that are looking to reduce the complexity and frustration of moving to a new operating system can use virtual desktops to lessen the pain. Using the proper persona-management tools, the user's profile can be brought into the new virtual desktop. The ability to try/test the new operating systems before they are deployed is possible by creating new pools with the new OS. Going to a new OS is never easy, but View can ease the transition.

- **Technology/hardware refresh**: The daunting task of replacing outdated desktops during a hardware refresh cycle can create significant operational costs and reduce productivity. This is an opportunistic time to migrate users to a VDI solution. After the users are moved off the physical desktop, the old desktops can be repurposed as thin or thick clients, extending their usable life.

- **Bring Your Own Device (BYOD)**: View allows for the current movement of users to bring their preferred device and allow it to connect back into a managed VDI. The Horizon Client, which has versions for several types of devices, would be needed, or the View desktops can be accessed directly with an HTML5-compliant browser.

- **Remote connectivity in times of crisis**: Pandemics, mass-influenza cases, border-crossing contagion — all bring thoughts of fear to the company. What about snow storms and other natural disasters that can prevent you from traveling to work? If you ask yourself, "Are we really prepared to effectively continue operations in emergency situations?", and are not sure of the answer, then VDI can help. View allows workers to continue to work when they can't physically get to their place of work. These same solutions that allow a BYOD solution can also help with an emergency situation that keeps workers out of the office.

Regardless of your driving reason, VDI is a technology that has gained a lot of traction across many verticals worldwide. This book will guide you through the necessary steps to begin your VDI/View journey and provide a solution that can address some or all the issues mentioned based on your needs.

What this book covers

Chapter 1, Components of VMware Horizon View 6, introduces the basic concepts of VDI along with the core components of the VMware View 6 platform. This chapter will cover VMware vSphere components and how they work together with the Horizon View solution.

Chapter 2, Solution Methodology, covers a defined methodology, including assessments, use case definitions, and a VDI hierarchy to establish a common framework of solution design.

Chapter 3, Persistent or Nonpersistent vDesktops, will explain an important design decision of a VDI solution, that is desktop persistency. It provides guidance on making the decisions along with the benefits and drawbacks to each approach.

Chapter 4, End Devices, will discuss the various endpoint choices that can be implemented to connect to the Horizon View VDI. It also provides guidance on selecting the appropriate devices based on the environment and organizational needs.

Chapter 5, The PCoIP Protocol, will explain the Horizon View protocol behind Teradici's PCoIP. It will cover performance tuning, provide information on the APEX offload card, and review the best practices around implementing a solution with PCoIP.

Chapter 6, Sizing the VDI, will focus on Horizon View's core component sizing, including Connection Servers and VMware vCenter Servers. It will discuss the designing of solutions based on VMware vSphere's maximums.

Chapter 7, Building Redundancy into the VDI Solution, will provide guidance on building a robust and, just as important, resilient VDI solution. It explains how a full redundant solution can be planned and delivered, along with design considerations and overall environmental impact.

Chapter 8, Sizing the Storage, covers another important and complex component of the VDI design, the underlying storage environment. It will discuss both high-level and in-depth technical options and design characteristics of the storage system that is supporting the VDI solution.

Chapter 9, Security, will focus on the hardening of the VDI environment and the robust authentication mechanisms. It will review the security considerations for specific environments, such as government agencies.

Chapter 10, Migrating User Personas, will cover techniques used to successfully migrate a user base from the physical desktop to a virtual desktop solution. It will also focus on user persona management and abstraction.

Chapter 11, Backing Up the VMware View Infrastructure, provides guidance on scheduling appropriate backups of a Horizon View environment.

Chapter 12, *Exciting New Features in Horizon View 6*, introduces some of the new and important developments in Horizon View 6. This includes Cloud Pod Architecture, application publishing, unified workspaces, and integration with Virtual SAN technology.

Appendix, *Additional Tools*, provides additional tools, online references, and suggested Twitter personalities, which may prove helpful in designing a VDI solution.

What you need for this book

As this book is technical in nature, you need to have a basic understanding of the following concepts:

- VMware vSphere
    - Hypervisor basics
    - vMotion
    - Cluster capabilities such as HA, DRS, and DPM

- Active Directory
    - Types of authentication
    - Encryption with certificates
    - Group policy objects
    - Folder redirection
    - Roaming profiles
    - DNS

- Virtual machine basics
    - VMX and VMDK files
    - Snapshots
    - VMware tools

- Networking
    - VLANs
    - DHCP
    - Port types
    - Routing
    - LAN and WAN basics

Who this book is for

Ideally, you should have a sound understanding of VMware vSphere fundamentals and should have been involved in the installation or administration of a VMware environment for more than two years. You should also have a basic understanding of VDI concepts and terminology.

Conventions

In this book, you will find a number of styles of text that distinguish between different kinds of information. Here are some examples of these styles, and an explanation of their meaning.

Code words in text, database table names, folder names, filenames, file extensions, pathnames, dummy URLs, user input, and Twitter handles are shown as follows: "Configure the ODBC connection and use <vCenter Server>/SQLEXP_VIM for the connection string. Replace <vCenter Server> with the appropriate information for your environment."

A block of code is set as follows:

```
enableRevocationchecking=true
allowCertCRLs=true
crlLocation=<URL_OF_CRL>
```

Any command-line input or output is written as follows:

```
keytool -import -alias view4ca -file certnew.cer -keystore trust.key
```

New terms and **important words** are shown in bold. Words that you see on the screen, in menus or dialog boxes for example, appear in the text like this: "This information can be found by opening the **Properties** tab from within **Device Manager** with the applicable device highlighted."

> Warnings or important notes appear in a box like this.

> Tips and tricks appear like this.

Reader feedback

Feedback from our readers is always welcome. Let us know what you think about this book—what you liked or may have disliked. Reader feedback is important for us to develop titles that you really get the most out of.

To send us general feedback, simply send an e-mail to feedback@packtpub.com, and mention the book title through the subject of your message.

If there is a topic that you have expertise in and you are interested in either writing or contributing to a book, see our author guide on www.packtpub.com/authors.

Customer support

Now that you are the proud owner of a Packt book, we have a number of things to help you to get the most from your purchase.

Errata

Although we have taken every care to ensure the accuracy of our content, mistakes do happen. If you find a mistake in one of our books—maybe a mistake in the text or the code—we would be grateful if you would report this to us. By doing so, you can save other readers from frustration and help us improve subsequent versions of this book. If you find any errata, please report them by visiting http://www.packtpub.com/support, selecting your book, clicking on the **errata submission form** link, and entering the details of your errata. Once your errata are verified, your submission will be accepted and the errata will be uploaded to our website, or added to any list of existing errata, under the Errata section of that title.

Piracy

Piracy of copyright material on the Internet is an ongoing problem across all media. At Packt, we take the protection of our copyright and licenses very seriously. If you come across any illegal copies of our works, in any form, on the Internet, please provide us with the location address or website name immediately so that we can pursue a remedy.

Please contact us at copyright@packtpub.com with a link to the suspected pirated material.

We appreciate your help in protecting our authors, and our ability to bring you valuable content.

Questions

You can contact us at questions@packtpub.com if you are having a problem with any aspect of the book, and we will do our best to address it.

1
Components of VMware Horizon View 6

Virtualization, a technology of abstracting the logical capabilities from the underlying physical resources has become a cornerstone of the data center architecture. Virtualization allows organizations to run not just one operating system per physical server in the data center, but tens, dozens, or even hundreds, on a single physical server. The benefits of virtualization are many, including a reduction in hardware, power, and cooling costs. In addition to these, virtualization allows new techniques of distribution and resilience to be applied, such as **VMware Distributed Resource Scheduler** (**DRS**) and **VMware High Availability** (**HA**). Server virtualization, the virtualization of server operating systems on server hardware, is now a mainstream technology that is readily accepted, adopted, and implemented in organizations across the world.

Virtual Desktop Infrastructure (**VDI**), the virtualization of desktop operating systems on server hardware, is another story.

The reason for the slower adoption of virtual desktops was originally due to many factors, including an immature technology, cost of storage, lack of general understanding of a comprehensive solution, a proven delivery methodology, and a clear understanding of the success criteria of a given virtual desktop project. Another key hurdle for the adoption of VDI has been the Microsoft VDA licenses, which many consider a desktop tax. Today, many of these hurdles have been removed. The supporting technologies from communication protocols to computing density, platform stability, and desirable end devices now exist. Design methodologies have been built by some of the largest integrators in the world; yet virtual desktop projects continue to fail, falter, or stall.

This book will provide the architect, the engineer, the project manager, the freelance consultant, or the contractor with a proven blueprint for success. More importantly, this book will teach the key success criteria to measure the most important design considerations to make and tip the probability of the project's success and sign-off in your favor.

This book assumes a familiarity with server virtualization, more specifically, **VMware vSphere**.

Before these concepts can be covered in depth, it is important to understand the components of a **virtual desktop (vDesktop)** solution.

> The technology in this book focuses on VMware Horizon View 6, which is a market leader in VDI. While some concepts in this book apply specifically to VMware View-based solutions, many of the topics will help a VDI architect of any technology plan and build for success.

This chapter will review improvements on:

- VMware vCenter Server
- View Connection Server
- View Manager
- View Agent
- Horizon Client
- View Composer
- Snapshot and linked clones
- Types of disks
- View Composer Array Integration (VCAI)

The core components of VMware Horizon View 6

The following figure shows the Horizon View 6 architecture that includes the core components explained in this chapter:

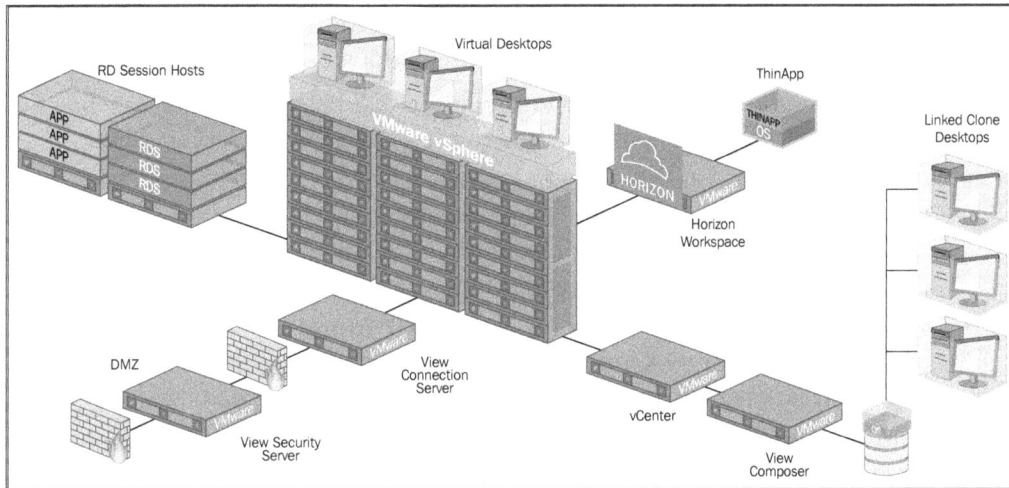

vCenter Server

VMware vCenter is a required component of a VMware View solution as the View Connection Server interacts with the underlying **Virtual Infrastructure** (**VI**) through **vCenter Web Service** (typically over port 443). vCenter is also responsible for the complementary components of a View solution provided by VMware vSphere, including vMotion and DRS (used to balance the virtual desktop load on the physical hosts). When a customer purchases View, VMware vCenter is automatically included and does not need to be purchased via a separate **stock keeping unit** (**SKU**). In the environments that leverage vSphere for server virtualization, vCenter Server is likely to already exist.

> It would *not* be a good idea to use the same vCenter that manages the servers to manage your View environment.

To ensure a level is set on the capabilities that VMware vCenter Server provides, the key terminologies are listed as follows:

- **vMotion**: This has the ability to live-migrate a running virtual machine from one physical server to another with no downtime.

- **DRS**: This has the vCenter Server capability that balances virtual machines across physical servers participating in the same vCenter Server cluster.

- **Cluster**: This is a collection of physical servers that have access to the same networks and shared storage. The physical servers participating in a vCenter cluster have their resources (for example, CPU, memory, and so on) logically pooled for virtual machine consumption.

- **HA**: This is the vCenter Server capability that protects against the failure of a physical server. HA will power up virtual machines that reside on the failed physical server on available physical servers in the same cluster.

- **Folder**: This is a logical grouping of virtual machines, displayed within the vSphere Client.

- **vSphere Client**: This is the web-based user interface used to connect to vCenter servers (or physical servers running vSphere) for management, monitoring, configuration, and other related tasks.

- **Resource pool**: This is a logical pool of resources (for example, CPU, memory, and so on). The virtual machines (or the groups of virtual machines) residing in the same resource pool will share a predetermined amount of resources.

Designing a View solution often touches on typical server virtualization design concepts such as proper cluster design. Owing to this overlap in design concepts between server virtualization and VDI, many server virtualization engineers apply exactly the same principles from one solution to the other.

The first misstep that a VDI architect can take is that VDI is not server virtualization (it is client OS/desktop virtualization), and should not be treated as such. Server virtualization is the virtualization of server operating systems. While it is true that VDI does use some server virtualization (for example, the connection infrastructure), there are many concepts that are new and critical to understand for success.

The second misstep a VDI architect can make is in understanding the scale of some VDI solutions. For the average server virtualization administrator with no VDI in their environment, they may be tasked with managing a dozen physical servers with a few hundred virtual machines. In comparison, there are View deployments that are close to 60,000 desktops for a single company that go well beyond the limits of a traditional VMware vSphere design.

VDI is often performed on a different scale. The concepts of architectural scaling are covered later in this book, but many of the scaling concepts revolve around the limits of VMware vCenter Server. It should be noted that VMware vCenter Server was originally designed to be the central management point for the enterprise server virtualization environments. While VMware continues to work on its ability to scale, designing around VMware vCenter server will be important.

So why does a VDI architect need VMware vCenter in the first place?

VMware vCenter is the foundation for all virtual machine tasks in a View solution. It includes the following tasks:

- The creation of virtual machine folders to organize vDesktops
- The creation of resource pools to segregate physical resources for different groups of vDesktops
- The creation of vDesktops
- The creation of snapshots

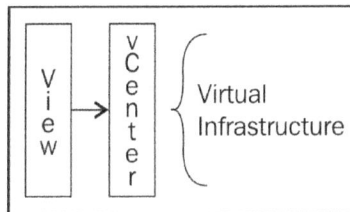

VMware vCenter is not used to break the connection of an end device to a vDesktop. Therefore, an outage of VMware vCenter should not impact inbound connections to already-provisioned vDesktops, but it should prevent additional vDesktops from being built, refreshed, or deleted.

Because of vCenter Server's importance in a VDI solution, additional steps are often taken to ensure its availability even beyond the considerations made in a typical server virtualization solution.

Later in this book, we will address the pros and cons of using the existing vCenter Server for an organization's VDI solution, or whether a secondary vCenter Server infrastructure should be built.

View 6 supports virtual appliance-based **vCenter Server Appliance (VCSA)** deployments that eliminate vCenter dependencies on Windows. VCSA also enhances View deployment flexibility and makes it easier to install and upgrade. The other advantage is the potential Windows license cost reduction.

Now, the question is, would you prefer VCSA or the Windows-based vCenter Server? The answer is… it depends. You still need to have a Windows host for the **Update Manager**. If you combine vCenter and Update Manager on one Windows host, then you don't gain any licensing advantage. If you are using **Windows Datacenter** licensing, then the number of Windows-based VMs is not an issue from a licensing perspective. Regarding the database compatibility, the built-in database is suitable for environments with a maximum of 100 hosts and 3000 VMs. If your environment was to grow beyond that, then you have to use Oracle DBMS.

You need to think about these issues, but when they appear in the future, VMware will move away from the Windows-based vCenter. The VCSA could be the right choice if you have to deploy a vSphere environment very fast for a demo or a testing solution. VCSA is the right choice, especially when the size of the environment is not too big.

View Connection Server

View Connection Server is the primary component of a View solution. If VMware vCenter Server is the foundation for managing communication with the virtual infrastructure and the underlying physical servers, then the View Connection Server is the gateway that end users pass through to connect to their vDesktops. In classic VDI terms, it is the VMware's broker that connects end users with desktops (physical or virtual). View Connection Server is the central point of management for the VDI solution and is used to manage almost the entire solution infrastructure. However, there will be times when the architect will need to make considerations for vCenter cluster configurations, as discussed later in this book. In addition, there may be times when the View administrator will need access to the VMware vCenter Server.

Types of VMware View Connection Servers

There are several options available when installing the View Connection Server. Therefore, it is important to understand the different types of View Connection Servers and the role they play in a given VDI solution.

The following are the three configurations in which View Connection Server can be installed:

- **Full**: This option installs all the components of View Connection Server, including a fresh **Lightweight Directory Access Protocol (LDAP)** instance.

- **Replica**: This option creates a replica of an existing View Connection Server instance for load balancing or high availability purposes. The authentication/ LDAP configuration is copied from the existing View Connection Server.

- **Security**: This option installs only the necessary components for the View Connection portal. View Security Servers do not need to belong to an Active Directory domain (unlike the View Connection Server) as they do not access any authentication components (for example, Active Directory). The Security Server is an instance of the Connection Server that adds a layer of security between the Internet and the internal network. It is located outside the corporate firewall in the DMZ. The Security Server acts as a portal to forward a connection request to the Connection Server.

> Our goal is to design the solutions that are highly available for our end customers. Therefore, all the designs will leverage two or more View Connection Servers (for example, one full and one replica).

All the View Connection Server types mentioned can be installed on the following operating systems:

- Windows Server 2008 R2 — Standard or Enterprise
- Windows Server 2008 R2 SP1 — Standard or Enterprise
- Windows Server 2012 R2

The following services are installed during a full installation of View Connection Server:

- VMware View Connection Server
- VMware View Framework Component
- VMware View Message Bus Component
- VMware View Script Host
- VMware View Security Gateway Component
- VMware View Web Component
- VMware VDMDS, which provides the LDAP directory services

View Manager

The View Manager user interface continues the new look and feel introduced in the previous version. The interface is streamlined and faster. View has also been localized to five different foreign languages (French, German, Japanese, Korean, and Simplified Chinese). The right-click functionality (as shown in the following screenshot) helps to streamline the process of managing desktop pools, entitlements, desktops, context menus, linking to saved View Administrator pages, and enhanced table column viewing. The overall feel continues to be faster and cleaner.

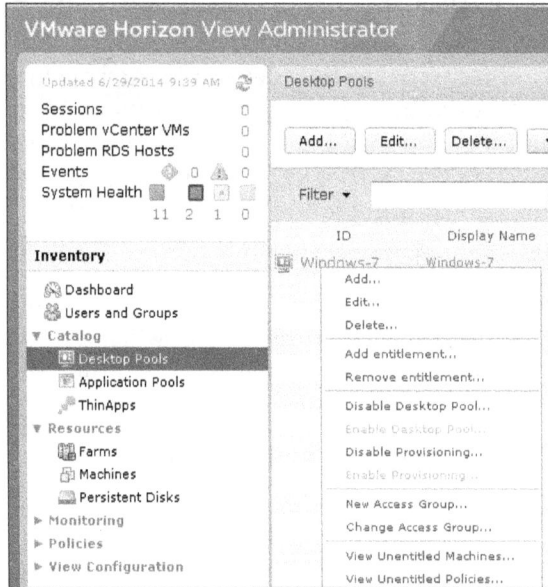

Precreated Active Directory machine accounts

The View Manager has the ability to provision View desktops with precreated Active Directory accounts. This addresses the need of locked-down Active Directory environments that have read-only access policies. Use precreated Active Directory accounts when provisioning View desktops in environments that require read-only access policies in your Active Directory.

This feature is a welcomed addition for companies that wish to create their own Active Directory computer accounts due to security/compliance requirements or because of an automated process used to ensure that Active Directory objects are created when users join the company.

Notice the pre-creation option in the following screenshot:

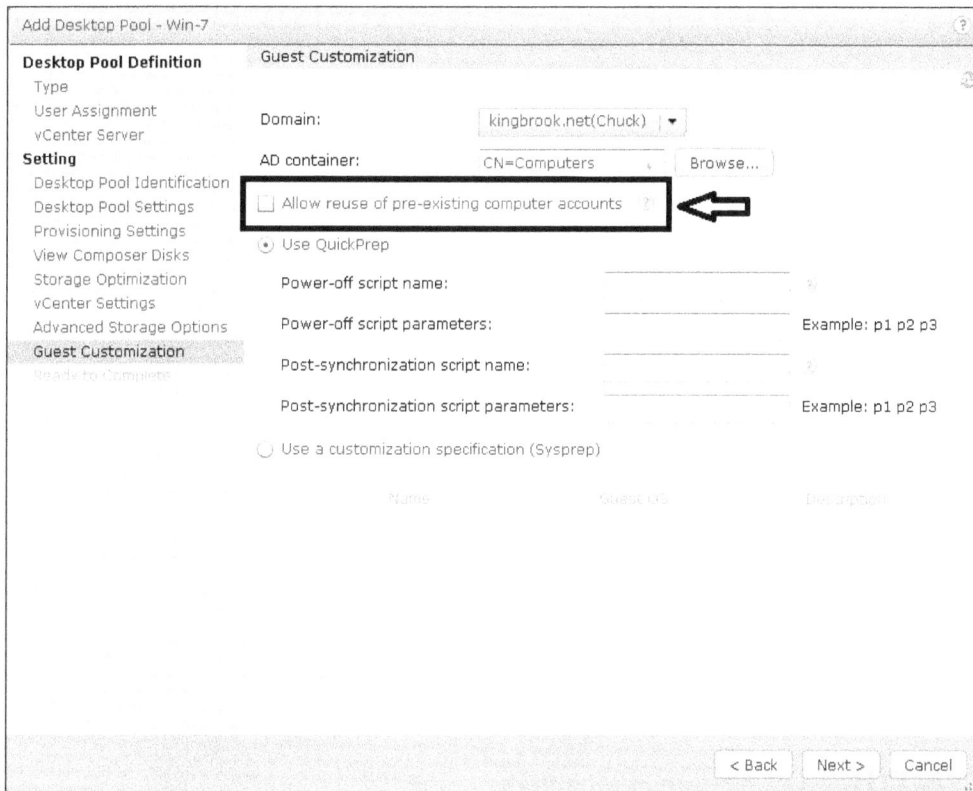

vCenter and View Composer's advanced settings

Changes to the VMware View UI allow administrators to specify the maximum concurrent number of provisioning and maintenance operations. Previously, only Power and vCenter concurrent operations were available for configuration using this user interface. You could *hack* into the **Active Directory Application Mode** (**ADAM**) and vCenter databases to increase the number of concurrent operations for higher scalability (completed unsupported). It is recommended not to change the default settings in the production environment as it could affect user experience if IOPs or throughput go beyond the limits supported by your storage subsystem.

The following screenshot includes the new options for the maximum concurrent number of provisioning and maintenance operations:

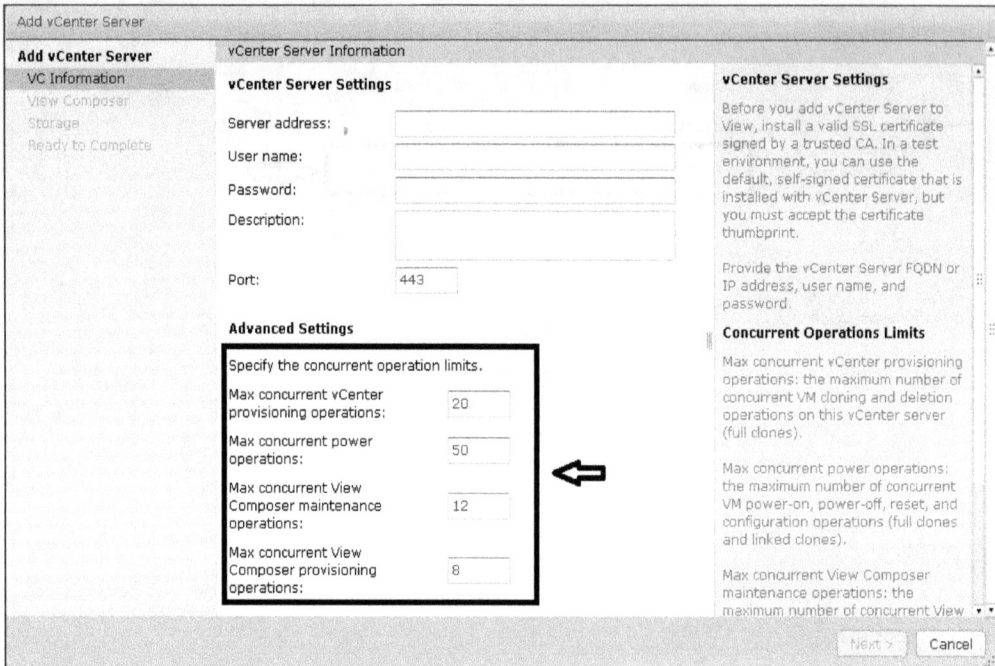

The Phone Home option

Phone Home is an optional (opt-in) choice you make during the installation for anonymous View usage statistics collection. All data is anonymous and untraceable. The phone home will collect information on versions, features used, the system's architecture, and the deployment scale. VMware will use this information to provide better support and more enhancements to popular features. In addition, VMware believes the data collected will allow for better alignment of the View product with R&D priorities and help match the way the customer is actually using View.

You could choose the **Send anonymous data to VMware** option on the screen, as shown in the following screenshot:

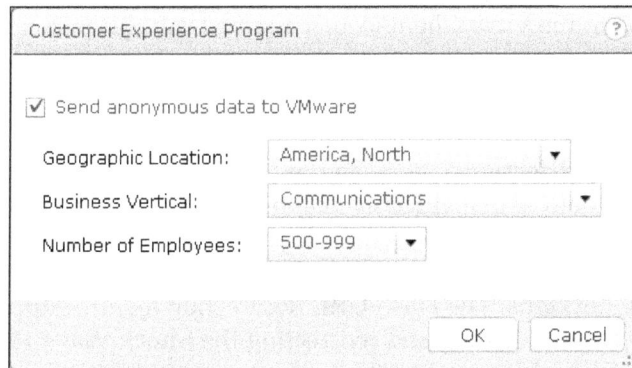

Feature Pack

The Feature Packs are fully integrated into the View Connection Server installer and do not require a separate installation. The Feature Packs provide the following features and components:

- **HTML Access Agent**: This allows users to connect to virtual desktops from their HTML 5 web browsers without having the Horizon View Client software installed on their systems. The HTML Access Agent runs on Horizon View desktops, and is the component that enables your users to connect to their desktops using HTML Access. You must install the Remote Experience Agent with the HTML Access Agent on the desktops on which you want to allow HTML Access.

- **Unity Touch**: This enhances the way mobile client (tablets) users access a desktop. Instead of trying to manipulate a full desktop image designed for a keyboard and mouse, on a small device screen, users can browse between apps and documents in a native mobile user interface without seeing the desktop. The Horizon Client documents for mobile devices will provide more information about end user features provided by Unity Touch. With this update, you can now add a favorite application or file from a list of search results and use the Unity Touch sidebar to minimize a running application's window. This requires users to connect to their desktops from Horizon Client for iOS 2.1 or later, or Horizon Client for Android 2.1 or later.

- **HTML Access installer**: This installer configures the View Connection Server instances to allow users to select HTML Access to connect to desktops. After you install HTML Access, the View Portal displays an HTML Access icon in addition to the View Client icon. You must run this installer if you want to use HTML Access to connect to desktops in a Horizon View deployment. Running this installer is also required if your users are using Horizon Workspace and they select HTML Access to connect to the desktops.

- **Flash URL Redirection**: Users can now use Adobe Media Server and multicast to deliver live video events in a VDI environment. To deliver multicast live video streams within the VDI environment, the media stream should be sent directly from the media source to the endpoints and bypass the virtual desktops. The Flash URL Redirection feature supports this capability by intercepting and redirecting the **Shock Wave Flash** (**SWF**) file from the virtual desktop directly to the client's endpoint.

- **Real-Time Audio-Video**: This allows View users to run Skype, WebEx, Google Hangouts, and other similar online conferencing applications on their virtual desktops. With Real-Time Audio-Video, the webcam and audio devices that are connected locally to the client system are redirected to the remote desktop. This feature redirects video and audio data to the desktop with a much lower bandwidth than can be achieved by using USB redirection. Real-Time Audio-Video is compatible with standard conferencing applications and supports standard webcams, audio USB devices, and analog audio input.

> For information about configuring these settings on Horizon View clients, see *Setting Frame Rates and Resolution for Real-Time Audio-Video on Horizon View Clients* on VMware KB 2053644.
>
> For information about using this feature with third-party applications, see *Guidelines for Using Real-Time Audio-Video with 3rd-Party Applications on Horizon View Desktops* on VMware KB 2053754.
>
> For more information about the Feature Pack, go to
> `https://www.vmware.com/support/view52/doc/horizon-view-52-feature-pack-2-release-notes.html`.

View Agent

View Agent is a component that is installed on the target desktop, either physical (seldom) or virtual (almost always). View Agent allows the View Connection Server to establish a connection to the desktop. The Remote Experience Agent is integrated with the View Agent. Before this release, the Remote Experience Agent, which contains HTML Access, Unity Touch, Real-Time Audio-Video, and Windows 7 Multimedia Redirection, needed a separate installation. View Agent also provides the following capabilities:

- **USB redirection**: This is defined as making a USB device, which is connected locally appear to be connected to vDesktop

- **Single Sign-On (SSO)**: This is done by using intelligent credential handling that requires only one secured and successful authentication login request, as opposed to logging in multiple times (for example, on the Connection Server, vDesktop, and so on)

- **Virtual printing via ThinPrint technology**: This has the ability to streamline printer-driver management through the use of ThinPrint

- **PCoIP connectivity**: This is the purpose-built VDI protocol made by Teradici and used by VMware in their VMware View solution

- **Persona management**: This is the ability to manage a user profile across an entire desktop landscape; the technology comes via the **Recovery Time Objective (RTO)** acquisition by VMware

- **View Composer support**: This has the ability to use linked clones and thin provisioning to drastically reduce operational efforts in managing a mid-to-large-scale VMware View environment

Horizon Client

The new Horizon Client is available for Windows, MAC, Ubuntu, iOS, and Android, to allow the connection to an entitled desktop resource. When the Horizon Client is installed on selected endpoint devices, a user can access the virtual desktop sessions from different devices such as smartphones, thin and zero clients, Windows, Macs, iOS, and Android devices. With the Unity Touch feature, the users can run Windows apps much easier on their mobile devices.

In addition to providing the functionality of being able to connect to a desktop, Horizon Client talks to View Agent to perform tasks such as USB redirection and Single Sign-On.

The View administrator can allow users to download the Horizon Client directly from the VMware download center (`https://my.vmware.com/web/vmware/info/slug/desktop_end_user_computing/vmware_horizon_view_clients/2_0#drivers_tools`).

The administrator can also control the Horizon Client for each user by storing the client software on a local storage device using a Horizon portal.

Improved end user experience

The new release of the Horizon Client has improved several features that pertain to the end user experience, as follows:

- **Expanded Windows Support**: Horizon Client now supports the following Microsoft Windows releases:
    - Windows 8/8.1 Desktop
    - Windows 7 Desktop
    - Windows Vista Desktop
    - Windows XP systems

- **Unmatched performance**: The adaptive capabilities of the PCoIP display protocol are optimized and normally improved with each client release. This is designed to deliver the best user experience, even over low-bandwidth and high-latency connections. Your desktop is faster and more responsive regardless of where you are.

- **Very simple connectivity**: Horizon Client for Windows is tightly integrated with Horizon View for simple setup and connectivity.

- **Secure from any location**: At your desk or away from office, your data is delivered securely to you wherever you are. The SSL/TLS encryption is always used to protect user credentials, and enhanced certificate checking is performed on the client. The View Client for Windows also supports optional RADIUS and RSA SecurID authentication (RADIUS support was added with VMware View 5.1 and View Client for Windows 5.1).

Real-Time Audio-Video

Other improvements with the Horizon Client are focused on Microsoft Lync 2013 and Flash URL redirection. This requires the current version of Horizon Client, which now includes the Remote Experience options, as follows:

- **Microsoft Lync 2013**: This supports use on a remote desktop to allow Unified Communications (UC) VoIP (Voice over IP) and video chat calls with Lync-certified USB audio and video devices. A dedicated IP phone is no longer required. The architecture design requires the installation of the Microsoft Lync 2013 client on the remote desktop, and it uses a Microsoft Lync VDI plugin on the Windows 7 or 8/8.1 client. The Microsoft Lync 2013 client can be used for presence, instant messaging, web conferencing, and Microsoft Office functionalities. When a Lync VoIP or video chat call occurs, the Lync VDI plugin offloads the media processing from the data center server to the client's endpoint, and then encodes all media into Lync-optimized audio and video codecs. This architecture is highly scalable and results in lower network bandwidth. It also provides point-to-point media delivery with support for high-quality and real-time VoIP and video.

> Recording audio is not yet supported. This integration is supported only with the PCoIP display protocol.

- **Flash URL redirection**: Streaming Flash content from Adobe Media Server directly to the client's endpoints reduces the load on the data center's ESXi host. It also removes the extra routing through the data center and reduces the overall bandwidth required to simultaneously stream live video events to multiple clients. The Flash URL redirection feature will use a JavaScript that is embedded inside the web page by a web page administrator. Whenever the virtual desktop user clicks on the selected URL link from within the web page, the JavaScript will intercept and then redirect the Shock Wave File from the virtual desktop to the client's endpoint. The endpoint will open a local VMware Flash Projector outside of the virtual desktop session and then play the media stream locally.

View Composer (an optional component)

The components covered earlier in this chapter belong to the set of mandatory components in a View solution. The major component that is optional in a View solution is the View Composer. It should be noted that when some third-party solutions such as Unidesk or storage-based cloning are used in conjunction with View, View Composer is not used. This is because solutions such as Unidesk or storage-based cloning have their own approach for handling mass provisioning of vDesktops.

View Composer is used in majority of View-based solutions today, but there are valid scenarios and solutions that do not require the use of View Composer. As this book focuses on VMware View solutions and not View with third-party components, View Composer will be discussed heavily throughout this book.

Understanding View Composer

View Composer is the component responsible for creating linked clones, described later in this chapter, for desktop VMs from a single base snapshot.

View Composer uses a separate database to store the information regarding mapping, deployment, and so on, of the linked-clone desktops. This database can reside on the same database server as the existing vCenter database, assuming that it is a supported platform. It also can be installed as a standalone server. This move is aimed towards creating a more highly-scalable Horizon View architecture. Another reason to allow the standalone option for View Composer is that you can use the VCSA. Having options is normally a good thing.

However, the database itself must be unique to View Composer. This means that the View Composer database cannot use the existing vCenter Server database (but it could use the same server with a separate database instance).

In addition, a separate **Open Database Connectivity** (**ODBC**) connection must be set up on the vCenter Servers with the appropriate information for the View Composer database connection.

> When View Composer is installed, automated pools are the only pools that need to use View Composer. Manual pools or terminal Services pools can still be used, but they do not use View Composer.

Using SQL Express installation for View Composer

Small **Proof-of-Concept** (**PoC**) environments may want to leverage the existing SQL Express installation on their VMware vCenter Server. It is possible to leverage the same SQL Express instance as long as a separate database is created. To create a separate database, perform the following steps:

1. Download and install SQL Server Management Studio Express.

2. Connect to the vCenter Server instance of SQL Express.

3. Right-click on the instance name and add a new database (for example, View_Composer).

4. Configure the ODBC connection and use <vCenter Server> / SQLEXP_VIM for the connection string. Replace <vCenter Server> with the appropriate information for your environment.

Snapshots and linked clones

A snapshot saves a point-in-time state of a given virtual machine. Changes beyond the snapshot of the point-in-time state are written to a delta disk while the original virtual disk (.vmdk) is marked as read-only. This preserves the point-in-time state of the virtual machine until the snapshot is deleted by an administrator. Multiple snapshots of a given virtual machine can be taken, and it is these point-in-time snapshots that are used as the basis for View Composer linked clones.

A **linked clone** is a copy of a virtual machine based on a specific snapshot of that virtual machine (known as the **parent**). When a linked clone pool is created, View Composer creates a replica.

A **replica** is the original read-only base virtual machine disk merged with a specific point-in-time snapshot chosen to be the point of deployment for a given View desktop pool. Replicas are always thin-provisioned.

A View desktop pool can only point to one specific snapshot at a time, but this can be changed easily through techniques discussed later in this book. A virtual machine can have multiple snapshots; thus, a single virtual machine with multiple snapshots could be the foundation for all the View desktop pools in an environment. This allows each pool to be based off of their own (or the same) point-in-time snapshot. This is possible because View desktop pools using the linked clone technology do not actually use the base virtual machine snapshots; instead, they use a replica (base virtual machine plus snapshot).

While linked clones are based off of an original parent VM, each linked clone still has a unique name, **Media Access Control** (**MAC**) address, and a virtual machine **Universal Unique Identifier** (**UUID**).

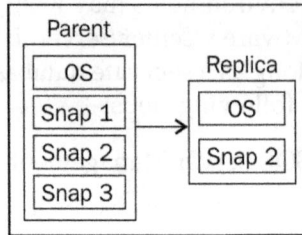

```
┌──────────────────────────────┐
│ Parent                        │
│ ┌────────────┐  Replica       │
│ │    OS      │ ┌────────────┐ │
│ ├────────────┤ │    OS      │ │
│ │  Snap 1    │→├────────────┤ │
│ ├────────────┤ │  Snap 2    │ │
│ │  Snap 2    │ └────────────┘ │
│ ├────────────┤                │
│ │  Snap 3    │                │
│ └────────────┘                │
└──────────────────────────────┘
```

The preceding figure illustrates a parent virtual machine with three snapshots (**Snap 1**, **Snap 2**, and **Snap 3**). Each snapshot represents a different point-in-time of the virtual machine. For example, the Snap 1 snapshot may have Office 2007 installed, the Snap 2 snapshot may have Office 2010 installed, and the Snap 3 snapshot may have Office 2010 and Visio 2010 installed. In this example, the Snap 2 snapshot was chosen for virtual desktop deployment. Once this snapshot has been selected and the desktop pool has been enabled for provisioning, a replica is created. The replica does not copy the other Snap 1 or Snap 3 snapshot states.

The use of a replica that preserves the original parent vDesktop's snapshot state allows the parent vDesktop to be powered on, patched, or altered without impacting the state of the vDesktop using the replica. Again, this is because the replica is a copy of a parent vDesktop's snapshot and not the actual parent vDesktop itself.

View Composer uses the linked clone technology. A virtual desktop using this technology contains a pointer to a replica of the original gold snapshot. To clarify, the pointer is not pointing to the original (parent) vDesktop but to an exact copy (replica) of the parent vDesktop from a specific point in time. View Composer uses this technology so that each vDesktop doesn't need its own full-sized virtual disk. The pointer uses the replica only for read-only access and writes all changes to a secondary disk, called the delta disk.

Delta disks can be viewed as a change of record. Instead of defiling a gold snapshot, all changes (deltas) to the original disk are recorded outside of the gold snapshot to the delta disk. This leaves the original gold snapshot in pristine condition while still ensuring a usable operating system that accepts changes made by the user and other applications.

Templates

A **template** is a virtual machine that has been marked read-only by converting it into a template. A template is simply a virtual machine, which has had its `.vmx` configuration file converted into a `.vmxt` configuration file. Virtual machines are read-only virtual machines that are then used for cloning purposes. A virtual machine created from a virtual machine template is a direct copy of the original template. However, customization specifications can be used to alter certain aspects (for example, SID, hostname, IP address, and so on) of the newly-created virtual machines. Customization specifications are created by using the **Customization Specification Wizard** in the vSphere Client when connected to a vCenter Server.

Full provisioning versus linked clones

View has the ability to use both full clones and linked clones. A **full clone** is a 1:1 independent copy of an existing VM template. This follows the same procedure as deploying a virtual machine from a template in VMware vCenter. A template is selected as the base for the vDesktops, and (likely) a customization specification is also chosen.

A vDesktop that has been deployed using full provisioning (for example, a virtual machine template) does not require access to the original template once it has been built.

A linked clone uses one master VM and then creates a delta disk for each additional VM. The additional VMs have a pointer back to the master VM when they need to talk to their base image (for example, to access the core Windows OS components), but use their delta disk for any unique data for that particular VM or user (for example, `...\Documents and Settings\`). A desktop built using the View Composer technology will have read-only access to the replica VM and read/write access to its delta disk.

> Full clones are based off a VM template, whereas linked clones are based off a VM snapshot.

Types of disks for vDesktops

There are several types of disks—OS disk, secondary OS disk, user data disk, and temp data disk.

OS disk

The OS disk stores the system data (for example, Windows 7) and provides the base for a functional desktop.

Secondary OS disk

The secondary OS disk stores OS data that must be preserved during certain View Composer activities (such as Refresh or Recompose). Each virtual desktop will have a secondary OS disk. These disks are typically 10 MB in size and are not configurable.

The secondary OS disk can only be stored on the same data store as the OS disk.

User data disk

A persistent user data disk is an optional component of a View virtual desktop. The user data disk stores the user profile information. By storing this information on a persistent disk, View Composer actions such as Refresh and Recompose will not affect the user profile data. The alternative is to store this information inside the OS disk, which would cause user profile data to be lost during a Refresh or Recompose task.

The size of the user data disk is configurable. In addition, the persistent user data disk can be stored on the same data store as the OS disk or on a separate data store.

Temp data disk

A non-persistent temp data disk is an optional component of a View virtual desktop. It is also referred to as the disposable disk. The temp data disk stores the OS swap file as well as temporary data that is created during a user session. By storing this information on a non-persistent disk, View will delete all data stored on the disk whenever the virtual desktop is powered off. This can help minimize the growth (in MB) of the virtual desktop as disposable user interaction is discarded and does not become part of the standard OS disk for each respective user.

The size of the temp data disk is configurable. The temp data disk can only be stored on the same data store as the OS disk.

Many options of disk types and redirection

The following is a list of the available options of the disk types and the redirection:

- OS disk: For an OS disk, there are following options:
    - ° Linked clones (1)
    - ° Full clones (2)

- User data: For a user data disk, there are following options:
    - ° OS disk (3)
    - ° Persistent disk (4)

- Temp data: For a temp data disk, there are following options:
    - ° OS disk (5)
    - ° Non-persistent disk (6)

The following figure illustrates the preceding disk types and their redirection. Note that the secondary OS disk is not illustrated as it is not a configurable option within View.

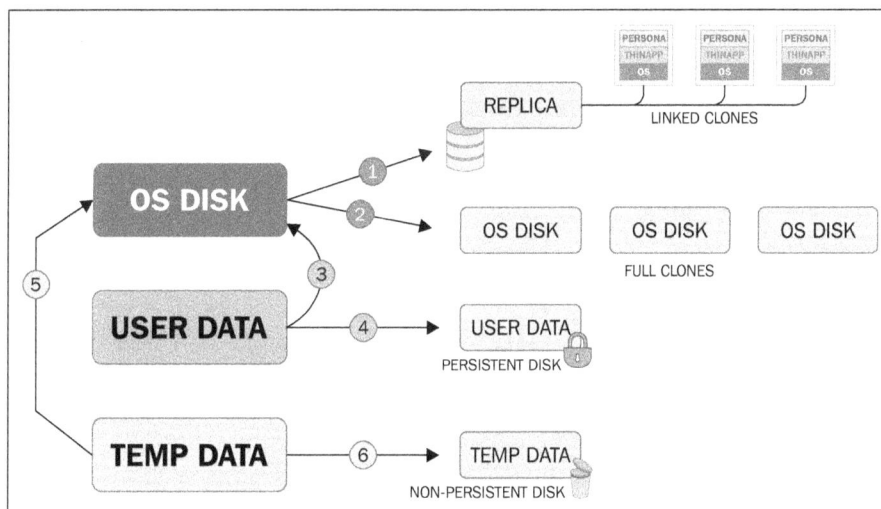

Thin provisioning versus thick provisioning

When a virtual disk is created using **thin provisioning**, the disk only occupies the actual data size on the disk. For example, a virtual disk (.vmdk) that is 20 GB in size but has only 8 GB of data will occupy only 8 GB on the data store. Two virtual desktops that have a 20 GB virtual disk but only 8 GB of data per disk will occupy 16 GB on the data store.

When a VM that is using thin provisioning needs to write new data to the virtual disk (and thereby increase the size of the virtual disk), it does so in the blocks defined by the data store's block size. The data store's block size is defined prior to being formatted in the **Virtual Machine File System** (**VMFS**) format. In VMware vSphere 5, the newly created data stores (versus the ones upgraded from vSphere) use a unified block size of 1 MB.

For example, if the VM is located on a 500 GB VMFS-3 block, which is the data store that was formatted using a 2 MB block size, a 10 MB new write operation will require the write of 5 blocks (10 MB file/2 MB block size), which results in a less efficient usage of the overall storage space.

> Thin provisioning makes it possible to over-allocate the available storage and can introduce significant issues if not monitored and managed properly.

When a virtual disk is created using **thick provisioning** (default), the disk occupies its entire allocated size on the disk. For example, a virtual disk that is 20 GB in size but has only 8 GB of data will occupy 20 GB on the data store. Two virtual desktops that have a 20 GB virtual disk but only 8 GB of data per disk will occupy 40 GB on the data store.

Actions for linked clones – Reset, Refresh, Recompose, and Rebalance

When using linked clones, there are several actions that can be performed on the clones themselves. These actions are discussed in the following sections.

Reset

The Reset action is equivalent to hitting the **Reset** button on a virtual machine. This is an ungraceful restart of a virtual machine that is equivalent to pulling the power cable out of a desktop and then plugging it back in.

Refresh

The Refresh action is an action that resets the delta disk back to its original state. An OS delta disk bloat can happen as a user continues to write changes to their delta disk over time. Data inside the OS delta disk is lost during a Refresh action.

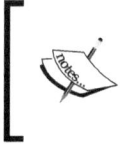

> The Refresh option is only available when using the persistent and automated linked clone desktop pools. During this action, data (for example, user data) can potentially be lost if it is not redirected elsewhere (for example, a non-persistent disk).

Recompose

The Recompose action is an action that is used to change the snapshot and/or a parent VM that is used by the desktop pool. In the following figure, number 1 is the original mapping to a base snapshot, and number 2 represents the available options during a Recompose action.

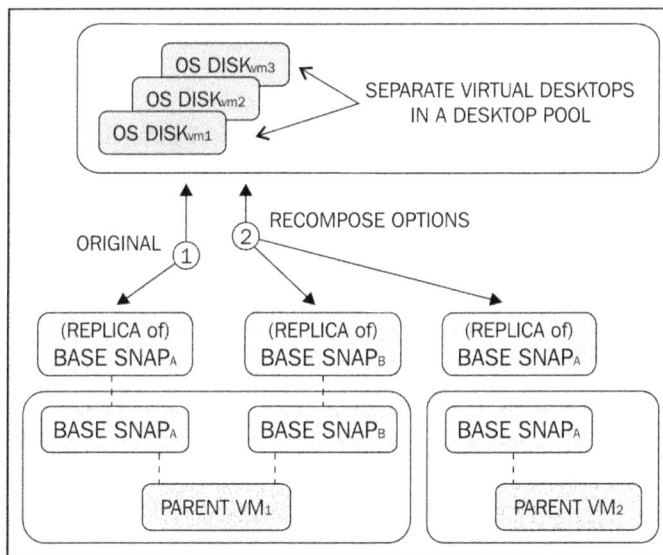

Administrators can use the Recompose action in the following scenarios:

- To change the linked clone pool to use a different snapshot (for example, **Snapshot_B**) of the original parent (for example, **ParentVM_1**) instead of the current one in use

- To change the linked clone pool to use a snapshot (for example, **Snapshot_A**) of a different parent (for example, **ParentVM_2**) instead of the current parent in use

> The Recompose option is only available when using the persistent and automated linked clone desktop pools.

Rebalance

The Rebalance action is an action that will evenly distribute desktops across all of the available data stores in the desktop pool. The desktop must be in the ready, error, or customizing state (with no pending tasks or cancellations) to be rebalanced.

A Rebalance action automatically executes the Refresh action on the desktop as well, which resets the OS disk back to its original state.

During a Rebalance action, the administrator can set whether to rebalance the desktop once the users log off of their desktop or to force all of the active users to log off.

The Rebalance action is also the only supported way to move linked clones to a new data store.

View Composer Array Integration (VCAI)

VCAI leverages the native cloning abilities in a storage array to offload the storage operations within the View environment. This option improves provisioning speeds and the management regarding View Composer along with offering another solution to customers who want to leverage their other storage options.

The feature allows the creation of linked clones to be offloaded to the storage array. VCAI expands the capability to deliver faster provisioning of View pools and proper alignment of linked clones on your storage array. It allows you to use Array Native Clones with View deployments on most NAS storage solutions such as NexentaConnect View Edition and Hitachi NAS 4000 Series. This means that the array takes over the creation of the clones and relieves the CPU on the vSphere server.

VMware Horizon editions

The new VMware Horizon View is available in three editions: View Standard, Advanced, and Enterprise. All three editions include all components needed for a comprehensive virtual desktop solution. The following table shows the editions and their components for both named users and concurrent users (CCU):

Product	Description
Horizon View Standard (CCU)	This contains the following: • View • ThinApp Client and Packager • Workstation (one Admin license) • vSphere Desktop • vCenter Desktop
Horizon Advanced Edition (named)	This includes Horizon View Standard edition and the following: • Virtual SAN • Hosted apps
Horizon Advanced Edition (CCU)	This includes Horizon View Standard edition and the following: • Virtual SAN • Hosted apps
Horizon Enterprise (named)	This includes Horizon Advanced edition and the following: • vCenter Operations Manager for View • vCenter Orchestrator and Desktop Plugin
Horizon Enterprise (CCU)	This includes Horizon Advanced edition and the following: • vCenter Operations Manager for View • vCenter Orchestrator and Desktop Plugin

Summary

This chapter has provided a solid introduction to the components of a VMware View VDI solution, including VMware vSphere fundamentals. Without an understanding of the basic concepts of the View architecture as well as the underlying VMware vSphere architecture, it will be very difficult to build a proper View solution. For additional reading on either View or VMware vSphere, please refer to the administration, evaluation, and installation guides from VMware on the desired product set (`https://www.vmware.com/support/pubs/view_pubs.html`).

This chapter reviewed the components that make up the View environment and highlighted some of the new features of version 6 along with the new edition purchasing options.

The next chapter will cover how to collect an organization's inputs to ensure that a VMware View design meets the requirements for success. Collecting the requirements is a phase many VDI architects either skip or do in haste, resulting in a less-than-ideal end product. Once a VDI architect has performed several discovery engagements with an organization, it is certainly possible that he simply asks the likely pitfall questions (for example, "Will you be using a bidirectional audio?"), but until this level of comfort has been reached, performing a full discovery is advised.

2
Solution Methodology

This chapter will focus on the solution approach required to design successful View environments, including the gathering of inputs, their digestion, and the production of a View design or project output.

A **Virtual Desktop Infrastructure** (**VDI**) implementation can have various project drivers, including cost reduction, increased security, and end device flexibility. When participating in a VDI endeavor, it is important to define the project success criteria. For example, if an organization is looking to decrease the login time for roaming physicians, it is important to incorporate a streamlined login process (for example, **Single Sign-On**) into the overall solution.

> A robust VDI solution that doesn't address the organization's key criteria might still be judged as a mediocre success, instead of being embraced as a significant improvement to the end users' work environment.

Also, for solution providers and architects that are designing View solutions for multiple organizations, it is important to take a scientific and organized approach to design these solutions. Designing the solutions for separate organizations in tandem can be very confusing. By taking the same approach to each project, the VDI architect can minimize errors, and more importantly, streamline the amount of effort required to produce a design.

When designing a solution, there are several methodologies that can be used. For example, use the Waterfall method comprising the following steps:

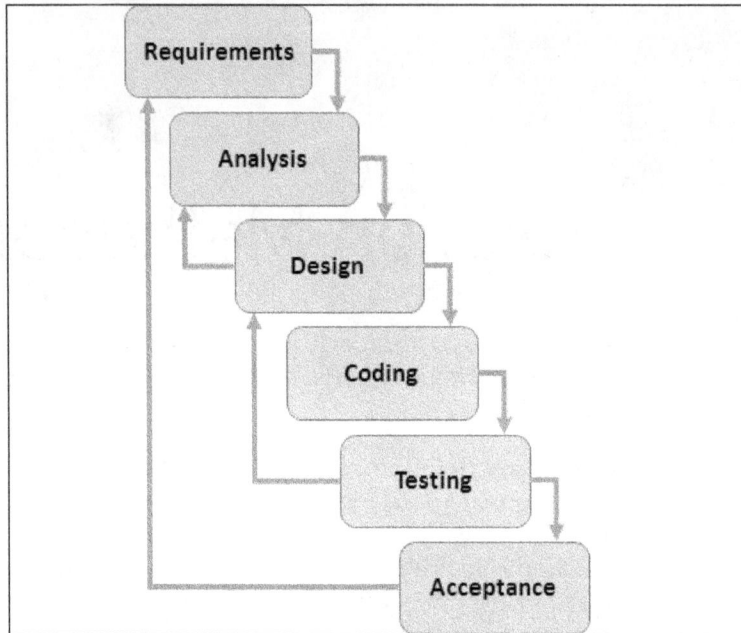

This book will not review all the methodologies or try to choose which is better, but it will stress the use of a methodology that helps put a repeatable structure around providing a VDI solution.

The key phases used in this book, and by the authors, in designing a VMware View solution are:

- Assessment
- Plan (define use cases)
- Design
- Pilot
- Implement
- User migration
- Hand-off/manage

The following is a diagrammatical representation of these phases:

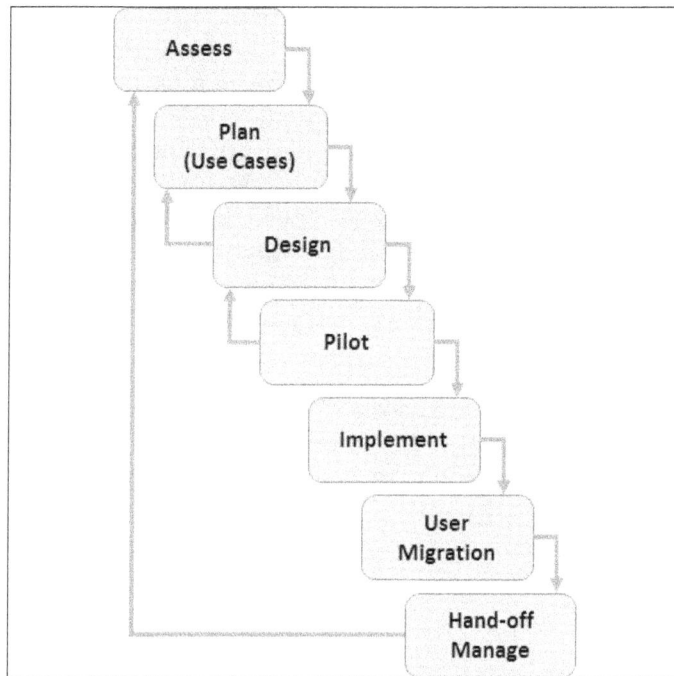

As noted in *Chapter 1, Components of VMware Horizon View 6*, this book focuses on designing the solutions based on VMware View 6. The chapter will cover assessment through the pilot steps in some detail, with an overview of implement, user migration, and hand-off. In a full solution, the implementation phase, which follows the pilot phase, includes subtopics such as defining the project timeline and key milestones; operational readiness is also incorporated. Nevertheless, these topics are outside the scope of this book.

As an example, a case study that refers to a successful VDI project can be found at `http://searchitchannel.techtarget.com/unassigned/VDI-project-success-VMware-View-installation-at-collection-agency`.

This book is a guide for architects to design solutions with the highest probability of success.

Assessment

A View solution may replace existing physical desktops and require a migration phase, or it may be a completely new solution to an organization. In either case, a proper assessment is required to understand how to scope hardware requirements, storage needs, and additional solutions that might be required (for example, a profile management solution). Many times, an organization that skips the Proof of Concept / pilot phase and goes right into the building and deploying of a VDI solution is able to meet the immediate tactical need, but then it often stalls when these factors scale because larger needs of the solution have not been fully planned out. It is extremely important to establish a baseline and run tests to validate your estimates for hardware, memory, storage, and networking, which will be required for the full-scale solution.

An assessment is used to collect the necessary information in order to design the solution properly. An assessment is the process of collecting both technical as well as organizational information. Typically, there are three components of an assessment:

- A questionnaire
- Metric collection
- A discussion

Questionnaire

A **questionnaire**, whether filled out manually or electronically, is a valuable tool you can use to collect the necessary data to help you put together a solid View design. A questionnaire is also a useful tool that helps an organization feel involved in the design, which helps increase the chances of success.

An organization that participates actively in the VDI design will feel more invested in its success. An organization that was handed a VDI solution with little input will likely enter into their solution with skepticism.

Providing a questionnaire is the first great step in the assessment of a possible VDI environment. A search on the Internet will provide several results that can be used as a starting point to develop the questions. Reviewing several questionnaires allows you to come up with a good comprehensive list of items. If you are an architect and are going to provide solutions for several projects, then the experience you gain with each project will help in building a list based on that experience.

Assessment worksheet for VMware View desktops

The following table can be used for the assessment planning of the solution around VMware View desktops. The **Value** column is used to record the information collected.

The following table provides the questions, values, and descriptions for the desktop pool input:

Question	Value	Description
What is the maximum number of vDesktop users in the environment?		It provides the total number of vDesktops for a persistent vDesktop solution.
What is the maximum number of concurrent users that will connect at any given time?		It provides the total number of vDesktops for a nonpersistent vDesktop solution.
What are the desired desktop operating systems for the VDI?		It determines the baseline of memory and vCPU required for the vDesktops.
Is there a requirement for a Single Sign-On (SSO) solution?		It determines access methods to the desktops.
What is the full size of the existing desktop images?		It determines how much disk space is required.
How often do you want the vDesktops to be refreshed?		It determines the desktop pool settings (refresh immediately, refresh after n minutes, refresh at n percent disk bloat, and so on).
What are the number of point-in-time snapshots to maintain the base image?		It determines how much disk space is required.
What is the full highly available solution?		It determines whether redundant View Connection Servers, vCenter Servers, and so on will be used.
Is there a need for load balancing?		It determines whether the connection servers will sit behind a load balancer.
Are there any special business continuity needs?		It provides a plan for special recovery methods.
Will any of the vDesktops be considered mission-critical?		It determines possible additional protection methods.

Question	Value	Description
Will remote workers be supported?		It determines whether View Security servers are required.
Will users be classified based on where they are connecting from?		It determines whether View Connection Server tags are required.
Should external users connect to a VDI that's different from internal users?		It determines whether View Connection Server tags should be used.
Will smart cards, CAC cards, proximity badges, and so on be used for authentication?		It determines the settings of View Client, View Agent, and the necessary certificates.
Do you adhere to FIPS 140-2 compliance?		It determines the advanced settings of the View environment.
Do you use two-factor RSA authentication?		It is used to configure advanced authentication options.
Are there special needs around compliance or regulatory requirements?		It can affect the set of special desktop pools.
Are your remote users primarily in a connected state?		It determines whether the solution requires VMware View Local mode.
Are USB drives allowed?		It determines the advanced View configuration settings.
Does the environment have shift workers?		It determines the desktop pool settings.
What is the average work day of an employee in hours?		It determines the desktop pool settings.

The following table provides the questions, values, and descriptions for the storage input:

Question	Value	Description
What is the amount of available space in the desktop images?		It determines the thin size of the image (full space free is equal to thin size).
How many desktop base images exist in the environment today?		It is used as an input for the number of desktop pools in the solution.

Question	Value	Description
Connection type and speed.		It determines parameters for the solution.
Does a SAN currently exist?		It determines the solution for a particular model.

The following table provides the questions, values, and descriptions for the landscape input:

Question	Value	Description
How are desktops patched today?		It determines the patching solution for vDesktops.
What is your existing server infrastructure?		It is used to understand the technical landscape.
What is your existing storage infrastructure?		It is used to understand the technical landscape.
What is your switching infrastructure?		It is used to understand the technical landscape.
Which group manages your virtual server environment?		It is used to understand the political landscape.
Which group manages your physical desktop environment?		It is used to understand the political landscape.
Who do you foresee managing your VDI?		It is used to understand the political landscape.
How technical are the people that will manage the solution once it's implemented?		It is used to understand the level of operational readiness that should be performed.
What is the current Microsoft desktop licensing agreement?		It determines whether the necessary Microsoft licensing exists.
What is the current asset-tracking solution for physical desktops?		It determines the existing technology landscape.
Will new end devices be purchased for this solution?		It determines whether new devices (for example, zero clients) can be used or the existing hardware will be repurposed.

The following table provides the questions, values, and descriptions for the network input:

Question	Value	Description
Will CD or DVD burners be used?		It is used to understand the PCoIP bandwidth considerations.
Will microphone jack headsets be used?		It is used to understand the PCoIP bandwidth considerations.
Will Dragon Naturally Speaking or Dragon Medical be used?		It is used to understand the PCoIP bandwidth and storage IOPS considerations.
Will USB handsets, dictaphones, and so on be used?		It is used to understand the PCoIP bandwidth considerations.
Will videos be streamed on a regular basis?		It is used to understand the PCoIP bandwidth considerations.
Will a VOIP solution be required?		It is used to understand the PCoIP bandwidth and end device considerations.
How far from the VDI will the majority of the users reside?		It is used to understand the network requirements and topology.
Will the solution reside on a sensitive or classified network?		It is used to understand the advanced configurations of the overall solution.
How many VLANs are currently used by your physical desktop networking environment?		It is used to understand the existing network layout.
Will you be supporting the remote offices?		It determines whether a remote office solution needs to be incorporated.
Number of remote site networks.		It determines access to desktops.
What is the current number of Dynamic Host Configuration Protocol (DHCP) scopes (and size) available for desktops?		It determines the existing network topology.

The following table provides the questions, values, and descriptions for the profile management input:

Question	Value	Description
What are you using today for profile management?		It determines whether profile management is required, and/or if there is a solution already in place.
Where are the users' home directories located?		It determines the existing profile management solution.
Is there any solution around roaming profile and/or file redirection?		It determines whether the current solution needs to be incorporated into the new VDI solution.

The following table provides the questions, values, and descriptions for the success criteria:

Question	Value	Description
3 months after the solution is live, how will you know you chose the proper solution?		It elicits the success criteria for the VDI project.
What is your primary motivation to implement a VDI solution?		It elicits the success criteria for the VDI project.

The following table provides the questions, values, and descriptions for the clients:

Question	Value	Description
Having/planning use of thin clients?		It determines client needs and possible solutions.
Primary thin client make?		It determines client needs and possible solutions.
Primary thin client model?		It determines client needs and possible solutions.
Thin client OS?		It determines client needs and possible solutions.
Using Windows PC as clients, and how many?		It determines client needs and possible solutions.
Apple Macs and how many?		It determines client needs and possible solutions.

Question	Value	Description
Any Linux PCs and how many?		It determines client needs and possible solutions.
Having/planning use of zero clients?		It determines client needs and possible solutions.
Web interface (HTML) required?		It determines client needs and possible solutions.
Use of tablets/ smartphones		It determines additional needs and possible solutions.

A **kiosk** is used to identify an end device that will be configured to automatically connect to a vDesktop in the VMware View environment.

Metric collection

Once the questionnaire has been completed, it is time to begin collecting real-world data from the organization's existing physical landscape. By completing the questionnaire before collecting the usage data, the metric collection phase can focus on the areas of concern.

For example, if it was revealed during the questionnaire that the View solution will support surgeons who work 10 hour days and use bidirectional audio (for example, Dragon Medical) often throughout the day, it will be beneficial to collect data such as CPU, memory, and network usage of these surgeons, even if they are a very small subset of the overall end user population. The collection of worst-case scenarios is also very important to predict performance requirements for exceptions to the standard types of solutions.

Assessments can be performed on an existing physical desktop infrastructure and VDI solution (for example, an organization looking to migrate from Citrix XenDesktop to VMware View).

A performance-monitoring tool will help gather the necessary basic information. There are several tools, including third-party tools such as VMware's Capacity Planner, Liquidware Labs' **Stratusphere FIT™**, and Lakeside Software's SysTrack, which are out there and can assist with this process.

In addition, Windows 7/8 comes with another option, the Performance Logs and Alerts tool, called **PerfMon**. PerfMon allows administrators to capture and graph various performance statistics from local and remote computers.

Additional information on PerfMon and the key attributes to monitor can be found at `http://www.vmware.com/files/pdf/view/Server-Storage-Sizing-Guide-Windows-7-TN.pdf`.

It is extremely important to establish a baseline for the existing environment, build a Proof-Of-Concept infrastructure, and run tests to validate your estimates for hardware, memory, and storage that will be required.

In this example, Liquidware Labs' Stratusphere FIT™ will be used.

FIT uses the software running on the desktop that reports back to a central location (**Stratusphere Hub**). Some of the key metrics collected are as follows:

- CPU and memory usage (total and per application)
- Average login delay
- Average **Input/Output Operations Per Second (IOPS)**
- Network latency
- Peripherals

In addition to metric and inventory collection, FIT can be used to rate users on their suitability for a vDesktop solution.

> There are plenty of successful VDI solutions implemented that have never undergone a metric collection phase. However, these are most likely implemented by very seasoned VDI professionals. If available, it is encouraged to execute the metric collection phase as it will drastically increase the project's chance of success as well as give the data to support both good and bad results as the project progresses.

The goals of the metric collection phase are as follows:

- Establishing a baseline average user
- Establishing the top 10 applications used in the environment
- Identifying the current pain points
- Identifying the potential pitfalls for VDI
- Classifying the users into use cases

FIT can also be used to organize the future vDesktop users into use types, which translates into desktop pools within the View infrastructure.

For example, if FIT determines that the vast majority of users are allocated 2 GB of RAM on their physical desktop (and use 80 percent of the allocated memory), but a small contingent of users have 4 GB of memory (and use 80 percent of their allocated memory), then two different linked clone desktop pools (at a minimum) are needed. The first pool will have a base desktop image with 2 GB of memory, whereas the second pool will have a base desktop image with 4 GB of memory.

The following figure demonstrates that the data must first be collected and then analyzed. After analysis, the design can begin.

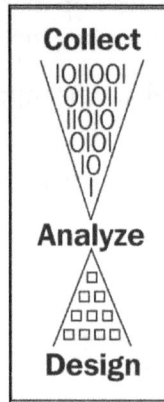

To properly determine how much physical hardware is needed to procure, as well as how to logistically divide the user population into the desktop pools, it is important to collect the information based on the real-world end user activities. Some of the key metrics to collect the information include the average and peak numbers of the following:

- Memory usage
- CPU usage
- CPU ready / wait time
- Network throughput
- Network latency
- Disk throughput (MBps)
- Disk activity (IOPS)
- Disk read/write percentage
- Most frequently used applications

- Number of monitors
- Unique peripheral requirements
- Unused applications
- Graphics intensity

With most collection utilities, an agent must be installed on the desktops to be surveyed. The most efficient way to install such an agent is typically through existing mechanisms such as group policy objects, Microsoft System Center Configuration Manager, logon scripts, or a variety of other methods.

> While data-collecting tools are often forbidden on the sensitive or classified networks, Liquidware Labs has taken the necessary steps and certifications to be able to run them on many sensitive networks.

FIT generates unique reports that help a VDI architect properly understand the existing physical desktop environment so that a robust View solution can be designed and implemented, as shown in the following screenshot:

	Machine	Unique Users	Time In Use(%)	Login Delay Avg.(s)	System CPU Avg.(%)	User CPU Avg.(%)	Total Memory Avg.(MB)	Total Memory Avg.(%)	Disk IOPS Avg.	Disk Used Avg.(GB)	Network Avg.(KB/s)
▼	COLW7VM4	1	100	13	8.26	28.71	2,412.51	58.92	11.63	38.45	307.16
▼	COLW7VM63	1	100	24	4.2	15.65	2,217.29	54.15	12.09	37.83	48.03
▼	COLW7VM64	1	100	33	4.84	16.76	2,154.05	52.61	15.13	40.12	54.8
▼	COLW7VM5	1	100	n/a	7.48	13.13	2,663.11	61.44	13.69	37.49	73

It is recommended to collect data between the second and fourth weeks to ensure that enough time has passed to capture the most typical business cycles. If the organization that is being assessed has known peak work periods (for example, end of quarter closeouts), it might be helpful to collect the data during this period. However, it is advised to not let the collection of outlier data slow down the overall project's process. Careful analysis is important, but just as prolonged capacity planning assessments can bring a server virtualization project to its knees, so can an overly prolonged VDI assessment.

Processing the data

Once the end user data has been collected, it is important to properly comprehend and analyze the information that has been collected from the customer's environment, as shown in the following table:

Metric	Input	Output
Memory usage (in MB)	This is the total memory consumed (both active and peak) by the end users. The summation of this metric does not yield the total memory required for the VDI solution.	It helps to determine how much memory is required by the physical environment. The formula is *MB required for vDesktops + MB required for supporting infrastructure + MB overhead of hypervisor + MB for swap space = total MB required.*
CPU usage (in GHz)	This is the total CPU usage consumed (both active and peak) by the end users. In a VDI environment, total CPU usage is less important than the users per core.	This helps determine the total CPU usage required by the physical environment and is used to determine which users may require multiple vCPUs.
Network throughput (in KBps)	This is used to determine potential bottlenecks in both an on-site and/or a remote solution. As the VDI solutions are often implemented in a central location, the network throughput can be used to determine the required bandwidth between a remote office and the location of the VDI.	For example, an environment with minimal network throughput between the end users at a remote site and the centrally located VDI might choose to implement VDI at the remote office and manage it from a central location (one solution to limited network throughput). It is also important to understand the unusual network bandwidth requirements of the VDI users.

Metric	Input	Output
Network latency (in milliseconds)	This is used to determine the potential bottlenecks in both an on-site and/or a remote solution. As both the **Microsoft Remote Desktop Protocol (RDP)** and VMware's PCoIP protocol are latency-sensitive, it's important to understand the round trip time for data transmissions between the end users and the location of VDI.	For example, an environment with high network latency might choose to implement policies optimizing the PCoIP protocol at both the end device and within the vDesktop. The policies may limit advanced graphics capabilities and use compression to maximize an end user's experience.
Disk throughput (in MBps)	This is used to determine potential bottlenecks in the underlying storage environment supporting VDI from a bandwidth perspective.	For example, an environment with a class of users requiring large amounts of disk throughput (for example, recording audio) might need to have their vDesktops reside on a separate data store when compared to other vDesktops users. This not only suggests and promotes the tiering of the storage platform but also prevents low disk throughput users from being impacted by high throughput users.
Disk activity (in IOPS)	This is used to determine potential bottlenecks in the underlying storage environment supporting VDI from a performance perspective.	Disk IOPS is one of the most important metrics of a VDI design, and as such, a chapter later in this book is dedicated to the fundamental concepts of storage in a VDI solution. Collecting a disk IOPS consumed by end users before migration to a View solution will provide an idea about the overall number of disk IOPSes that need to be supported in the solution. However, as discussed later in this book, storage design plays a paramount role in the overall success of a View solution.

Metric	Input	Output
Disk read/write percentage	This is used to determine a suitable storage environment for the VDI.	More on designing a suitable storage environment for the VDI can be found later in this book.
Most frequently used applications	This is a list of common applications used on a daily basis by the majority of users in a given user class.	Understanding the most frequently used applications can help determine a candidate list for a given application virtualization (AppVirt) solution, for example, VMware ThinApp. The most frequently used application list might also be helpful to determine what applications will be included in a desktop pool's parent image.
Number of monitors	This is used to determine how many monitors a given user is using.	As supporting additional monitors will change the memory settings of the vDesktop (and all vDesktops in a given pool when using linked clones), it might be useful to separate multimonitor users from single-monitor users. With a growing number of environments, using two monitors is the standard, and four monitors is not abnormal. In this case, separating the four-monitor users may prove beneficial.
Unique peripheral requirements	It is used to determine potential compatibility issues with a Horizon View solution.	For example, a class of users might require the use of webcams for collaboration.

Metric	Input	Output
Unused applications	This is used to determine applications that are never or seldom used in a desktop environment.	For example, an environment might have several applications that are included in the current gold image. However, it might make sense to not include such applications in the base image for the View vDesktop deployments.
Graphics intensity	This is used to determine potential bottlenecks in the underlying storage environment supporting the VDI from a bandwidth perspective.	For example, it is used to determine which users might need additional hardware (for example, blade PC) to provide the level of graphics required by an end user. In some environments, a vDesktop will not be able to provide the level of graphics capabilities required by a class of users. In these environments, a solution that integrates a blade PC solution into a VDI (for example, a solution from ClearCube) will be ideal.

Why users per core?

Calculating users per core is more important than trying to determine the total number of MHz needed by a given user. The two key CPU-related metrics are CPU Ready and CPU Wait.

CPU Ready is the time in milliseconds that a machine spends waiting for a CPU to become available. If the design implements too many vDesktops per core, the end users will experience a high CPU Ready time and their vDesktops will be sluggish as they wait for one another to free up the CPU time for their own processing needs.

CPU Wait is the time in milliseconds that a CPU spends waiting for an I/O to complete. A high CPU Wait time is usually indicative of either a disk or a network bottleneck. For example, a particular vDesktop may be running a process that reads and writes a large amount of data to the local filesystem. If the underlying storage is unable to meet the performance needs of the vDesktop's process, a high CPU Wait time might be realized.

Discussion

When having your discussions, make sure to emphasize and reference how key business factors are paramount and influential in this process. The implementation should align with both business and users' needs and expectations.

Plan (define use cases)

Once sufficient data has been collected during the assessment phase, the data can be analyzed to determine the specific use cases.

A use case is a collection of connection, performance, peripherals, and other characteristics for a group of vDesktop users. It is important to use the data collected in the assessment phase as well as observations (if possible) of the users in action to determine the primary use cases for a given environment.

For example, through a diligent assessment phase consisting of 300 vDesktop users, the following might be determined:

- 50 require two monitors
- 25 have high performance needs that are fulfilled with two vCPUs and 6 GB of RAM
- 200 have average needs that are fulfilled with two vCPUs and 1.5 GB of RAM
- 25 require four monitors

If the design attempts to support all of the preceding requirements in a single desktop pool, the desktop pool will have support for four monitors and vDesktops with 6 GB of RAM. This type of design will lead to a waste of a lot of physical resources (for example, 4 GB of additional memory for 175 vDesktops, totaling 700 GB of waste).

Therefore, a proper design will be as follows:

- A desktop pool of 25 desktops based on a gold image of two vCPUs and 6 GB of RAM
- A desktop pool of 50 desktops supporting up to two monitors
- A desktop pool of 25 desktops supporting up to four monitors
- A desktop pool of 200 desktops supporting the bulk of the user environment, which is based on a gold image of two vCPUs and 1.5 GB of RAM

Some key questions that can help determine use cases are as follows:

- What are the minimum performance requirements needed to provide a favorable vDesktop experience?
- Are there bidirectional audio requirements?
- How many monitors must be supported?
- Will the desktops be disposable (nonpersistent)?
- How will the user profiles be managed (if applicable)?
- Are there any unique security or compliance needs?
- Are there special peripheral or I/O devices and physical connection requirements (USB dongles, special video cards, advanced biometrics authentication devices, point of sale hardware, and so on)?

By determining the various use cases supported by the VDI solution, the ultimate design doesn't only support the required use cases but also ensures that the underlying physical infrastructure is optimized.

At the end of the use case definition phase, the input required to design a solution has been collected, discussed with the organization, and agreed upon.

Design

A VDI solution builds on the complexity of a typical server virtualization solution by adding requirements for connection infrastructure, persona management (if applicable), desktop pool infrastructure, end devices, and so on, as shown in the following diagram, which shows the VMware View solution stack:

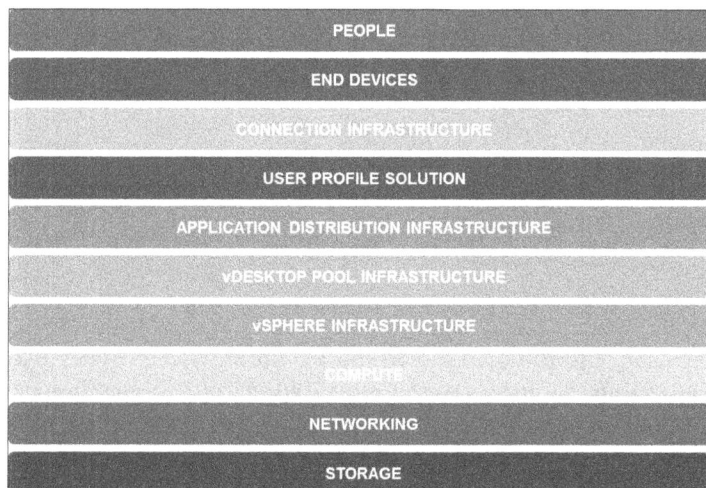

In addition, for experienced server virtualization architects, the requirements of a VDI solution are often significantly different (for example, the way a vSphere cluster may be designed), so it is important to respect the importance of a sound VMware vSphere design while recognizing the new implications of a View solution. For example, a VDI solution will most likely have greater virtual machine density than physical machine density when compared to a classic server virtualization solution. In addition, the compute and storage demands have higher peaks and shorter durations as opposed to a classic server virtualization solution.

While many of the following subsections (for example, storage and user persona management) will be covered in much greater detail later in this book, an overview of the methodology used for each design is briefly provided for each component in the following section.

Storage

Storage is an area of high impact in regards to the overall View solution. Without a properly designed storage infrastructure, the entire solution may ultimately fail. Again, this is an area where it is extremely important to establish a baseline for the existing environment, build a Proof-Of-Concept, and then run tests to validate your estimates for storage size and performance.

This book focuses primarily on View solutions that leverage the linked clone technology afforded by View Composer. In designs using linked clones, a single replica disk is used for all vDesktops in a given pool. Therefore, storage considerations, for example, read IOPSes are extremely important when designing the storage subsystem for a VDI solution.

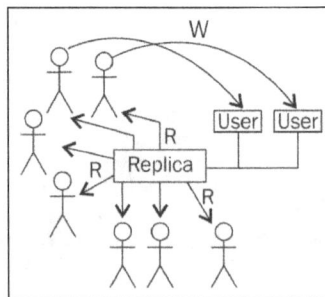

In the preceding diagram, the heavy read load is illustrated as every user in a given desktop pool is reading from the same replica disk. However, each user will write to his or her own OS disk (and persistent user data disk and/or nonpersistent temporary data disk, if applicable).

In addition, understanding the application environment of the end users is important as applications such as Nuance's Dragon Medical can place a heavy load on the disk when performing transcription tasks. For users that require heavy storage I/O, it is advised to place them in their own desktop pool:

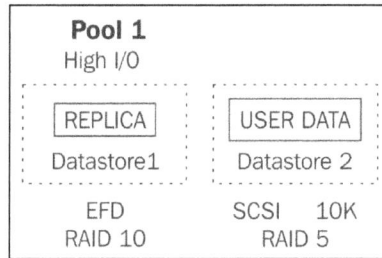

```
┌─────────────────────────────────────────┐
│  Pool 1                                  │
│  High I/O                                │
│                                          │
│  ┌ ─ ─ ─ ─ ─ ─ ┐   ┌ ─ ─ ─ ─ ─ ─ ─ ┐    │
│  : ┌─────────┐ :   : ┌───────────┐ :    │
│  : │ REPLICA │ :   : │ USER DATA │ :    │
│  : └─────────┘ :   : └───────────┘ :    │
│  :             :   :               :    │
│  :  Datastore1 :   :  Datastore 2  :    │
│  └ ─ ─ ─ ─ ─ ─ ┘   └ ─ ─ ─ ─ ─ ─ ─ ┘    │
│                                          │
│        EFD           SCSI    10K         │
│       RAID 10        RAID 5              │
└─────────────────────────────────────────┘
```

As shown in the preceding diagram, linked clones allow the use of storage tiering. In the preceding example, the replica disk (a high read I/O load) is placed on **Enterprise Flash Drives** (**EFDs**) protected with RAID 10. The user data virtual disks are placed on SCSI 10K drives protected with RAID 5. Linked clones allow the storage subsystem to be tailored economically, technically, and functionally, matching the needs of the VDI.

Isolation at the data store level

When designing a View solution, especially one leveraging linked clones, it is important to understand the inherent advantage of being able to separate desktop pools, user classes, and performance requirements on separate data stores.

In the following diagram, **Pool 1** supports heavy users requiring an I/O intensive application, **Pool 2** supports the general user population, and **Pool 3** supports kiosks for walk-in customers:

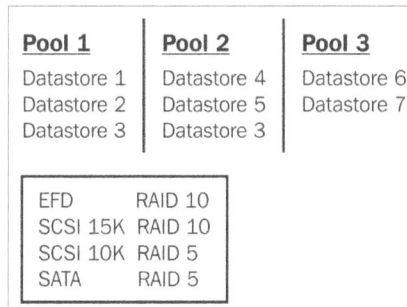

```
┌────────────────────────────────────────────────┐
│  Pool 1      │  Pool 2      │  Pool 3           │
│              │              │                   │
│  Datastore 1 │  Datastore 4 │  Datastore 6      │
│  Datastore 2 │  Datastore 5 │  Datastore 7      │
│  Datastore 3 │  Datastore 3 │                   │
│                                                 │
│  ┌──────────────────────────┐                   │
│  │ EFD       RAID 10        │                   │
│  │ SCSI 15K  RAID 10        │                   │
│  │ SCSI 10K  RAID 5         │                   │
│  │ SATA      RAID 5         │                   │
│  └──────────────────────────┘                   │
└────────────────────────────────────────────────┘
```

In Pool 1, for example, the replica disk can reside on performance optimized EFDs (extremely high IOPS supported) or SSD (solid state drives), with the user's write activity (for example, OS disk) occurring on SCSI 15K disks in a RAID 10 set (high IOPS supported), and the user's nonpersistent data residing on SATA RAID 5 (low IOPS supported) disks.

Furthermore, for Pool 2, the replica disks can reside on a separate EFD/SSD-based data store with the user's write activity occurring on a separate SCSI 10K RAID 5 data store. Pool 2 can also use the same data store for nonpersistent temporary data, if so desired.

Finally, Pool 3 can use separate data stores, as compared to Pool 1 and Pool 2, for its replica disks and user OS disks.

Why is isolation beneficial?

Isolation is beneficial for the following reasons:

- **Cost savings**: In this solution, an entire storage array doesn't need to be populated with expensive EFDs; instead, only enough EFDs need to be purchased to support the desired replica disks. On the contrary, for nonpersistent and performance-insensitive data, cheap SATA disks can be used.

- **Performance tuning**: In this solution, the appropriate technology (for example, EFD) is used to deliver an optimized end-user experience. By using tiered storage, the disk optimized for heavy I/O can be used when necessary, but it doesn't have to be used for all disk activities.

- **Performance segregation**: In this example, extremely heavy use (for example, login storm, application batch processing, and so on) in Pool 1 should not impact end users in Pool 2 (assuming that the storage array network is not a bottleneck). Therefore, high I/O users (for example, bidirectional audio physicians) can be separated and segregated from moderate I/O users (for example, administrative staff).

- **Service-level agreements**: In this example, each pool uses its own data store for replica disks. However, if each pool uses the same data store for its replica disks, it will be possible for the actions and activities in one desktop pool to impact another, making adhering and enforcing **service-level agreements (SLAs)** extremely difficult.

vStorage API for Array Integration (VAAI)

vStorage API for Array Integration (VAAI) is an application program interface framework that enables certain storage tasks, such as thin provisioning, to be offloaded from the host to the storage array. Offloading these tasks reduces the processing workload on the virtual server hardware. The manufacturer of the storage system must build support for VAAI into the storage system.

The most notable functionality addresses thin provisioning of storage systems and expands support to network-attached storage (NAS) devices. VAAI's thin provisioning enhancements allow storage arrays that use thin provisioning to reclaim blocks of space when virtual disks are deleted, to mitigate the risk of a thinly provisioned storage array running out of space.

View Storage Accelerator

VMware View Storage Accelerator (formerly known as **Content Based Read Cache**) optimizes storage loads and improves performance by caching the common image blocks when reading the virtual desktop images, which helps reduce the overall total cost of ownership in View deployments. The storage accelerator is an in-memory (ESXi Server Memory) cache of common blocks. It works with stateless (nonpersistent) and stateful (persistent) desktops, and it is completely transparent to the guest virtual desktops.

Since the cache can handle peak read workloads, it is configured for the steady state workloads rather than the peak workloads. This reduces the cost of VDI deployment by decreasing the amount of storage that customers need to buy to address peak workloads. It improves the end user experience, creates faster boot times, improves application performance, and can reduce network bandwidth. It does not require any special storage array technology and provides additional performance benefits when used in conjunction with other storage array technologies.

Networking

There are several core networking components that must be considered when designing VDIs, **Dynamic Host Configuration Protocol** (DHCP) leases, **Domain Name System** (DNS) resolutions, load balancing solutions, and virtual switch technologies. This is addressed in detail later in this book, but it is worth noting that engaging the organization's network team early in the conversation is highly recommended.

Compute

As addressed earlier in this chapter, users per core are the primary measurement of consideration in the compute layer of a View solution. With an ever-increasing processing power and processing density becoming available, compute is becoming a layer that requires less attention, especially when using processors with six or more cores.

VMware vSphere and View desktop pool infrastructure

As discussed in more detail later in this book, a sound VMware vSphere infrastructure is extremely important to a robust View solution. For seasoned vSphere architects, many of the concepts of a sound vSphere infrastructure will be familiar and practiced. However, View solutions will likely exceed some of the maximums allowed, as defined by VMware.

For example, in the current version of VMware vCenter, the maximum number of powered-on virtual machines is 10,000. In some large-scale VDI implementations, this number will easily be surpassed. Regardless, it is important to understand that 10,000 vDesktops may not be an acceptable notion from the management's perspective. This book will cover how to properly design a VMware vSphere infrastructure for large-scale View solutions.

Pod architecture

As mentioned earlier, View solutions might exceed the maximum allowed by VMware vSphere, the underlying virtual infrastructure platform. As such, collections of VMware vSphere environments, called pods, are used to provide modular building blocks for the VDI. A **pod** is a collection of physical servers running VMware ESX, one or more VMware vCenter Servers, and the supporting storage and networking infrastructure to provide *n* number of vDesktops. This number will vary with design, unique customer requirements, and the data gathered during the assessment phase.

In the following diagram, the pod consists of a VMware vCenter environment managing two clusters of eight hosts per cluster:

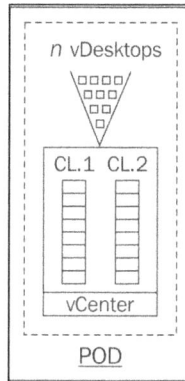

Application distribution infrastructure

Whether VMware ThinApp, Citrix XenApp, Microsoft App-V, Horizon Hosted Apps (now in View 6), or another solution is used to deliver applications to the desktops in an environment, understanding where the environment is located, how it is used, and its impact on the overall solution (for example, network implications) is important. This book will cover the key concepts of application virtualization as it relates to a View solution. However, this book does not dive deep into the technical components of application virtualization.

What is a user persona?

A **user persona** is a collection of settings, favorites, shortcuts, wallpapers, customizations, desktop icons, printers, and other settings unique to a given user.

As illustrated previously, vDesktop is composed of three abstract layers. These layers are OS, APPS, and Persona.

The OS layer is the execution environment for the vDesktops. This is primarily either Microsoft Windows 7 (or planned to be Microsoft Windows 8) with some legacy Microsoft Windows XP.

The APPS (applications) layer can either be a separate layer by using an application virtualization solution (for example, VMware ThinApp) or can be included inside the OS layer, as shown:

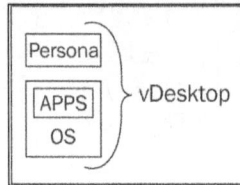

In the preceding diagram, the APPS layer is not separate and is instead nested within the OS layer. This means that to update a single application for a desktop pool, the entire parent image must be updated:

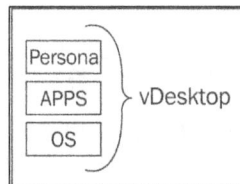

In the preceding diagram, the APPS layer is independent of the OS layer, and it thus can be updated independently. This allows administrators to update a single application without massive changes to the composition of a View desktop pool. In most instances, there are strong advantages to using an AppVirt solution for some or all of the applications for the VDI. The user base and performance characteristics of the applications might play a part in your overall decision on how you decide to deliver your applications.

VMware's Horizon Mirage is a solution that provides centralized image management for your Windows desktops/laptops (endpoints) with advanced levels of backup and operation system migration capabilities. While Horizon View is used to build out the virtual desktop infrastructure, Mirage can manage the content that resides inside the endpoints (OS, applications, and user profiles and settings). So, it makes a great deal of sense to manage View desktops with Mirage. This gives a single desktop management solution for both physical and virtual desktop environments.

The book *VMware Horizon Mirage Essentials, Packt Publishing*, can be found at http://www.packtpub.com/vmware-horizon-mirage-essentials/book.

User persona management

There are many options, such as Microsoft Folder Redirection, User State Migration Tool, Liquidware Labs ProfileUnity, and AppSense, when it comes to managing the user persona in a VDI solution.

VMware's acquisition of **RTO** now provides an integrated persona management solution with View. User persona management will be addressed later in this book as it is important to understand how they integrate (especially) in a nonpersistent desktop pool as well as potential network implications that user profiles may add.

Connection infrastructure

The connection infrastructure includes brokers or View Connection Servers, an optional load balancer, an optional WAN optimizer, a DNS solution, and any advanced routing capabilities (for example, **Cisco Global Site Selector**).

In most cases, incoming connections will initially route to a View Connection Server. Normally, it makes sense to keep at least one View Connection Server available to end users at all times. One of the useful features of VMware Horizon View (since 5.3) is the ability for a View Client to connect directly to a Horizon View desktop without going through the View Connection Server. The **View Agent Direct-Connection Plugin** enables some new possibilities and flexibilities in the way that Horizon View desktops can be used, as follows:

- **DaaS**: These are multitenant **Desktop-as-a-Service** (**DaaS**) deployments used with Horizon DaaS

- **Branch offices**: These are where VMware vSphere hosts running View desktops are deployed

- **Brokerless Horizon View desktops**: These are simple deployments where full brokering from a Connection Server is not needed

Once a connection has been successfully authenticated, the View Client directly connects to the View Agent within the vDesktop; this is referred to as a **direct connection**. For direct connections, a failure of the View Connection Server once a user has already connected to their desktop does not impact existing connections. However, it does impact future connection requests.

It is possible to use the Microsoft RDP protocol with View. Microsoft RDP uses a tunneled connection. This tunneled connection opens a second HTTPS connection with the View Connection Server or View Security Server. In this scenario, the failure of the View Connection Server or View Security Server providing the secondary HTTPS connection will cause the end user to be disconnected.

End devices

As detailed later in this book, there are various end devices that offer various benefits (and trade-offs). It's important to understand the multitude of devices available in the market to understand how they are incorporated into a View solution. This book will cover the major categories of end devices, including thick clients, thin clients, zero clients, Apple iPads, Chrome Books, and forward-looking end devices.

People (the end user experience)

People is the one of the most important layers of any VDI solution. It is important for the VDI architect to always understand that a project's success will very likely be measured by the people using the solution, their experiences, their perceptions, and their transitions to a vDesktop environment.

Not keeping the end user experience at the forefront of the solution can have catastrophic consequences. Everything from end devices to desktop pool configuration should be chosen with the happiness of the end user in mind.

Keeping the end user happy is a major concern, but do not forget that the VDI solution must meet the needs of the business too.

Pilot and validate

Once a design has been formulated, vetted, and approved, then comes the time to validate the solution. Validation is normally performed on a representative subset of the full-scale solution. For example, in a solution that leverages two fully populated HP c7000 Blade chassis, a single half-populated chassis may be used to test the provisioning, basic functionality, and underlying storage performance. In some scenarios, disposable hardware is used simply to test the software components.

Leveraging an economically scalable hardware platform, such as the Nutanix converged virtualization appliance (http://www.nutanix.com/) or Pivot3 vSTAC (http://pivot3.com/), can help both prove out the design with a low cost of entry as well as support a production solution in the future.

One of the best ways of validating a solution is to build a pilot environment according to the specifications detailed in the design document. Once the pilot environment is built, a pilot group of users can be enrolled to test user experience, functionality, and apply a load on the underlying hardware.

The VMware View Planner tool (formerly VMware RAWC)

The **VMware View Planner** tool, formerly known as the **Reference Architecture Workload Simulator (RAWC)** tool, is the best way to simulate end user connections and activity in a View environment. For organizations looking to stress test VMware and competing solutions side by side, the **Login VSI** tool (http://www.loginvsi.com/) will support comparison testing. The VMware View Planner tool is for View environments only.

The VMware View Planner tool comprises the following:

- **Session launcher virtual machine**: This virtual machine launches the actual vDesktop sessions. Each session launcher virtual machine can support up to 20 concurrent sessions.

- **Controller virtual machine**: This virtual machine hosts the View Planner interface and the network share for the configuration and logfiles.

- **Target vDesktops**: The vDesktops used for stress testing have the View Planner code residing on each of the vDesktops (or as part of the parent image).

- **E-mail server virtual machine (optional)**: This virtual machine is only necessary if Microsoft Outlook is used as part of the View Planner testing and there is no Microsoft Exchange Server available for testing purposes.

View Planner can be tailored to perform end user tasks using the following applications:

- **Microsoft Word**: This is used to insert text, save modifications, resize window, and close application.

- **Microsoft Excel**: This is used to insert numbers, insert and delete columns and rows, copy and paste formulae, save modifications, resize windows, and close applications.

- **Microsoft PowerPoint**: This is used to open a presentation, conduct a slideshow presentation, resize a window, and close applications.

- **Microsoft Outlook**: This is used to set up a mailbox, send e-mails, resize windows, and close applications.

- **Internet Explorer**: This is used to browse a web page, resize windows, and close applications.

- **Windows Media Player**: This is used to view a video and close applications.

- **Adobe Acrobat Reader**: This is used to open a PDF document, scroll through the document, resize windows, and close applications.

- **Java Runtime**: This is used to run a Java application and close applications.

- **McAfee AntiVirus**: This is used to execute a real-time virus scan and close applications.

- **7-Zip**: This is used to compress files and close applications.

With this extensive list of capabilities, a variety of tests can be executed to test the overall VDI performance, login storms, boot storms, storage performance, and so on.

> **Boot storm versus login storm**
>
> When researching, designing, discussing, and planning the VDI solutions, the terms **boot storm** and **login storm** will appear often; however, the two terms cannot be used interchangeably.
>
> A boot storm is a significant enough number of vDesktops booting (or resuming from a suspension) to cause a decrease in the overall VDI performance. This can be caused due to one or more data stores that are unable to handle the I/O load, a file lock conflict with too many vDesktops/data stores, a DHCP lease request flood, and so on.
>
> A login storm occurs when a significant number of end users log in to the vDesktops, causing a decrease in the overall VDI performance. This can be caused due to creating initial profiles, streaming a user's persona, slow Active Directory performance, misaligned disks (for example, Windows XP without the proper offset), and so on.

Using RAWC in conjunction with a monitoring solution, such as Liquidware Labs Stratusphere UX (User Experience) or RTO PinPoint, can allow a VMware View architect to identify bottlenecks during the validation phase instead of during the implementation phase.

Comparing storage platforms

As RAWC View Planner provides a scientific approach to testing a canned (or random) series of tailored tests, the tests can become the control in an experiment where the storage platform is the variable.

For example, if the true advantages of EFD in an RAID 10 (over SCSI 15K RAID 10) are needed to be quantified, a saved RAWC test can be run against a desktop pool using EFD in the first iteration and SCSI 15K in the second iteration.

This technique can be used not only to test, quantify, and optimize a storage array and its configuration, but also to compare the storage arrays from multiple vendors.

Many thanks to Fred Schmischeimer, for all his help with the RAWC tool and information guide and Workload Considerations for Virtual Desktop Reference Architectures.

Implementation

A successful implementation depends on a well thought out and tested design. The implementation phase should begin after the design and pilot cycles. After the initial design, the pilot can expose flaws that require changes in the design, and then, the pilot should prove out the changes. Only after the cycle is complete, the project should move to the implementation phase.

User migration

The user profile migration phase turns out to be one of the most critical and sensitive activities in VDI projects. A good migration plan must be strategized to provide a seamless user migration of data and profiles. In this phase, moving user information from existing physical desktops to virtual desktops might be an opportunity to use third-party tools.

Hand-off and manage

After the completion of successful implementation and user migration, the next phase is to monitor and manage the new VDI environment. This is a critical stage to ensure user satisfaction and increase productivity. The operational performance should be monitored and maintained to ensure high service uptime and avoid costs associated with downtime. This will be an ongoing phase, and it involves maintenance of the user profile, desktop pools, user entitlements, and access. This is where the process of keeping the desktop images updated will also occur. The organization must identify the right level of skills and efficient processes, and it can decide to use automated tools for an efficient management of the VDI environment.

Summary

The VDI solution design is complex; by taking a measured approach that involves hard data (metric collection), organizational input (questionnaire), and technical expertise, the chances of a suitable design increase drastically. This chapter discussed the layers involved in a View solution, some of the pitfalls to watch out for, and some of the industry tools to use to help support the overall design and validation process.

The next chapter discusses one of the most important design considerations a VDI architect can make: persistent or nonpersistent. The answer to this is the cornerstone of the View design, and as such, it needs to be fully understood to ensure the best possible design outcome.

3
Persistent or Nonpersistent vDesktops

One of the most fundamental decisions that must be made early in the design process is whether to use persistent or nonpersistent vDesktops. This decision of the vDesktop type may impact many areas of the overall VDI, including storage, desktop pools, and management.

In this chapter, we will cover the following topics:

- Persistent desktops
- Nonpersistent desktops
- Multisite solutions
- The best choice for your organization

Persistent desktops

A **persistent desktop** is a vDesktop that is assigned to a specific end user and whose state is saved after they log off:

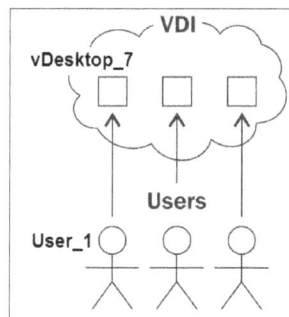

For example, in the preceding figure, if User_1 signs in to a View environment for the first time and is automatically assigned vDesktop_7, they would connect to vDesktop_7 today, tomorrow, and until the assignment is removed. If vDesktop_7 has an issue and is unavailable, User_1 will not have a functioning work environment and will be unable to be productive.

When using persistent desktops, View does not automatically reassign the end user to an available vDesktop if their assigned vDesktop is unavailable.

A persistent vDesktop has persistent data until:

- The vDesktop is unassigned from the specific user
- The desktop pool that the vDesktop is a member of is refreshed (linked clones), unless you are using a persistent disk to preserve the Profile and AppData information
- The desktop pool that the vDesktop is a member of is recomposed (linked clones)

Historically, persistent vDesktops that have been used in VDI implementations as persistent vDesktops mostly resemble the physical world, and allow both end users and IT administrators to be able to relate to the virtual world. This 1:1 relationship (that of an end user to a vDesktop) is likely the most simplified deployment option available, but its design and cost considerations should be properly understood.

Persistent vDesktops are often the easier political sale to an organization, as each user still maintains possession of an individual (virtual) desktop asset. The following table explains areas related to the persistent vDesktops:

Area	Implications
Desktop pool sizing	This requires a vDesktop for every end user.
Availability	If a user's assigned vDesktop is unavailable, the user is unable to connect.
Recoverability — OS failure	VMware HA can be used to monitor a vDesktop's response to a *heartbeat*. If a vDesktop does not respond, it can be automatically restarted by VMware vSphere.
Recoverability — site failure	There is no easy way to recover from a site failure. There are third-party options such as **ByteLife** that can help with this issue (`http://www.bytelife.com/`).
Cost	The VDI must support vDesktops for the entire target user population; this includes compute and storage requirements (storage requirements may be higher as well).

Example scenario

For this example, consider that Customer_A has 6,000 end users. They are targeting to move to a View solution. Customer_A operates three shifts a day with 2,000 end users working at any given time.

The customer has asked for help in scoping the hardware required for the solution (for example, in the form of a bill or a list of materials).

The platform will be Windows 7, with one vCPU, 2 GB of RAM, and a 50 GB C:\.

The hardware platform is determined to consist of 2U servers with two 6-core processors per server (a total of 12 cores per server).

Using an average and a conservative estimate of 10 VMs per core yields 120 vDesktops per server. Using 2 GB of RAM per vDesktop, 240 GB of RAM would be required to support 120 vDesktops. Adding in RAM for overhead and for amounts that can be easily ordered from any vendor rounds up 240 GB of RAM to 256 GB of RAM per server.

Therefore, the server specification used for this solution includes a 2U server with two 6-core processors and 256 GB of RAM. The following table explains the server specifications and the costs related to the persistent vDesktop:

Area	Description
Physical server specification	A 2U server with two 6-core processors and 256 GB of RAM
Number of vDesktops/physical servers	120
Total end user population	6,000
Total number of end users that require a vDesktop at any given time	2,000
Total number of vDesktops that must be provisioned and be made available	6,000
Total number of physical servers required without *n + 1* considerations	50
Estimated number of racks required	3
Cost per individual physical server	$40,000
Subtotal for physical server costs	$2,000,000

Area	Description
Total number of processors	100
Estimated cost of VMware View licenses per vDesktop	$250
Subtotal for VMware View licensing	$1,500,000
Total cost	$3,500,000

Even though Customer_A only has 2,000 end users online at any given time, the fact that Customer_A has 6,000 unique end users indicates that to support this environment with persistent vDesktops, the VDI must have 6,000 vDesktops. It is possible to use extremely strict timeout values and logoff parameters to decrease the total number of supported vDesktops (perhaps from 6,000 to 5,000), but it does add risk to the overall solution and may or may not be feasible in a given environment.

Using rough estimates of $40,000 per physical server, the estimated total cost, including server costs and rough estimates for VMware vSphere and VMware View Standard, is $3,500,000. You could use a concurrent license to save the cost, but for now, we are using a named user.

This estimate does not include costs for the additional ports needed for this configuration. For example, if each server required only two network connections (for example, using **10GbE**), then an additional of 99 switch ports would be required for the production network connections and a single out-of-band management connection (for example, HP iLO).

This estimate also does not include financial considerations for cooling and power costs associated with the servers along with the cost of the storage to have all the desktops running.

Operationally, it's also harder to manage from the perspective of human resources. As people leave and enter the company, vDesktop sprawl could potentially eat up resources as there is no easy way to track and maintain the user data disks in conjunction with user accounts.

A final consideration is the amount of physical U-space the persistent solution requires. For environments that require minimal footprint (for example, tactical installation), every U is of significance.

There might be additional ways to configure the solution, but the point to be made is that persistent desktops can be an inefficient solution for most environments, especially those of a significant scale.

Nonpersistent desktops

A **nonpersistent desktop** is a vDesktop that is not assigned to a specific end user, and instead, is made available to the end user population.

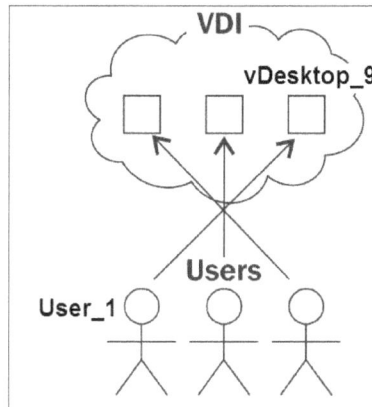

For example, in the preceding figure, if User_1 signs in to a View environment, they are assigned one of the available vDesktops (for example, vDesktop_9). When they log off and then log back in to the View environment, they are randomly assigned another available vDesktop from the pool.

A vDesktop may only have a maximum of one owner at any given time.

There are several settings that can be manipulated from the **View Admin** console that dictate how fast a nonpersistent vDesktop is unassigned from a user that executes a disconnect command (this is different from logging off).

Nonpersistent vDesktop solutions are starting to become more common as the VDI is not only adopted more within the industry but also implemented at a larger scale. As persistent vDesktops often require vast amounts of additional resources, including technical, human, and financial, this book will focus primarily on solutions leveraging on nonpersistent vDesktops.

While persistent vDesktops are still what most people think of when they think of VDI, it's important to demonstrate the advantages and cost savings realized by leveraging a nonpersistent solution, or in most cases, a hybrid solution that contains both persistent and nonpersistent desktops. This creates the right solution for the right reason.

VDI is less about ownership of a particular virtual machine in the data center and more about the availability of a desktop resource when needed, which is customized for the user (via that user's specific profile). While there are plenty of solutions that do not require customization of the vDesktop (for example, a kiosk solution in a hotel), a large percentage of VDI implementations will be for unique users with potentially unique desktops in an organization. The following table explains the areas related to the nonpersistent vDesktops:

Area	Implications
Desktop pool sizing	This requires a vDesktop for the maximum number of concurrent users.
Availability	A user will be able to connect to a vDesktop as long as there is an available vDesktop in the pool.
Recoverability — OS failure	A user will be able to connect to a vDesktop as long as there is an available vDesktop in the pool.
Recoverability — site failure	While it isn't still out of the box to recover from a site failure, a nonpersistent vDesktop forces the user's persona to live outside the vDesktop, thereby making the replication and recovery of a viable vDesktop environment much easier (there are third-party options such as ByteLife that can help).
Cost	The VDI must support vDesktops for the maximum target concurrent users; this includes compute and storage requirements for peak load and not for theoretical maximum users based on the total number of users.

Example scenario

To continue from the example earlier in this chapter, Customer_A has 6,000 end users. They are targeting to move to a View solution. Customer_A operates three shifts a day, with 2,000 end users working at any given time. The following table explains the server specifications and the costs related to the nonpersistent vDesktops:

Area	Description
Physical server specification	A 2U server with two 6-core processors and 256 GB of RAM
Number of vDesktops per physical server	120
Total end user population	6,000
Total number of end users that require a vDesktop at any given time	2,000

Area	Description
Recoverability — site failure	2,000
Total number of physical servers required without *n + 1* considerations	17
Estimated number of racks required	1
Cost per individual physical server	$40,000
Subtotal for physical server costs	$680,000
Total number of processors	34
Estimated VMware View Standard per vDesktop	$250
Subtotal for VMware View licensing	$500,000
Total cost	$1,180,000

The advantages of a nonpersistent solution are clearly evident. For example, in a persistent solution, 50 physical servers were required (versus 17 in a nonpersistent solution) to meet the demands of the user load. By saving a significant number of physical servers from being procured (and the associated software licensing), the overall VDI solution requires one-third less of funding. These savings come from having to support only the maximum concurrent user load instead of having a named vDesktop for every user that will connect to the VDI.

Notes and considerations for nonpersistent vDesktops

A nonpersistent vDesktop solution should be viewed as volatile. It means that when a user logs off, anything written to the local disk of the vDesktop will be inaccessible or even destroyed.

As such, for solutions that require a user to maintain a profile, custom applications, unique device mappings, and so on, a persona management and application management solution will need to be used as part of the overall VDI. Also, solutions that pertain to record retention, disposition, data retention policies/compliance, DLP, data governance, IS, and forensic implications may exist in that nonpersistent context and may need to be addressed.

Another potential benefit of nonpersistent vDesktops, if designed correctly, is that they can potentially reduce the number of help desk calls. This is because the solution focuses less on the availability of an individual's vDesktop and more on the availability of a set number of vDesktop resources available in a pool.

With an emphasis placed on desktop pool health (and likely user persona health), there's less worrying about a specific user's vDesktop as resources are assigned randomly at login for each end user. The nonpersistent desktop can also address benefits on the information security side as it fixes malware infections, resolves program malfunctions, and makes local data corruption issues easier.

The potential drawback is that there could be an increase in support of the persona management layer, depending on the solution chosen, its design, and implementation.

Multisite solutions

A View solution that spans multiple sites is fairly typical. College campuses, large corporations, and even small businesses, may have requirements to deliver vDesktops from more than one physical location.

In these scenarios, there are a few qualifying questions to ask the organization. They are as follows:

- Should the desktop experience be unique for each end user?

  Essentially, should end user persona be saved to include changes to the desktop environment, customizations to applications, and so on?

- If the answer to the preceding question is a yes, should the user persona be consistent across all the sites?

  For example, if Liliana logs in to Site_A and makes modifications to her desktop, should those settings be reflected if Liliana were to log in to the VDI at Site_B?

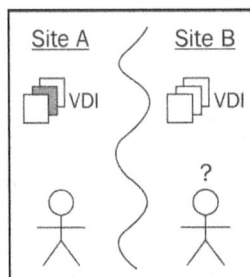

The preceding figure shows a multisite VDI with View persistent vDesktops, and it is based on a real-world scenario. In this example, Site_A and Site_B are owned by the same organization, **Acme Corp**. Acme must support worker mobility as two of their locations (Site_A and Site_B) are used by their entire workforce.

A user could be working at Site_A in the morning and then at Site_B in the afternoon for meetings.

The user, as shown in the preceding diagram, connects to the VDI in Site_A in the morning, and as persistent vDesktops are being used, they get their assigned vDesktop. Remember, when using persistent vDesktops, a user is assigned a specific vDesktop and will keep this assignment until unassigned by the View administrator.

When the user leaves Site_A and drives over to Site_B, the following two cases are possible:

- They do not have a vDesktop assigned
- They have a second vDesktop assigned in the completely independent VDI running at Site_B

Why isn't the user's vDesktop in Site_A copied to Site_B? This is because View persistent vDesktops are independent virtual machines assigned to an individual user.

If we are using View persistent vDesktops, replicating the changes to a peer persistent vDesktop in one site (for example, Site_A) to another site (for example, Site_B) is not an out-of-the-box supported use case. Making persistent View vDesktops to behave in such a manner would require the following:

- Significant scripting
- A deep understanding of the underlying storage platform
- A deep understanding of the View **ADAM database**
- An understanding of how to manipulate objects using PowerCLI

It would also add too many variables to make it a sustainable VDI model to have proper support.

The user could connect their desktop in Site A via WAN, for example, using a global load balancing solution. This would be an additional cost for the company. The point is that there could be several solutions possible with View, given enough time, a deep knowledge of vSphere and View, and ample time to test. However, View was not designed to support multisite-persistent vDesktops.

Third-party add-on solutions (for example, Unidesk, `http://www.unidesk.com`) are potentially helpful in these scenarios.

Why is a nonpersistent vDesktop best for a multisite?

The following figure shows a multisite VDI with nonpersistent View vDesktops and persona replication:

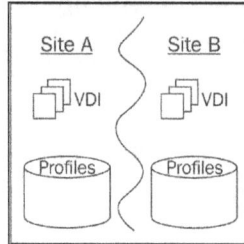

Imagine the same scenario that we previously mentioned. An organization has two sites, Site_A and Site_B. A user works at Site_A in the morning, connects to their vDesktop running on the VDI in Site_A, and then heads to Site_B for afternoon meetings. When at Site_B, the user connects to the VDI local to that site.

How can the VDI architect make the VDI experience consistent across both sites?

By using nonpersistent vDesktops, the user's persona is naturally separated from the underlying desktop operating environment. By using the View profile management, or a third-party solution such as AppSense or Liquidware Labs ProfileUnity, a nonpersistent vDesktop can have the same look and feel of a persistent desktop (for example, customizations are retained) and yet offer the advantages of nonpersistent vDesktops (for example, greater flexibility).

In the preceding figure, the user profiles are stored on a file share system that is replicated between the two sites.

> This could add other problems such as making sure the user connects only to one site at a time. If this is not enforced, replication errors and profile inconsistencies could occur if the user is logged in to both sites at the same time.

It does not matter which site's VDI the end user connects to, as long as their profile has been replicated. If a nonpersistent vDesktop solution with replicated profiles is implemented, it is important to ensure that there are no unnecessary files in the user persona. Proper filtering techniques (within the persona management solution) can ensure that gigabytes of MP3 songs or downloaded movies are not considered as part of the user's persona, and prevent them from congesting the replication transmission.

Replication (why distance and size matters)

Replication is a function of physics. The size (throughput), speed (latency), and integrity (dropped packets) of the connection between sites as well as the amount of data that needs to be replicated help determine the total time required to replicate a set of profiles. If the goal is for users to not notice any difference when they log in to Site_A or Site_B, the replicated copy of a given user's persona will have to be ensured.

This guarantee can only be provided if the underlying network, storage, and replication solution can meet the requirements.

Typically, the closer the two sites and the smaller the replication dataset, the easier it is to meet these requirements.

Nevertheless, if a multisite VDI solution is to be implemented, it is important to perform an adequate network survey to recognize any potential hurdles before an actual implementation begins.

Profiles in the cloud

Multisite VDI solutions with local copies of the user profile are likely the most common types of multisite VDI solutions. This is because the technologies are likely to be already known by the VDI architect, and the supporting technical personnel are also familiar with similar solutions, even if not related to VDI at least.

However, should there be a disruption or congestion in replication, it is possible for a user to log in to a site and not have their latest user persona. Even worse, it is possible to end up in a split-brain scenario, where changes are lost or corrupted because two master copies of the user persona now exist.

While this is rare and can be combated by proper replication design and monitoring of replication health, it is still possible.

Another type of multisite VDI solution still leverages nonpersistent View vDesktops and persona management, but instead of storing local replicated copies of the user personas, they are stored in the cloud.

The following figure shows a multisite VDI with the nonpersistent View vDesktops and the cloud-based persona storage:

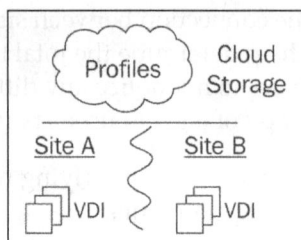

A **cloud**, in this sense, is any external storage platform that maintains the user profiles. This could be a VMware cloud solution, a local cloud provider, or a peer's community cloud offering, just to name a few.

In this scenario, there is no cross-site replication because the user profiles are always read and written to the cloud-based storage platform.

The advantage is that replication issues are no longer a concern, but the drawback is that a connection to the cloud (Internet, VPN, and so on) is required to load a user's profile. A lack of connectivity to the cloud storage means that user profiles cannot be read or saved. Check to make sure that it is within the company policy to have any sensitive user data saved in the cloud.

In addition, most cloud providers charge a fee for inbound and/or outbound traffic. Exceptions to this rule (for example, **Amazon Direct Connect**) do exist; however, they may come into play while deciding on a hosting partner.

A hybrid solution – persistent mixed with nonpersistent

Often, the first VDI use case at an organization will be clearly persistent or nonpersistent; as the VDI adoption increases, so does the amount of use cases that need to be supported.

For example, an organization can initially implement a View solution to support their 250-seat classroom environment. This is likely a nonpersistent solution. However, after seeing the benefits of View for its classroom, the organization may decide to roll out VDI on a larger scale. Now, instead of just supporting classrooms, the executive team has decided to adopt VDI to support its mobile lifestyle. In addition, the CEO has demanded that he needs to be able to use VDI from his Apple iPad.

In these types of situations, persistent vDesktops can make life a bit easier. There aren't any user profiles to worry about, per se, and the application distribution is conceptually the same as it is in the physical world. It may also be the easiest way to troubleshoot for the executive team, as you know which executive has which desktop quite easily.

View natively supports the ability to have both persistent and nonpersistent desktop pools side by side. There are no real design considerations to be made other than those found in their respective solutions. Profile management can be applied across nonpersistent and persistent vDesktops uniformly. One point of consideration is that in the preceding example of a classroom and an executive team, there may be different support personnel responsible for each group. If that is indeed the case, then the appropriate permissions will need to be defined in the View Admin console.

Choosing the right solution

Fortunately, with View, both persistent and nonpersistent vDesktops can be tested side by side, to see what works best with an organization's requirements. However, when designing a solution for an organization, some guidelines must be followed to help choose between persistent or nonpersistent vDesktops. The following are some questions with their suggested (not necessarily only) solution type. The suggestions assume that you will answer *yes* to the questions:

- Will users be installing their own native applications or a third-party solution? Persistent.
- Does the environment support a large percentage of shift workers? Nonpersistent.
- Will application virtualization be used? Nonpersistent.
- Will a roaming profile solution be used? Nonpersistent.
- Should the solution support a disaster-recovery event? Nonpersistent.
- Will users be assigned their own specific desktop for an application or operating system licensing restrictions? Persistent.
- Do record retention policies apply to local data in the organization? Persistent.

These high-level questions will help the architect steer the solution in the proper direction. It is important to keep in mind that the preceding suggestions are not steadfast answers. Finally, it is important to remember that almost all solutions will most likely have a need for persistent and nonpersistent solutions to cohabit in the same View environment.

Knowing your end users

You need to spend the time up-front to understand your end users. How many total virtual desktops are planned? What kind of endpoints are your users accessing their virtual desktop on? These are just a few questions that you need to know the answers to, before you decide which type of virtual desktop you are going to deploy.

Many POC/pilot programs start off with about 50 percent persistent and 50 percent nonpersistent desktop deployment. Your persistent desktops should be deployed to your power users, C-level executives, and other users that use the desktop in this manner. Your nonpersistent desktops will be deployed to the users who need or want less customization and are your typical daily workers. The last thing you need is your C-level executives dealing with "roaming" profile issues while accessing their desktops from various endpoints and locations. An executive should not feel like they are on a virtual machine at all; they need to feel like they are on their desktop and all of their customizations such as shortcuts, backgrounds, OS, and applications are consistent.

If you are in an education area or a call center, you want to be 100 percent nonpersistent as possible. You don't want changes made by the users left behind when they log off at the end of their session. If you are the IT administrator at a law office, you want to have 100 percent persistent desktops. You want each of the attorneys and/or partners to have all of their applications and personalization consistent in order to have the least distraction for their work environment. Anyone who makes profile changes in an almost-hourly basis should be considered a good persistent candidate. Most of the time, you would deploy a heterogeneous mix of persistent and nonpersistent desktops between the different types of users based on their working arrangements. I believe that most solutions will be a heterogeneous mix and is the most commonly deployed.

A note about applications

For the virtual desktop, alternative apps are generally deployed in one of the following two ways:

- Streamed to the desktop
- Included in the base image

For streaming, organizations generally use App-V or ThinApp. XenApp can also be used as well to provide applications to physical and VDI desktops.

With App-V, you have servers that stream virtualized applications to desktops. The desktop has a client with a large cache. The whole application is loaded at runtime or you can pre-cache the application to the desktops. The App-V concept of *sequencing* an application is where it figures out the files that are needed first when you run the application. Then, it streams those to the desktop first so that when the application is requested, the launch times are faster. App-V has a new feature called **Shared Content Store** (`http://blogs.technet.com/b/appv/archive/2013/07/22/shared-content-store-in-microsoft-app-v-5-0-behind-the-scenes.aspx`). This solution is explicitly developed to support RDSH and VDI scenarios.

ThinApp works slightly differently, in that it encapsulates the streaming file into an executable file that can be either executed from a file server or copied locally to the desktop and run.

These products isolate the applications from each other by default, which allows you to run conflicting applications side by side. If you want applications to integrate with each other, you have to know in advance and design it in the build. Another benefit of app streaming is that it provides dynamic assignment of applications to users as they log on. This allows the desktops to be generic with customization on logon.

There are applications that you will have to build into your base image because you won't be able to virtualize them. This indicates that as not all applications will be used by all users, you will have to build different images for different groups that require the different applications. Then, the issue is that you have to manage and patch many images that have lots of overlaps in the applications the users have installed.

If the solution calls for a persistent desktop, look for VMware Horizon Mirage to provide application layers to the desktop. This layering solution allows applications to be sent to the desktop, independent of the operating system, yet become fully integrated at the endpoint.

The applications you need for your VDI environment could also drive the type of desktop to provide a good understanding of the users' needs, and the application delivery methods will help provide a successful VDI implementation. Always remember to consider the licensing issues around application deployments.

The pros and cons of both persistent and nonpersistent desktops

The following are the pros and cons of persistent desktops:

- What you do from one session to the next stays with the user
- They can become a possible administrative nightmare to manage
- The amount of disk space needed to maintain these types of desktops will grow and performance can be an issue
- Updates and patching are needed for each image, which can lead to a lot of support hours

The following are the pros and cons of nonpersistent desktops:

- Patches and upgrades are easily applied to fewer images
- They reduce the amount of time IT spends on management
- They ensure that the profile changes are synced in a timely manner between the multiple user sessions
- Without a good profile-management tool, the time it takes to log on will gradually increase because of the number of changes that happen in each user's profile

Summary

The question of vDesktop type is one of the cornerstone decisions of any VDI design. The vDesktop type defines how volatile the vDesktops may be, how applications may be distributed, and the amount of underlying hardware required. For VDI architects, it is important to build a portfolio of proven designs. VDI is a complicated technology as there are a lot of moving parts. Reducing the number of variables for each project is important and this can be done by building some loose parameters. The following is an example mission statement taken from a real-world scenario:

I'm the Director of IT for Acme and I have a 2,000-seat classroom environment I need to support, with frequent turnover.

A VDI architect's formula in this scenario may be as follows: *View nonpersistent vDesktops + VMware ThinApp + zero clients.*

By already having an idea of what the solution should look like, the architect can focus on some of the key variables:

- How large is the desktop image?
- How will the applications be managed?

Building a View solution from scratch for every project is not efficient and more error-prone than building a stable one from a few solid VMware View designs. Having the knowledge to choose the right vDesktop type helps you build that solid design.

The next chapter discusses the end devices used to connect into the View solution. End devices are another important part in a VDI solution as choosing the right end device can drastically improve the probability of success. Understanding the limitations of each end device type is important in choosing the right device for a given organization, and this will be discussed in the next chapter.

4
End Devices

Horizon View is a solution that delivers a desktop experience to end user devices through the PCoIP protocol. The devices supported by View vary greatly and include thick client, thin client, zero clients, and other devices, for example, the Apple iPad. This chapter will cover the various types of clients as well as the features that they do and do not support so that proper design considerations can be made in an overall solution.

Something to keep in mind while evaluating client devices for a View solution is that most people associate the quality of their work computer with the size and appearance of their monitor.

For example, Jenson has a dusty HP workstation under his desktop connected to a 17-inch monitor. If the IT department replaces Jenson's dusty HP workstation with a zero client and 24-inch monitor, then he is likely to already have a positive impression. Extend the positive perception by giving Jenson, who previously ran a Windows XP workstation, a Windows 7 vDesktop, and Jenson is likely to rave about his "new computer".

The device selection is important for the success of a VDI project as it is the gateway for users to connect to their vDesktops.

In this chapter, we will cover the following topics:

- Thick and thin clients
- Teradici PCoIP-powered zero clients and other clients
- Choosing proper devices for your organization

Thick clients

A **thick client** is a laptop or desktop running a full version of a workstation operating system, for example, Windows 7. The thick client has a fully usable operating system and uses a natively-installed VMware View Client to connect to the VDI.

A few examples of thick clients are as follows:

- A Dell OptiPlex workstation
- A Lenovo laptop
- An Apple MacBook Pro

One of the most common advantages of thick clients is that they provide high performance from a graphics offloading perspective.

Often, during a migration to a virtual desktop solution from an existing physical desktop environment, the organization will be interested to phase-in thin or zero clients. This approach is common in organizations that have recently purchased new thick clients (for example, workstations) and/or organizations that are not up for an upgrade for several years to come. However, by phasing-in thin or zero clients, the organization will still be forced to manage the underlying OS of the thick client.

If the decision to continue with an underlining OS is taken, the organization can use **VMware Horizon Mirage** to manage the images of the thick clients, reducing the operational cost. Note that Mirage can not only manage your thick client Windows image but also manage your physical and virtual images, allowing you to reduce the total number of images to update.

In addition to forcing an organization to manage the underlying OS, the organization might be forced (depending on its particular OS license agreement) to license the OS on the thick client in addition to the OS of the virtual desktop. This could quickly increase the license count needed for an organization as well as the overall capital expenditure of the virtual desktop initiative, depending on the licensing model in use.

Finally, a thick client is typically a machine that boots from a writeable partition. This means that the device might come up in a slightly different state on every boot. The consistency of a thin client or a zero client does not come into play; therefore, maintenance tasks such as reimaging thick clients are likely to be incurred and thus increase the operational expenses associated with each thick client.

The drawbacks of thick clients are as follows:

- They need another workstation to keep themselves patched, maintained, and in compliance
- They have the potential of having data at the edge (as the device is still a fully functional desktop by itself)
- They have a possible additional operating system to license
- They have a volatile endpoint
- They have a higher target of theft (again, because the device is a fully functional device by itself)
- The users require additional training as they might be confused about when they are navigating their vDesktop and when they are actually on the native OS

Repurposing thick clients

Repurposing is the process of taking a thick client (for example, a Dell OptiPlex workstation with Windows 7 installed) and turning it into a purpose-built VMware View endpoint. Some vendors offer a solution that allows you to do this. Repurposing typically involves the following:

- Installing a streamlined operating system (such as Windows 7 embedded or a Linux distribution)
- Installing a few additional applications on the repurposed thick client other than the VMware View Client
- Preventing changes to the thick client's configuration

An alternative to reimaging thick clients with a new, purpose-built image is to use a bootable solution. For example, by creating a Live CD with a Linux desktop operating system and the necessary components to run the VMware View Client, thick clients can simply be booted off a CD (read-only). This ensures a uniform experience each and every time a user turns on their device. The newly-released VMware View Client for Linux makes repurposing even more appealing for many organizations without the capital to invest in PCoIP zero clients.

Repurposing thick clients is often viewed as a stop gap measure to a zero client implementation as well as a means of prolonging the life of aging desktop hardware.

Thin clients

Thin clients are referred to as purpose-built devices that run a streamlined OS (for example, Microsoft Windows 7/8 Embedded, SUSE Linux, or the new Chromebooks) meant to deliver a minimal desktop environment to the end user. From this minimal desktop environment, the end user launches the VMware View Client and is then connected to their virtual desktop. Thin clients often have a write-protected or write-filtered system partition.

A few examples of thin clients are as follows:

- ClearCube I8520
- Wyse R50
- Dell Latitude 13 mobile

Let's see another example. By mid-2013, basic Chromebooks, which are web thin clients, had become relatively popular among US buyers looking to buy an affordable laptop. With their lower entry price, high security (due to the secure design of their browser-based operating system and Chrome OS), and simplicity, the Chromebook might be a desirable choice.

A Chromebook could be a good platform to use when you want quick access to a Windows application through a Horizon View virtual desktop. Now, with View 6, users can access their Horizon View desktops from an HTML 5-compliant browser such as the Google Chrome browser, as shown in the following screenshot. Horizon View HTML Access includes video playback, text copy and paste, and audio from the desktop. Using web access has some limitations compared to a full desktop experience, and provides an easy option without the need for a client setup on the endpoint.

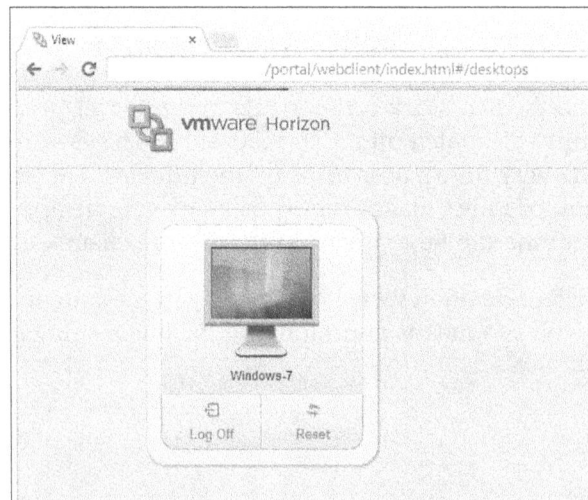

If you decide to choose a Chromebook, consider the following for the best possible end-user experience:

- Choose Chromebooks with X86 chips; the performance is better than with ARM chip systems.
- Turn off Aero Vista on the Windows 7/8 virtual machine.
- Enable copy and paste through the Horizon View Administrator console if your company policy allows copying between the virtual machine and the Chromebook desktop. When copy and paste is enabled, the user selects **Get Copied Text** and then **Paste Text** from the drop-down menu in the upper-right corner of the virtual desktop.

The common advantages of thin clients are as follows:

- They provide a consistent desktop environment
- They allow third-party software (such as a VPN client) to be installed
- They have a smaller footprint than thick clients
- Typically, they consume less power than thick clients
- They are also easier to manage because of purpose-build management tools

As thin clients are typically locked down OSes with a write filter (not allowing any writes to the system partition, or only allowing writes in specific subdirectories), the end user will have a consistent experience during every boot process. This can help reduce operational expenses associated with patching, maintaining, and reimaging thick clients.

In addition, thin clients allow the installation of third-party software to create a streamlined OS image specific to an organization's needs.

The drawbacks of thin clients are as follows:

- Cost
- Performance
- Potential vendor lock-in for upgrades (for example, Wyse)

While thin clients often have less features and a lower specification in terms of the hardware platform, their cost is typically equal to that of thick clients for most organizations. This is partly due to the high volume orders typically associated with thick client purchases and the healthy discounts that go with such an order. This is also due to the fact that thin clients are still a lower volume business overall, and the manufacturing costs are typically higher than that of traditional thick clients.

Also, as thin clients are often trying to use and deliver the minimum possible for the end user to have a favorable experience (and ultimately connect back to a virtual desktop with sufficient horsepower for a user's needs), the overall experience can suffer if the thin client's processor can't handle multimedia redirection.

For organizations that want to lock down the end devices, thin clients provide a consistent experience and require a VPN connection. Thin clients are a solid choice for an end device when compared to zero clients, which will be covered next. Currently, zero clients do not support a **virtual private network** (**VPN**) connection as there is no client built into the PCoIP firmware.

Thick clients typically have extremely good performance as they are often ordered with more than 2 GB of RAM, a multicore processor, and a moderate-to-high performing local disk. With some entry-level thin clients, running multimedia applications might cause the thin client's CPU to reach 100 percent as it struggles to handle the multimedia redirection. Multimedia redirection causes the media to be rendered at the end device, placing importance on the end device's horsepower capabilities.

Changes to thick and thin client solutions

View 6 has changed the approach for certain solutions around thick and thin clients. Earlier, solutions required the usage of thick clients with Lync 2013. If you want to use Horizon View 6 and Microsoft Lync 2013 together, you can provide the solution on a thin client. This combination will enable the following features:

- Presence
- Instant messaging
- Desktop sharing
- Application sharing / PowerPoint sharing
- Whiteboards
- File transfers
- Online meetings

  A couple of disadvantages associated with online meetings are as follows:

    ° Communication modes for online meetings are limited by peer-to-peer communication modes. For example, if audio is not supported on the specified architecture, audio will not work in online meetings.

    ° Joining online meetings from a Microsoft Outlook meeting reminder and/or meeting invitation is not supported.

- Office integration
- VoIP

  A feature that is not supported for VoIP is as follows:

  - ° Audio is supported only in a VDI environment. Audio is not supported in a session-based desktop delivery environment such as Microsoft RDS.

- Video chat

  A feature that is not supported for voice chat is as follows:

  - ° Multiparty video chat

The solution works with Windows 7, Windows 8, Windows Embedded, and Windows Thin PC on a thin client such as Dell Wyse (Z90D7, R90L7, and X90m7) and two models from HP (t610 and t5740e). You can find the information on the solution at `http://blogs.technet.com/b/nexthop/archive/2012/07/31/microsoft-lync-2013-preview-in-a-virtual-desktop-infrastructure.aspx`.

Teradici PCoIP-powered zero clients

Zero clients refer to a device with an embedded Teradici PCoIP chip that allows the device to immediately boot to the VMware View Client without the need for an underlying OS. Zero clients have neither a writeable system partition nor a hard disk for that matter. Instead, zero clients boot off of a chipset embedded into the device.

This section specifically highlights Teradici PCoIP-powered devices as it is the authors' opinion that other zero clients on the market that do not adopt the PCoIP model are destined for obsolescence. At the very least, they will most likely not have the same levels of adoption within the VMware ecosystem.

A few examples of zero clients are as follows:

- Samsung NC240 monitor
- EVGA PD02
- ClearCube I9424
- Wyse P20

The common advantages of zero clients are as follows:

- Security
- Ease of configuration
- Cost
- Vendor diagnostics for management
- Often a smaller footprint than thick or thin clients
- Often less power consumption than thick or thin clients

Zero clients are the most secure end devices an organization can leverage for their VMware View solution as there is no hard disk inside a zero client. In a solution based on a zero client, there is no chance for sensitive data to reside on an end device because the end device is not capable of storing such data.

Zero clients are often thought to be on par or easier than thin clients to configure. This is because a zero client has very few settings (IP settings, VMware View Connection Server, and other minor settings) as the goal is to get the end users to their entitled virtual desktop as fast as possible.

Finally, zero clients are often viewed as not only the most secure but also the most affordable solution. This is because it is significantly less expensive for organizations to replace their desktops, for example, a Samsung NC240 with a keyboard and mouse, than replace a thin client (which still needs a monitor). For organizations looking to leverage existing monitors, a standard zero client (for example, EVGA PD02) might be one of the lowest cost options on the market.

The possible drawbacks of most zero clients are as follows:

- Currently, they do not support VPN inside a client
- Currently, they do not offer Wi-Fi support natively
- They do not offer client-side caching

For organizations that need their end devices to establish a VPN connection in order to connect to the VMware View Connection Server environment, a zero client will not suffice. This is because zero clients currently do not have a VPN client embedded into the firmware and have no means of establishing a secure connection to a remote peer.

It should be noted that a proper VMware View solution leveraging a security server should negate the need of a VPN connection.

Also, zero clients have no means to support a virtual desktop running natively in the local mode. There are no mobile-centric (for example, a zero client in a laptop housing) zero client solutions today, so mobile users who need to leverage the local mode might still be best served by a traditional thick client.

Other clients

Other clients can include items such as an iOS device (iPhones and iPads), Android-based tablets, and smartphones including Amazon Kindle Fire and Microsoft Surface tablets.

For organizations that deploy tablets as the end device, they are strongly encouraged to provide a keyboard solution with the tablets. Today, most of the users are native users of conventional keyboard and mouse solutions. Tablet devices offer a new type of input that many users are still growing accustomed to. While the user experience is often enjoyable, trying to type a long e-mail or perform some of the regular tasks in certain organizations can prove tedious.

The VMware Horizon Client for the iPad, for example, supports Bluetooth keyboards such as the **Zagg Mate** (`http://www.zagg.com/accessories/logitech-ipad-2-keyboard-case`).

Unity Touch for iPad and Android-based tablets

Unity Touch is a feature of Horizon View 6 and the VMware Horizon Client for iOS and Android. There is a lot of demand from end users who want Windows apps on their mobile devices. However, those applications are difficult to use on the smaller screens and without the native keyboard and mouse. Unity Touch makes it easier to run Windows apps on your iPhone, iPad, or an Android device.

With Unity Touch, users can browse, search, and open Windows applications (and files); choose favorite applications and files; and switch between running applications without using the Windows Start menu or taskbar, as shown in the following screenshot:

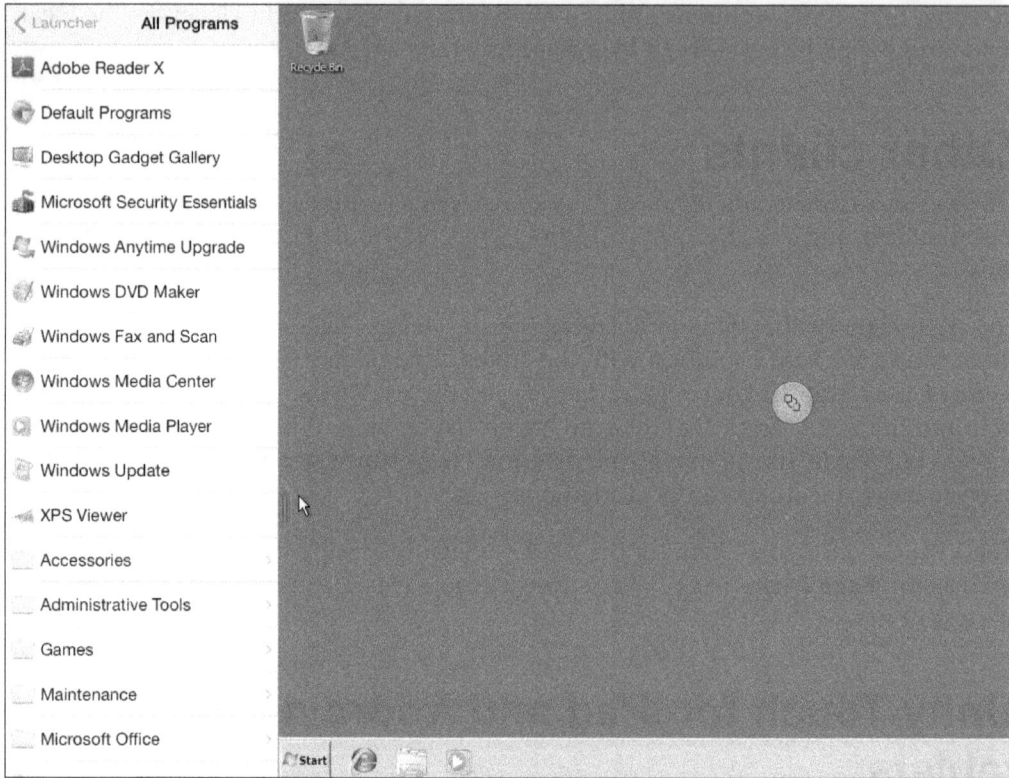

Some of the features of Unity Touch are:

- **Intuitive sidebar**: The Unity Touch sidebar will automatically open the first time your device connects to a Horizon View desktop that is enabled with Unity Touch. Then, the sidebar will make it easy to navigate the Windows All Programs and My Files folders from your iPad or Android device. After you find what you are looking for, the sidebar will automatically retract. To move back, just swipe left to right or click on the tab.

- **Favorite apps and files follow you from device to device**: You can create a custom list of favorite applications or files to access from the Unity Touch sidebar. Click on **Manage** under **Favorite Applications** or **Favorite Files** and select your items. Your favorites are remembered across all your mobile devices. When you switch from an iPad to a Galaxy Note to a Kindle Fire HD device, your favorite apps and files are the same across all the devices. You must be using the Horizon View Clients for iOS and Android on each device.

- **You can launch Windows applications**: When you select **All Programs** in the Unity Touch sidebar, it will find and launch your Windows applications, as shown in the following screenshot:

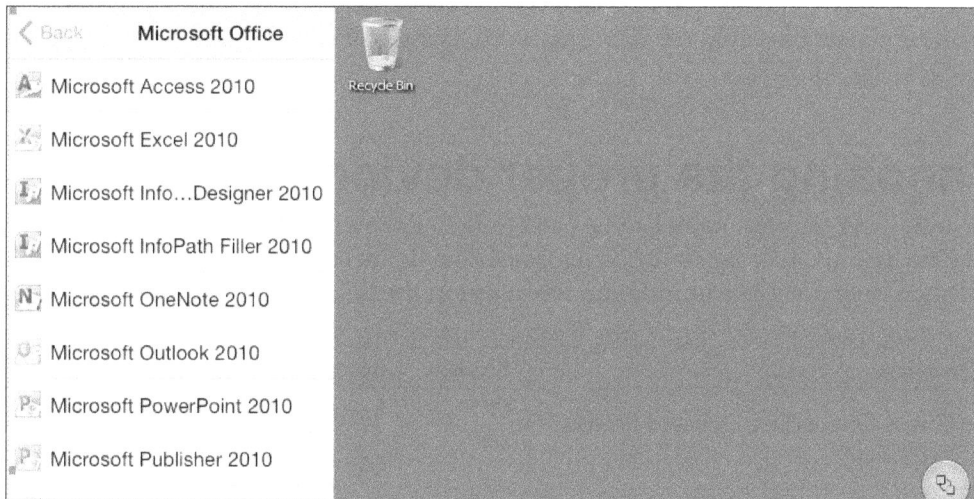

- **You can open files in your Horizon View desktop**: **My Files** opens the files and folders in your `Users` folder including `Documents`, `Desktop`, `Music`, `Pictures`, `Videos`, `Downloads`. By selecting **My Files** in the Unity Touch sidebar, you can navigate and open the files you want in your virtual desktop.

- **You can instantly search for applications and files**: Use the search bar and search for the applications and files on your remote desktop and get results that can be launched with a single touch. Use iOS or Android voice detection to search for applications and files in your Horizon View desktop.

- **You can switch between applications or quit apps from the Unity Touch sidebar**: Unity Touch makes it easy to switch between running applications. Open the Unity Touch sidebar and select the application or open the window under **Running Applications**. Then, Unity Touch will bring that application to the foreground. If you want to close apps or windows and find tapping the red close box **X** a pain, open the Unity Touch sidebar and perform a left-to-right swipe on the window or application in **Running Applications** and click on **Close**.

You need to have VMware Horizon Client with Horizon View 6 in order to invoke Unity Touch on the endpoint. Once you have installed Horizon View, your View environment will be enabled with Unity Touch. The latest Horizon Clients are available from the iOS App Store, Google Play Store, and Amazon AppStore for Android.

Choosing the proper device

The following questionnaire can be used to help determine the right device or devices for a given organization. This questionnaire is based on experience and should be used as a foundation when out in the field:

Question	Answer	Solution
Will new devices be purchased for this VDI project?	Yes	Use zero clients as primary with other devices/tablets as secondary.
Will new devices be purchased for this VDI project?	No	Repurpose existing thick or thin clients.
Is security of paramount importance?	Yes	Use zero clients as they do not offer a writeable hard drive in the unit.
Will the solution need to support regular video conferencing?	Yes	Investigate one of the upcoming integrated PCoIP zero client solutions from companies such as Cisco.
Will smartcard authentication be required?	Yes	Thick, thin, or zero clients will suffice; avoid tablets.
Is a minimal footprint and cable infrastructure desired?	Yes	Use a Samsung-integrated monitor (zero client) with a third-party Wi-Fi solution and a wireless keyboard and mouse. It requires one cable (power) from the solution to the wall.

Question	Answer	Solution
Are the majority of users going to be connecting from a fixed position?	Yes	Use a zero client.
Are the majority of users mobile or road-warriors?	Yes	Use a thick client (laptop).

The preceding table is simply a starting point. Ideally, several devices can be tested during the pilot and should include a thick and zero client. This will help an organization understand how the different endpoint choices could work for them (or potentially not work in unique circumstances).

A one-cable zero client solution

Cable reduction is a topic that comes up often in education environments, or any environment, where the client environment must be built and torn down quickly. A typical physical desktop solution includes the following:

- A power cable for the workstation
- A network cable for the workstation
- A USB cable for the keyboard
- A USB cable for the mouse
- A video cable
- A power cable for the monitor

This solution equals a total of six cables to have sprawled across a desk or conference room. It also includes three cables (monitor power, workstation power, and workstation network) that need to be connected to a wall jack.

The following solution requires just one cable to the wall and is based on the integrated PCoIP monitor solution from Samsung (NC190 or NC240):

- A power cable for the Samsung monitor zero client
- NETGEAR WNCE2001 Universal Wi-Fi Internet Adapter

    Its features are as follows:

    - This allows the zero client to connect to the VDI over Wi-Fi without requiring a patch cable to run from the device to a wall jack
    - The WNCE2001 can also be powered by USB (to remove a power cable requirement)

- Logitech MK520 wireless keyboard and mouse

  ° The transmitter occupies only one USB port and provides a wireless keyboard and mouse

This solution requires exactly one power cable and can be used in environments that require quick build up and tear down such as emergency response, training, and educational environments.

Summary

VMware View is an extremely flexible solution that can support a wide variety of end devices. This helps increase the overall success of a VDI initiative because it allows users to bring the device that works best for them in a given situation or state of connectivity. For example, a user can simply travel with an Apple iPad and use the VMware View Client to connect into their corporate vDesktop to perform lighter tasks such as Internet browsing, file management, and so on. When the user is back at their home office or their desk at work, they may have a full-blown desktop with the View Client to work from, allowing faster input.

From our collective experience, PCoIP zero clients are often the best way to move forward for an organization as it removes an unnecessary variable from the overall VDI solution. PCoIP zero clients are dependable, predictable, affordable, and secure.

The next chapter discusses how to properly size the VMware View solution, which is important to ensure a positive end user experience, redundancy, and cost effectiveness. Now that the ground work has been laid for VMware View, it is time to jump in and start designing the software and hardware infrastructure.

5
The PCoIP Protocol

The **PCoIP** protocol, developed by Teradici and licensed by VMware, is a purpose-built protocol for virtual desktop solutions on both LAN and WAN connections. PCoIP is a content-aware protocol, meaning that it has algorithms to differentiate between text and high-resolution pictures, and then performs delivery optimization depending on real-time network characteristics.

VMware's own testing has shown that PCoIP can reduce display latency by more than 50 percent compared to Microsoft's **Remote Display Protocol** (**RDP**) for common operations (VMware View PCoIP network sizing guide can be found at `http://www.vmware.com/files/pdf/view/VMware-View-5-PCoIP-Network-Optimization-Guide.pdf`).

In this chapter, we will cover the following topics:

- PCoIP tuning and configuration
- Why lossless quality is important
- Various PCoIP network fundamentals
- Multimedia redirection
- The Teradici APEX offload card

PCoIP has many differentiators when compared to other protocols in competing VDI solutions; one such differentiator is the fact that PCoIP is a host-rendered technology. Host rendering means that all pixels are rendered in the data center and then simply broadcasted to the end device. This means that there are no codecs to install on the end device.

One of the most touted features of PCoIP is the fact that the protocol can be built to a lossless quality.

Consider that an end user is connecting to their vDesktop over a latent connection and attempting to render a web page. The web page consists of both high-resolution graphics as well as text. In such cases, initially, the text is crystal clear while the graphics are significantly compressed to conserve bandwidth.

Assuming that the display isn't changed by the user navigating to a different web page, the visual will build to a perceptually lossless quality. This means that the human eye cannot tell the difference between what's displayed and the original version (with a higher number of pixels) rendered by the VDI. If there is still time before the user changes what they are trying to view, PCoIP will finally build to a fully lossless quality.

Why lossless quality is important

The protocol for the PCoIP display uses an encoding method called **progressive building**, which attempts to provide an overall optimal user experience during constrained network periods. Initially, the progressive build provides a highly-compressed initial image called a lossy image. The image is progressively built to a full state called lossless. The lossless state displays the image with the full fidelity intended. When displaying an image on a LAN, PCoIP always uses the lossless compression. If the bandwidth available per session drops below 1 Mbs, PCoIP will initially display a lossy text image and quickly "fill in" the image to a lossless state.

Using this approach will allow the desktop to remain responsive while still displaying the best possible image during changing network conditions. This method provides the optimal experience for users.

The attributes of the build-to-lossless feature are as follows:

- It reduces the image quality during network congestion
- It dynamically adjusts the image quality
- It provides responsiveness and reduces screen update latency
- It obtains maximum quality of the image quality when the network congestion subsides

The PCoIP protocol efficiently provides the build-to-lossless feature in most conditions, which means this feature can stay enabled. The build-to-lossless feature can be enabled or disabled by selecting the **Turn off Build-to-Lossless feature** options in the PCoIP group policy setting, as shown in the following screenshot:

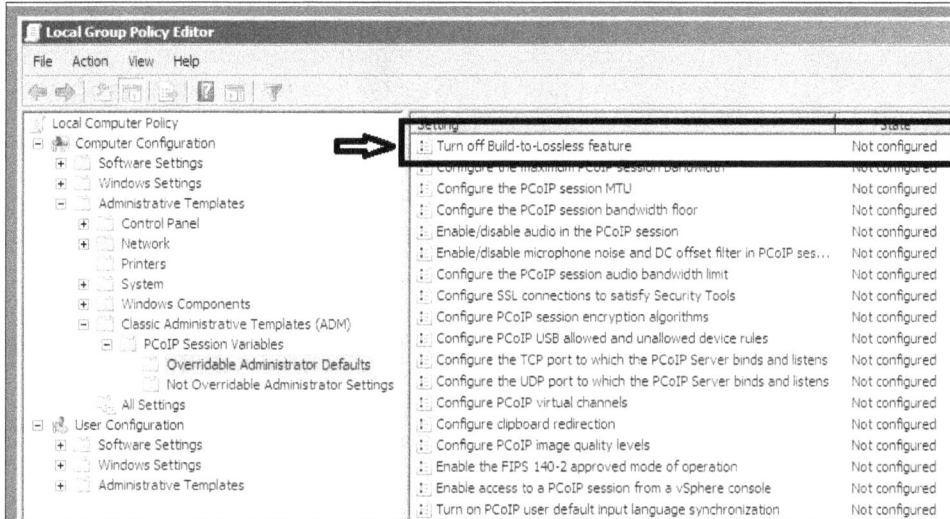

In the PCoIP policy, you will need to specify whether you want to disable the build-to-lossless feature (this is the default). When you choose to enable the setting, the build-to-lossless feature is disabled. Images and other content will not be built to a lossless state. In bandwidth-constrained network environments, disabling the build-to-lossless feature will provide bandwidth savings, as shown in the following screenshot:

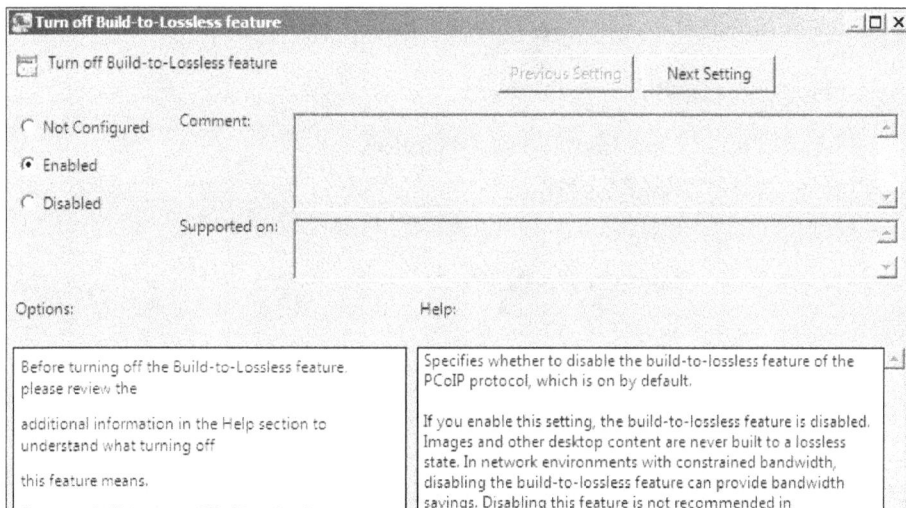

To understand why lossless representation is important, let's use an example. Whitney is a security agent tasked with screening packages that are entering a building. Her organization has implemented a VDI solution at her primary workstation. As packages enter the X-ray machine and the contents are displayed on her monitor, she has two seconds, as per the agency's policy, to determine whether it's a threat. If Whitney's agency is using a solution that is using a protocol that can't guarantee a lossless image at the end device, the visual representation on her screen may or may not be completely accurate. In this scenario, a lossless image delivered by PCoIP is of much greater value than a solution that leverages a solution, and a protocol that may have significant compression and may or may not be an exact visual representation of the virtual desktop.

Another example of where a lossless image is of critical importance is in a healthcare environment. For example, if VDI has been implemented at a hospital, where the clinicians are accessing their vDesktops from laptops, Apple iPads, and other end devices, it's important that the image being delivered is lossless. Without a solution capable of lossless rendering, a clinician could be looking at a **positron emission tomography** (PET) scan of a patient and be unable to determine whether the image suggests a particular diagnosis.

PCoIP network fundamentals

In order to understand how to size a network for PCoIP session delivery, it's important to know some of the key configurations and concepts of PCoIP. For example, the PCoIP protocol adds minimal overhead, with just 85 bytes of overhead in a standard 1,500 byte Ethernet packet.

For a PCoIP session to be established, a PCoIP-capable client must reside on the end device, and the destination must be a PCoIP-capable host.

PCoIP-capable clients include the following:

- VMware View Client for 32/64-bit Windows
- VMware View Client for Linux
- VMware View Client for Mac
- VMware View Client for Apple iPad
- VMware View Client for Android
- Thin and zero clients

PCoIP-capable hosts include the following:

- A Windows-based desktop operating system running the VMware View Agent software (physical or virtual)
- A Windows-based desktop operating system with a PCoIP hardware host card (physical)

Using PCoIP with Server Desktop Mode

Horizon View allows you to use the Windows Server 2008/2012 R2 and the Services RDS feature to create virtual machines that are managed by vCenter Server as desktops for a View deployment.

> Using this option does not require the Microsoft VDA license. There is always the chance of application interoperability using desktops running on a server operating system.

This feature is set up by the following steps:

- Installing the Remote Desktop Services
- Installing View Agent on the RDS Host
- Creating an RDS farm

Installing the Remote Desktop Services

Follow these steps to install the RDS:

1. Log in to the server as administrator.
2. Click on the **Server Manager** icon on the **Quick Launch**, or the **Start** menu under **Administrative Tools**.
3. Choose **Roles**.
4. Click on **Add Roles**.
5. On the initial screen of **Add Roles**, click on **Next** to continue.

6. Choose **Remote Desktop Services**, as shown in the following screenshot, and click on **Next** to continue:

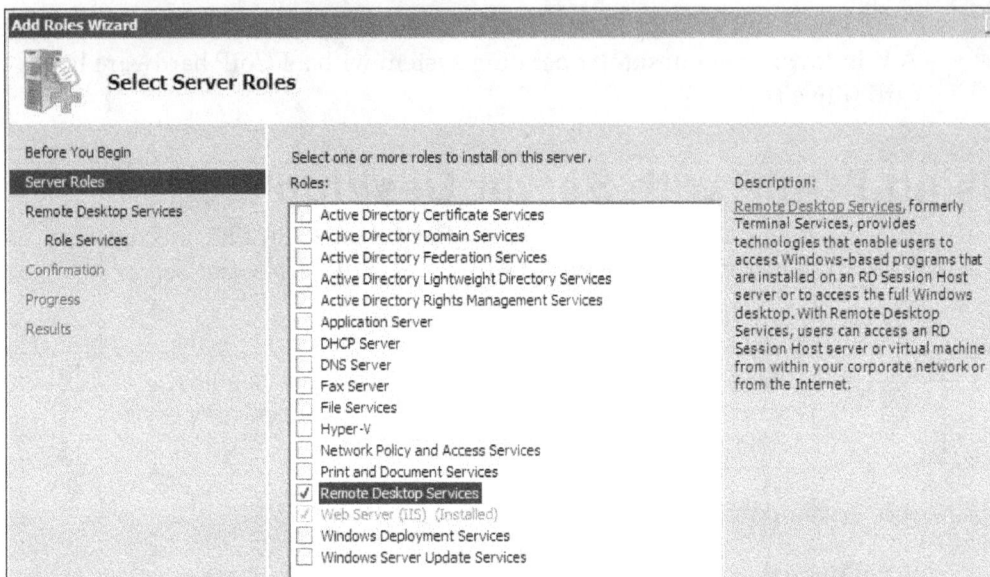

7. On the **Introduction to Remote Desktop Services** screen, click on **Next** to continue.

8. Under **Remote Desktop Services**, choose the role for **Remote Desktop Session Host** and click on **Next** to continue, as shown in the following screenshot:

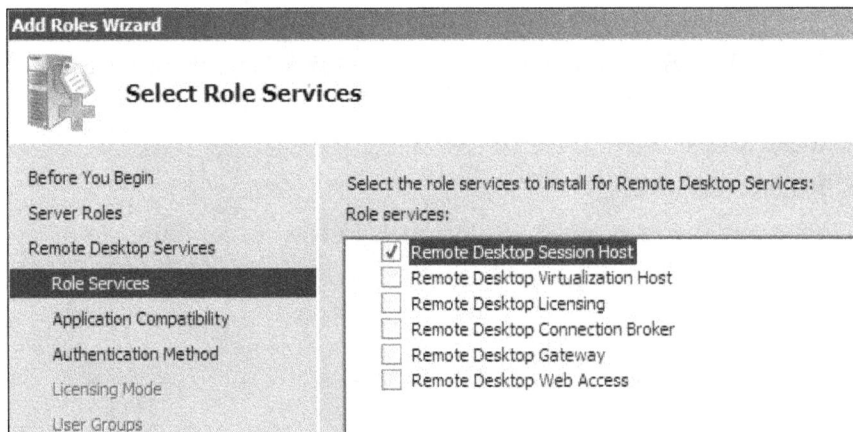

9. On the **Uninstall and Reinstall Applications for Compatibility** screen, click on **Next** to continue.

10. Select the desired method of authentication, and then click on **Next** to continue, as shown in the following screenshot:

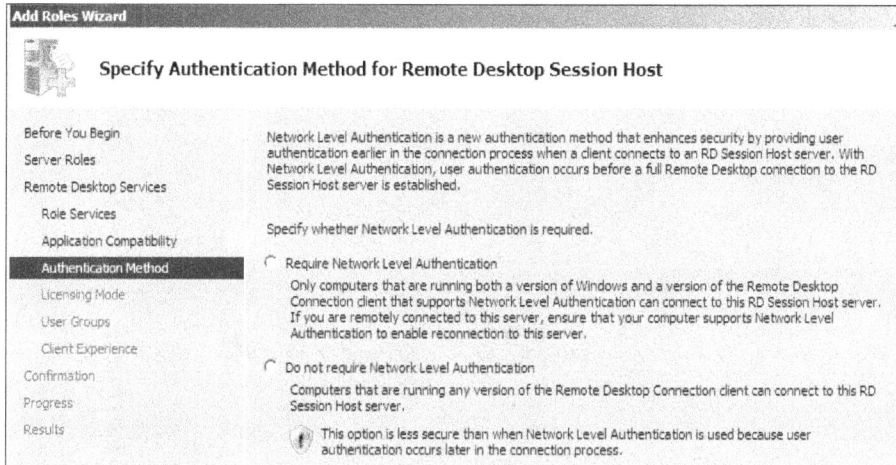

11. Choose the method of RDS Host licensing and then click on **Next** to continue.

12. Add the appropriate users/groups that will be authorized to access the RDS Host server, and then click on **Next** to continue (this can be added later), as shown in the following screenshot:

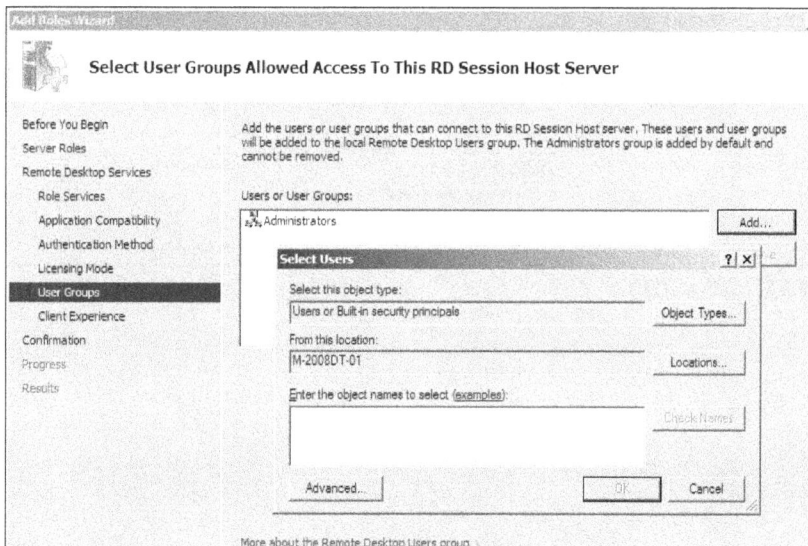

13. On the **Configure Client Experience** screen, as shown in the following screenshot, select the desired functionality, and click on **Next** to continue. The **Desktop Experience** features can be added after the installation.

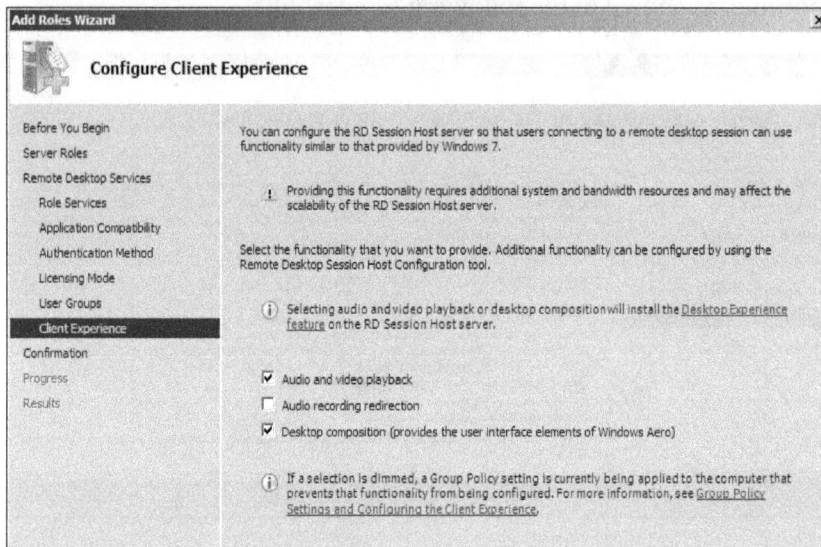

14. Click on **Install** to continue, as shown in the following screenshot. Click on **Close** and **Yes** to reboot.

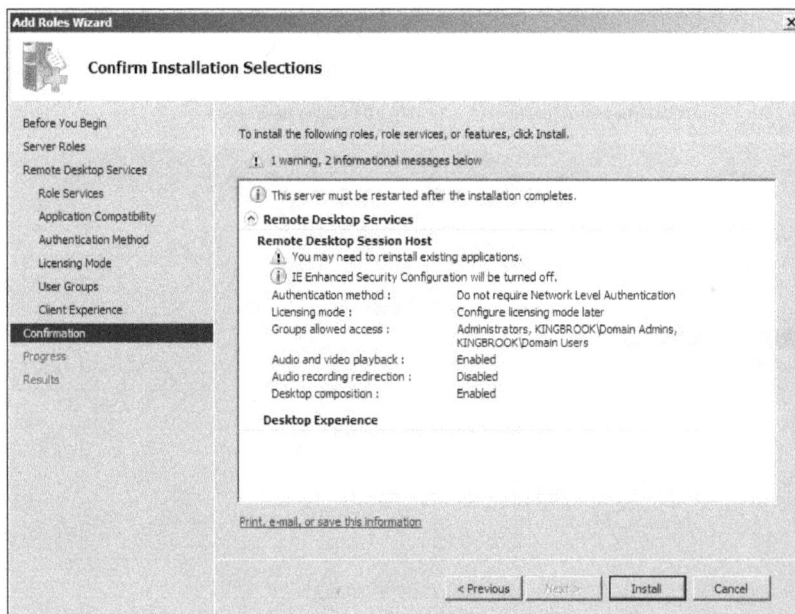

15. After the server has rebooted, log on as the administrator and click on **Close** to finalize the installation.

Installing View Agent on the RDS Host

After the Remote Desktop Services Host role is installed, perform the following steps:

1. Log on to the RSH Host server as the administrator.

2. Launch the **VMware Horizon View Agent** installation, accept the **End User Licensing Agreement**, and click on **Next**.

3. On the **Welcome** screen, click on **Next** to continue.

4. Change the installation path, if necessary, and click on **Next**.

5. Enter the FQDN or IP of a View Connection Server that the RDS Host uses. Specify the authentication credentials and click on **Next** to continue, as shown in the following screenshot:

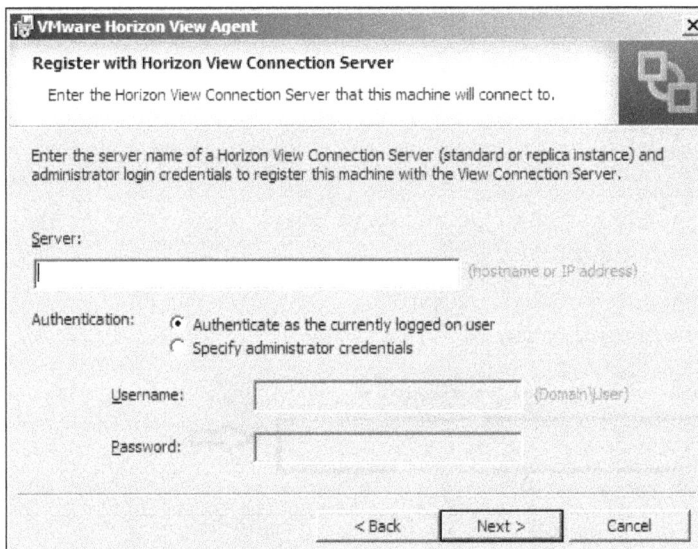

6. Click on **Install** to continue.

7. Click on **Finish**. If prompted, reboot the server.

Creating an RDS farm

To create a farm that gives users access to the RDS desktops, follow these steps:

1. In **View Administrator**, go to **View Configuration | Global Settings**.

2. Choose **Edit** in the **General Settings** window.

3. Select **Enable Windows Server 2008 R2 desktops**, as shown in the following screenshot:

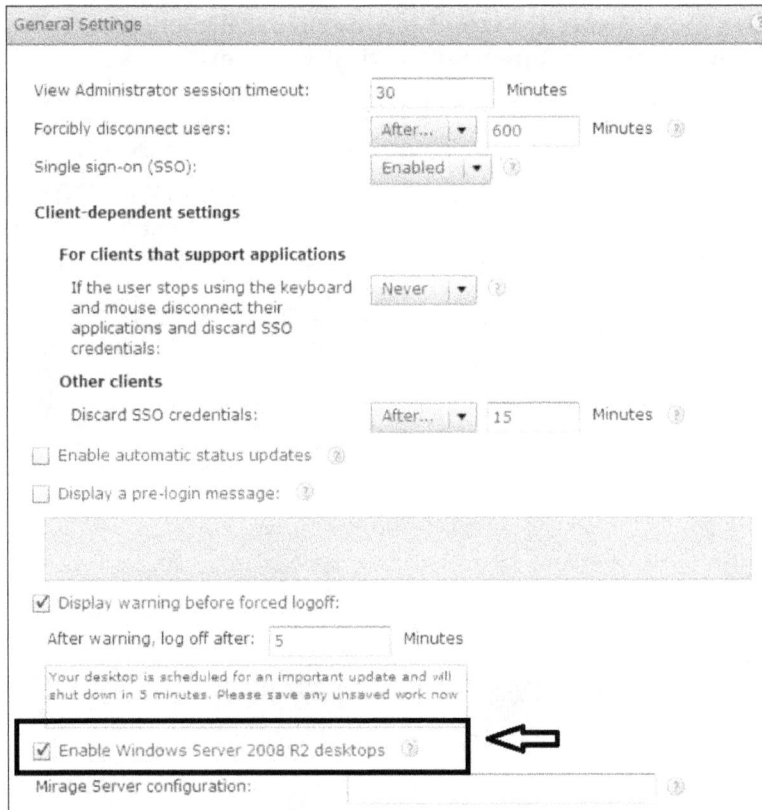

General Settings	
View Administrator session timeout:	30 Minutes
Forcibly disconnect users:	After... ▼ 600 Minutes ⑨
Single sign-on (SSO):	Enabled ▼ ⑨

Client-dependent settings

   For clients that support applications

      If the user stops using the keyboard and mouse disconnect their applications and discard SSO credentials: Never ▼ ⑨

   Other clients

      Discard SSO credentials: After... ▼ 15 Minutes ⑨

☐ Enable automatic status updates ⑨

☐ Display a pre-login message: ⑨

☑ Display warning before forced logoff:

After warning, log off after: 5   Minutes

Your desktop is scheduled for an important update and will shut down in 5 minutes. Please save any unsaved work now

☑ Enable Windows Server 2008 R2 desktops ⑨   ⇦

Mirage Server configuration: ⑨

4. Click on **OK** to enable the feature.

After you have enabled the Windows 2008 R2 desktops, use the following steps to create a farm for the remote desktop session hosts:

1. Again, in **View Administrator**, navigate to **Resources | Farms**.

2. Click on **Add** to enter the name of the farm and click on **Next**.

3. Specify the settings for the farm, as shown in the following screenshot, and click on **Next**:

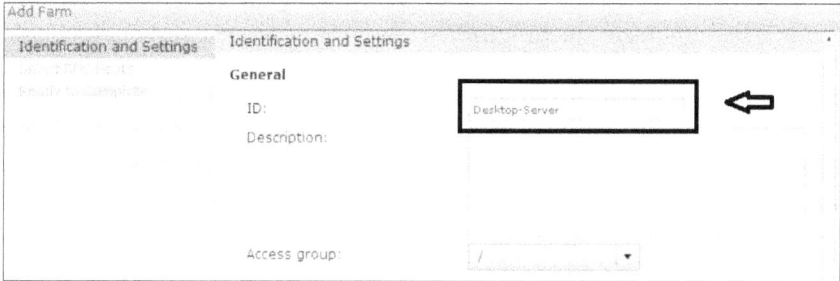

4. Choose the RDS hosts to be added to the farm and click on **Next**.

5. Click on **Finish**.

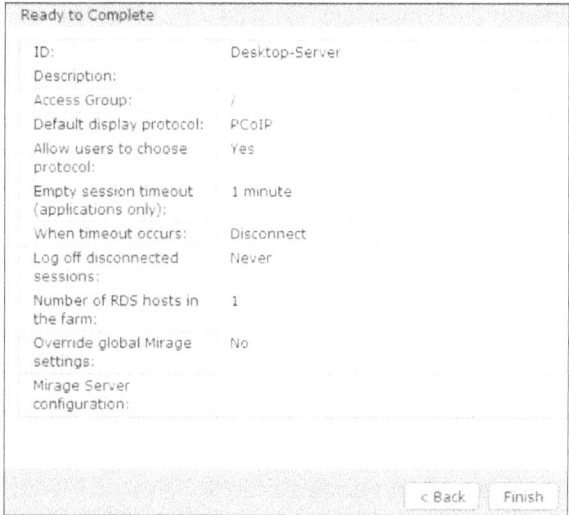

In **View Administrator**, you can now verify the farm by navigating to **Resources** | **Farms**.

PCoIP connections

There are two types of PCoIP connections: soft and hard.

Soft PCoIP is used when connecting to VMware View vDesktops. As a vDesktop cannot have a PCoIP host card, it uses a software implementation of PCoIP, and is referred to as a **PCoIP software host**. Soft PCoIP can tolerate up to 250 milliseconds of round trip latency without any negative end user experience. With the latency below 250 milliseconds, PCoIP is capable of displaying videos at 30 **frames per second (FPS)**.

Hard PCoIP is used when connecting to a physical device with a Teradici PCoIP host card. As the connection terminates in the PCoIP host card device, this is called **hard PCoIP host**. Hard PCoIP can tolerate up to 150 milliseconds of round trip latency. Hard PCoIP is capable of displaying videos at 60 FPS. The following table provides a summary:

Type of PCoIP	Round trip latency tolerance	Maximum frames per second for videos
Soft	250	30
Hard	150	60

> To test the network latency, use the ping -l 1400 <destination_ip>, where <destination_ip> is the IP address of the remote location. The -l 1400 switch forces the ping test to use a packet size of 1,400 bytes, which is the Teradici recommendation for testing network latency for PCoIP.

Both soft and hard PCoIP leverage local cursor technology, which ensures that cursor functionality for the end user is still favorable in high-latency situations.

Multimedia redirection

Multimedia redirection (MMR) is the process of redirecting a media file from the PCoIP host (typically a VMware View vDesktop on the server) to the end user device. The more typical approach, which is known as **host video decoding**, is a common practice with VMware View solutions.

MMR is only capable when the end device is an x86 (XP or Vista).

Additionally, the x86 end device must also have the appropriate codecs installed to support the type of media file being redirected. MMR is a technique that originally came to the market years ago to support terminal services. Earlier, thin clients were gaining popularity, primarily through the efforts of companies such as Wyse. As we learned in *Chapter 4*, *End Devices*, thin clients have a locked-down version of an operating system, for example, Windows XPe.

Media file types supported by MMR with PCoIP include the following:

- MPEG-1
- MPEG-2
- MPEG-4
- WMA
- MP3
- AC3
- WMV

PCoIP MMR does not support the redirection of Adobe Flash or Apple QuickTime. MMR does offer advantages by placing less of a demand on the server CPU that is hosting the vDesktops as the rendering of the media is done by one or more CPUs of the end device. In addition, MMR can potentially require less network bandwidth as already-rendered visual data is not sent to the end device, but instead to the media file to be rendered.

There are many disadvantages of MMR. For example, to use MMR, an x86 end device must be used. As previously discussed in this book, there are many advantages (for example, price and security) to using PCoIP zero clients in a VMware View solution. By using MMR in a solution, thin or thick clients become the only available options.

For solutions that are looking to support video editors or video editing software, a hard PCoIP solution is quite likely to be the best (and only) viable solution. While the PCoIP protocol has made significant improvements since its initial launch years ago, a hardware-based PCoIP solution is the best approach.

> PCoIP is a unique desktop delivery protocol in that it is not only available via software (soft), but also has the ability to leverage the advantages of hardware in the form of a host card.

The following table is an excerpt from a Teradici virtual desktop host presentation:

Description	MMR	Host video decoding
Server CPU load	Medium	Medium to high
Supports any video codec	No	Yes
Supports PCoIP zero clients	No	Yes
Requires application and patch management	Yes	No
Requires codec and patch management	Yes	No
WAN performance	Poor	Good
Operation below the native video bit rate	Video stutter	Smooth playback

As the server's CPU power and density increases, host video decoding will only become less concerning as the available horsepower in a given physical server increases with technology advancements.

The MMR perfect storm

One of the only legitimate reasons to use MMR in a VMware View solution is if there are requirements for frequent video use with a very specific codec. For example, if a public relations company watches videos of their clients frequently, and the video is delivered in a specific codec, such as an **audio video interleave (AVI)** file using **DivX**, it is possible that MMR to a thin or thick client with the DivX codec installed will outperform a solution that relies solely on PCoIP.

Most organizations rely less on files such as AVI with DivX and more on Adobe Flash and Apple QuickTime, which will perform best with host video decoding.

Windows 7 support for H.264-encoded Windows Media files

H.264/MPEG-4 is a standard used for video compression, and is currently one of the most commonly used formats in the recording, compression, and also distribution of high-definition videos.

View 5.3 has added Windows 7 support for MMR of H.264-encoded Windows Media files. The Windows 7 client end points will receive the original compressed multimedia stream from the server and then decode it locally for display. This will decrease the bandwidth usage since the data over the connection will be a compressed video instead of a sequence of bitmaps. Bandwidth usage remains the same when the video window is resized and also when it's played in the full-screen mode. Server resources are saved using this method, because the server no longer needs its CPU resources to decode the video content and then send it in bitmap from over PCoIP.

The MMR data is sent across the connection without application-based encryption and possibly could contain sensitive data, depending on what is being redirected. Administrators can control access to MMR by enabling or disabling the MMR policy in the View Administrator console.

Teradici APEX offload card

In 2011, Teradici announced the Teradici APEX 2800 offload card. The APEX card is a **PCIe** card that is used to offload the PCoIP protocol that is encoding from the physical server's CPU (abstracted as vCPU within the vDesktop) to the offload card. The PCoIP Hardware Accelerator reduces CPU overhead by offloading the 100 most active virtual displays to ensure its capabilities are used where most needed. This could increase server consolidation ratios by up to two times. The Hardware Accelerator in the Horizon View environment enhances and complements either shared GPU or GPU pass-through deployments. Combined with certain PCoIP zero clients, the accelerator doubles the frame rates to ensure a consistent user experience.

This offloading is for videos only and does not help offload the audio channels of PCoIP. The APEX offload card is an integrated solution with VMware View.

As mentioned earlier in this book, the fact that VMware View is capable of leveraging hardware solutions (for example, the PCoIP zero clients and the PCoIP host card) provides unique capabilities in the market.

In many, if not most, VMware View solutions, the APEX offload card can be used to effectively increase the vDesktops that can be run on a physical server. Increasing this user per core density should measurably reduce the overall costs of the VMware View solution, even with the price of the offload card built in.

There are three components in the Teradici APEX offload card solution:

- The Teradici APEX offload card itself
- The APEX driver for ESXi
- The APEX driver for Windows vDesktop

Without installing and configuring all three of the components properly, hardware offload is not possible. The following figure is an illustration that shows both the required ESXi driver and the Windows driver to support PCoIP offloading:

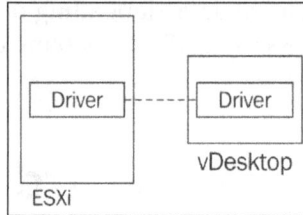

Hardware-assisted PCoIP protocol encoding is used to increase the number of users per core. Even in VMware View solutions that may be more memory-constrained than CPU (for example, an environment heavy in Java applications with poor memory management), there can still be significant benefits realized from using the APEX card. As a general rule of thumb, the benefits are as follows:

- Task workers equals 1.15x users per core
- Knowledge workers equals 1.5x users per core
- Video workers equals 1.75x users per core

For example, if a VMware View design that does not utilize the APEX card is capable of 10 knowledge works per CPU core, then using the APEX card will roughly increase the number to 15 knowledge workers per CPU. The following figure shows the encoding of a Windows 7 desktop with PCoIP without any previous encoding:

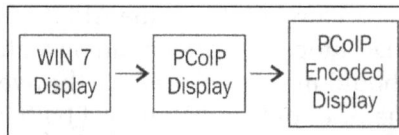

In the preceding figure, the display of the Windows 7 desktop is encoded using the VMware View Agent, and is done completely in software and by the virtual CPU of the vDesktop. The encoded display is then sent securely to the end device in use. With PCoIP, only the encoded display is sent to the device without any actual data of the desktop itself. The following figure is an illustration that shows the encoding of a Windows 7 desktop with PCoIP offload encoding:

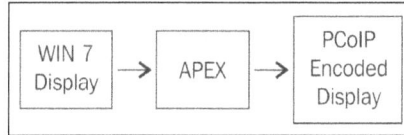

In the preceding figure, the display of the Windows 7 desktop is encoded using the APEX offload card. The encoded display is then sent securely to the end device in use. The offload card does not perform rendering; it performs encoding. Rendering is performed by the VMware View virtual graphics driver or virtual GPU.

The following table shows the maximum number of displays supported:

Display resolution	Portrait mode	Landscape mode
2560 x 1600	25	40
1920 x 1200	40	64
1680 x 1050	50	85
1280 x 1024	100	100

The offload process

The APEX 2800 ESXi driver monitors all vDesktops for image activity, irrespective of whether the vDesktop is using hardware offloading or not. There are several factors that the APEX solution uses to determine whether a vDesktop's display should be offloaded. They are as follows:

- **Eligibility**: Is the vDesktop eligible to have its display offloaded?
- **Imaging activity**: Is the vDesktop's imaging activity above the minimum threshold?
- **Priority**: Does the vDesktop currently have priority among its peers?

The following figure shows a Teradici PCoIP APEX offload decision tree:

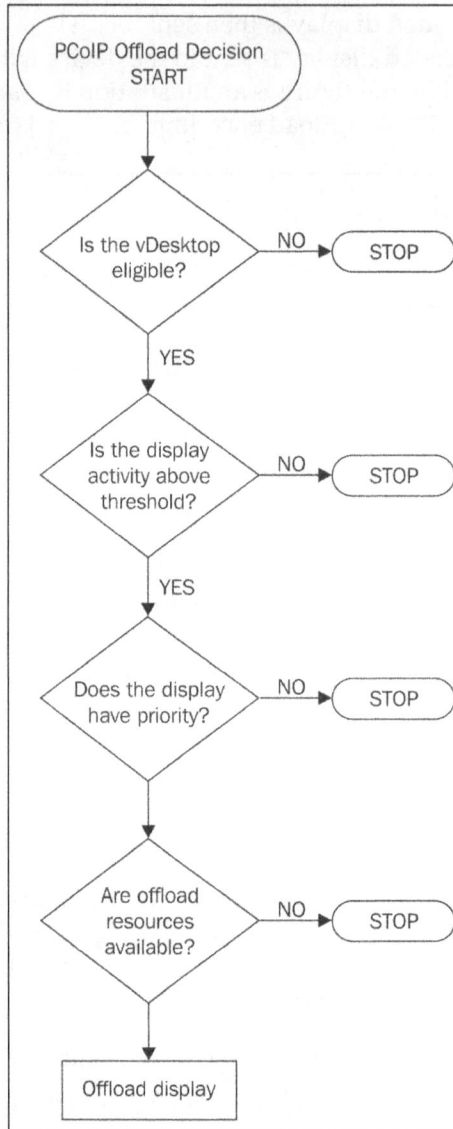

The switch between software and hardware encoding is a seamless process. In the current version of the solution, a tiny red dot appears in the upper-left corner of the display (can be disabled) to let the end user know that hardware encoding is being used. This should most likely be used only during the test and pilot phase and not during an actual production implementation.

Defining the offload tiers

The Teradici APEX offload card uses priority as one of the factors in determining whether a given vDesktop's display will be offloaded to the hardware card or not. Priority for a given desktop pool is defined within the VMware View Admin console under Policies. The offload priority is listed as PCoIP hardware acceleration priority. There are five priority settings available. They are as follows:

- Lowest
- Lower
- Medium (default)
- Higher
- Highest

In many designs, only one or two offload priority settings will be used. For example, a design may have an end user population that is separated from the executive team. The executives may receive a *Higher* priority setting while everyone else is configured for *Medium*.

The best practice is to use only *Highest* and *Lowest* if required by the number of priority groups defined for a given solution. By keeping *Highest* as an available option, if the need arises, a desktop pool can immediately be given priority over everyone else in an emergency.

Design considerations

The implementation of the APEX offload card is fairly straightforward; the driver installations are well documented, and enabling and configuring offload from the View Admin console is simple. Have a look at `https://www.evga.com/support/manuals/files/PCoIP_APEX_2800_AdminGuide.pdf`.

The major consideration to make when using PCoIP hardware offloading is with regards to its capabilities across a cluster that supports a given desktop pool.

If a desktop pool's underlying vCenter cluster has hosts both with and without the APEX card, the vMotion (whether manual or triggered by DRS) could need to disconnect and reconnect to allow the PCoIP to initiate.

The following figure shows one cluster without the APEX card and one cluster with the APEX card:

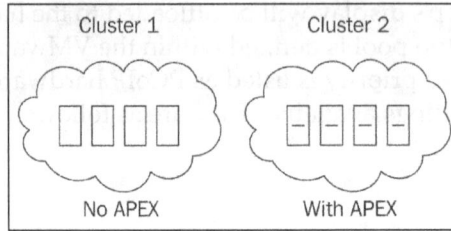

As vMotion tasks can prevent PCoIP offload from initiating, it is recommended that you use the Teradici APEX offload card across all hosts in a given cluster. That's not to say that all hosts in a given VMware View solution need the Teradici APEX card, but if the card is to be leveraged, it should be leveraged cluster-wide.

PCoIP Secure Gateway

The **PCoIP Secure Gateway** (**PSG**) is a way to provide the ability to use PCoIP connections from outside the firewall. The connections to the View desktops use port 4172 through the server that is running the PCoIP Secure Gateway.

The PSG service identifies an SSL certificate to use with the help of a server name and the certificate **Friendly name**. You can set the Friendly name value in the Windows registry of the View Connection Server or View Security Server where the PSG service is running. When the PSG service discovers a certificate that has a Friendly name that equals the Friendly name value in the Windows registry, it then uses that certificate only after a sequence of tests are passed by the certificate. Also, all of the certificates in the trust chain must be installed on the certificate store of the Windows local computer. There were a few problems that have been resolved by the current release. The items related to this functionality that have been resolved are as follows:

- All certificates had to be in the Personal certificates store on the Windows local computer. With the current release, the PSG service looks for the root certificate in the Trusted Root Certification Authorities store.

> If you fixed this problem in a previous release by moving the root certificate to the Personal store, the certificate will not be selected after the upgrade to 5.3. Move or copy the certificate back to the original Trusted Root Certification Authorities store.

- Previously, if you set the Friendly name value in the Windows registry to a substring of the certificate Friendly name, it could cause the PSG service to choose the wrong certificate. For instance, a Windows registry value of "Sam" could result in the selection of the certificate that had the Friendly name of "Sammy" instead of "Sam." With the release of 5.3, the PSG service will make an exact case-sensitive selection of the Friendly name.

Summary

As outlined in this chapter, the Teradici PCoIP protocol is the technology behind the delivery of the desktop to the end device. Whether that end device is an Apple iPad or IBM laptop, PCoIP uses its intelligence to ensure that the best possible user experience is delivered. Understanding how the Teradici PCoIP protocol works is important in understanding the network requirements of a given VDI solution. In the next chapter, sizing the network will be discussed, which includes the discussion of PCoIP considerations. A working knowledge of the Teradici PCoIP protocol is a requirement for anyone designing a VMware View solution; otherwise, the network could become a limiting factor in an otherwise well-designed solution.

6
Sizing the VDI

Sizing is the process of determining how much horsepower any given component of the VDI solution requires, which is ideally based on metrics collected during the assessment phase. In most situations, the challenge will not be the handling of the average daily VDI workloads, but the handling of the peaks. Peak loads in a VDI environment are often short in duration and may not be able to be mitigated through typical balancing techniques such as **VMware Distributed Resource Scheduler (DRS)** or manual **vMotion** balancing.

The components discussed in the earlier chapters of this book, for example, VMware View Connection Server, require minimal sizing considerations when compared to the hardware components that must be sized, the reason being that the software components are primarily performing relatively lightweight work and merely brokering connections or performing provisioning tasks, which, most likely, aren't happening constantly.

The following figure shows the sizing layers of a VDI solution:

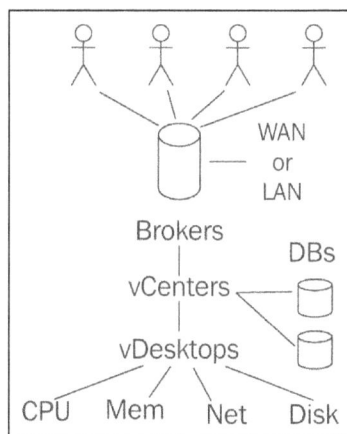

For example, having a properly-sized and performing database infrastructure is important, as slow database response times can impact both View Composer tasks as well as the tasks within vCenter. Also, it is important to ensure that the View Connection Server has adequate virtual or physical resources such as CPU and memory. However, the primary focus of this chapter is on sizing the physical components of the VDI.

To properly understand how to size a VDI, it's important to gather proper metrics during the assessment phase, which was covered in *Chapter 2, Solution Methodology*. Such metrics include the following:

- Number of concurrent users
- User classes and number of vCPUs, memory, and so on, per user class
- Network requirements
- USB redirection frequency

This chapter will focus on the following components from a sizing perspective and not necessarily from a redundancy perspective. This chapter is about the *n* in the *n + 1* formula. These components include the following:

- VMware View Connection Server
- VMware vCenter Server
- Server hardware
- Network infrastructure

Storage sizing is covered in *Chapter 8, Sizing the Storage*.

An improperly-sized VDI could experience any of the following problems:

- Slow logons
- Poor PCoIP performance
- Inability to power on vDesktops when vCenter maximums are reached
- Inability to log in to the VDI
- Authentication errors
- Random failures

All of the listed items have an effect on the end user experience, which is the most important measuring unit in VDI.

Network considerations

While understanding the networking connectivity between end users and the VDI is fairly obvious in a remote scenario, where the end user is removed geographically (for example, working from home) from the VDI, it's less obvious in a local scenario. While a local scenario may not blatantly cause a VDI architect to think about network sizing, it is still imperative to analyze and size the network component of a VDI solution even when all components reside on a **Local Area Network** (**LAN**). This is the only way to truly confirm that the end user's experience should be as positive as possible.

Sizing the network

As a general rule of thumb, a typical task worker requires approximately 250 Kbps of network throughput for a positive end user experience. By the generally accepted industry terms, a task worker is a user that has the following characteristics:

- They use typical office applications or terminal windows
- They do not require multimedia
- They do not require 3D graphics
- They do not require bidirectional audio

However, a task worker can potentially generate significant network bandwidth with the use of USB peripherals. If a task worker requires USB peripherals to perform their job, then it is imperative to perform a network analysis of the specific USB peripherals in action prior to full-scale implementation.

The list of the consumables is as follows:

- PCoIP baseline: 250 Kbps
- PCoIP burst headroom: 500 Kbps
- Multimedia video: 1,024 Kbps
- 3D graphics: 10,240 Kbps
- 480p video: 1,024 Kbps
- 720p video: 4,096 Kbps
- 1080p video: 6,144 Kbps
- Bidirectional audio: 500 Kbps
- USB peripherals: 500 Kbps
- Stereo audio: 500 Kbps
- CD quality audio: 2,048 Kbps

The network checklist is given at `http://techsupport.teradici.com/ics/support/default.asp?deptID=15164`. However, before that, you will be required to create an account at `http://techsupport.teradici.com`.

The other weights are as follows:

- Buffer: 80 percent
- Bandwidth offset: 105 percent

The minimum bandwidth to deliver acceptable performance is determined by the activity and requirements of the user's session. Some baseline numbers for the minimum bandwidth needed for a respective user type are shown in the following table:

Description	Kbps
Task worker – low activity without multimedia	250
Task worker – high activity without multimedia	315
Task worker – low activity with multimedia	340
Task worker – high activity with multimedia	375

The following figure is an illustration showing bandwidth provisioning of a given network connection:

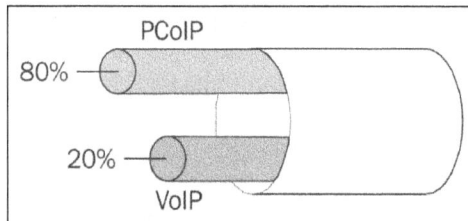

In most environments, the only network traffic that should have a higher network priority than PCoIP is network traffic related to **Voice over IP (VoIP)** communications. Giving PCoIP a higher priority than VoIP could cause poor quality or loss of connections in certain environments with an improperly-sized network. Therefore, it is recommended to give VoIP a higher priority than PCoIP (approximately up to 20 percent of the overall connection), give PCoIP traffic the second highest priority, and classify the remaining traffic appropriately.

Network connection characteristics

Teradici has made significant improvements in the ability of the PCoIP protocol to handle high-latency and/or low-bandwidth scenarios. Teradici's PCoIP protocol is a purpose-built protocol for delivering a native desktop experience. In order to deliver the best possible end user experience, PCoIP will consume as much bandwidth as is available at a given time, up to the point where it can deliver a favorable end user experience. PCoIP is dynamic in nature, and as the available bandwidth changes, so does the amount of bandwidth that PCoIP attempts to consume. PCoIP initially uses **Transmission Control Protocol** (**TCP**) to establish the connection and then uses **User Datagram Protocol** (**UDP**) to transmit the desktop experience.

PCoIP also has two primary settings that should be understood: the PCoIP maximum bandwidth and the PCoIP bandwidth floor.

The PCoIP maximum bandwidth is the maximum amount of bandwidth a given PCoIP session is allowed to consume. Configuring this setting can ensure that end users never exceed a certain amount of bandwidth themselves. In addition, properly configuring the PCoIP maximum bandwidth provides a sense of insurance in a solution. Without limiting consumptions per session (even if the maximum is configured to be very generous), it is possible to have a runaway PCoIP session consuming a disproportionate amount of the available bandwidth. This disproportionate consumption could negatively impact the other users sharing the same network connection.

The following figure is an illustration of the bandwidth floor and the bandwidth maximums:

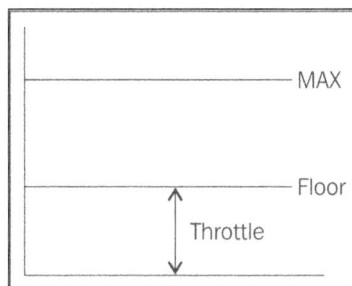

The PCoIP bandwidth floor is the minimum threshold of bandwidth that must be available for PCoIP to throttle the stream.

Here's an example.

An organization has 500 task workers, and is looking to understand how large a network pipe they need to provide for their VMware View solution. The VDI users only use basic office applications and require no other capabilities. Hence, the basic bandwidth consumption is:

Average Bandwidth Consumption = (Total Users * 250 Kbps) + (Special Need * Bandwidth Penalty) * Bandwidth Offsite * Buffer

So, substituting the values given in the preceding example gives us the following output:

Average Bandwidth Consumption = (500 * 250 Kbps) + 0 * 80 percent = 100,000 KBps (approximately 97 Mbps)

DHCP considerations

While it is possible to cobble together a VDI solution that uses static **Internet Protocol (IP)** addresses, it is not recommended, unless there is a business-defined reason. Due to the potential volatility of a VDI and for ease of management, **Dynamic Host Configuration Protocol (DHCP)** is the preferred method for managing the issuing of the IP addresses of the vDesktops. When using DHCP, vDesktops do not own a specific IP address, but rather, it leases itself from a DHCP server.

A single DHCP scope consists of a pool of IP addresses on a particular subnet. A DHCP superscope allows a DHCP server to distribute IP addresses from more than one scope to devices on a single physical network. Proper subnetting can ensure that enough IP leases exist in a particular scope to serve the number of end devices that require IP addresses. The following figure shows a DHCP workflow:

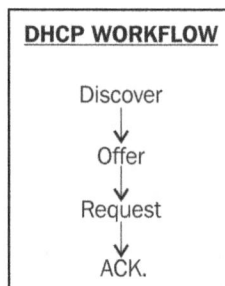

DHCP WORKFLOW

Discover
↓
Offer
↓
Request
↓
ACK.

The workflow of a DHCP lease allocation is as follows:

1. The client broadcasts a DHCPDISCOVER message on its physical subnet.

2. The available DHCP servers on the subnet respond with an IP address by sending a DHCPOFFER packet back to the client.

3. The client replies with a DHCPREQUEST message to signal which DHCP server they accepted the DHCPOFFER packet from. The other DHCP servers withdraw their offer for a DHCP lease.

4. The DHCP server in the DHCPREQUEST message from the client replies with a DHCPACK packet to acknowledge the completion of the lease transaction.

DHCP reallocation occurs when a client that already has an address within a valid lease expiration window reboots or starts up after being shut down. When it starts the backup, it will contact the DHCP server previously confirmed via a DHCPACK packet to verify the lease and obtain any necessary parameters.

After a set period of time (T1) has elapsed since the original lease allocation, the client will attempt to renew the lease. If the client is unable to successfully renew the lease, it will enter the rebinding phase (starts at T2). During this rebinding phase, it will attempt to obtain a lease from any available DHCP server.

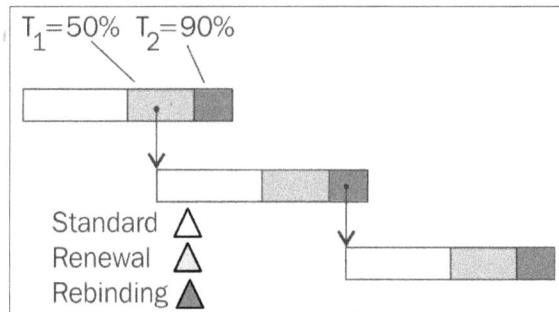

In the preceding figure, T1 is defined as 50 percent of the lease duration, and T2 is defined as 90 percent of the lease duration.

For this example, assume a lease duration of 120 minutes (2 hours).

A vDesktop boots and is successfully allocated a DHCP lease for a duration of 120 minutes from DHCP_SERVER_01. At T1 (50 percent of 120 minutes, that is, 60 minutes), the vDesktop attempts to renew its lease from DHCP_SERVER_01. During the renewal period, the vDesktop successfully renews its DHCP lease. The lease clock is now reset back to a full 120-minute lease since the lease renew was successful.

This time, the vDesktop is unsuccessful during the renewal period and enters the rebinding period. The vDesktop successfully obtains a new DHCP lease from DHCP_SERVER_03 with a lease of a fresh 120 minutes.

In most VDI scenarios, a DHCP lease time of one hour is sufficient. Typically, this is considerably less than the average DHCP lease time in default scopes used by most organizations.

If a desktop pool is set to delete a vDesktop after a user logs off, this could generate significant DHCP lease thrashing, and a very short DHCP lease time should be considered (depending on the frequency of vDesktop deletions).

The VMware View Composer tasks such as Recompose and Refresh should maintain the same MAC address throughout the process as the VMX (the virtual machine configuration file) settings related to vNIC should not be altered. Therefore, the original lease will attempt to be reallocated during the boot process. As a special note, you should consider that the availability of the DHCP server with it is used with a VDI solution.

Virtual switch considerations

Virtual switch design for VDI environments is another component that may prove challenging for those unfamiliar with large-scale virtual infrastructure, or those accustomed to designing solutions with potentially high virtual machine volatility.

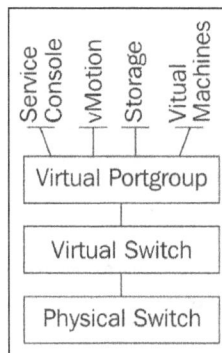

The preceding figure shows the network components of a VDI environment at a high level. The abstraction (that would reside in between the physical switch and the virtual switch) done by the hypervisor is not shown.

There are two types of virtual switches you can use when configuring the VMware environment including the VDI environment. The first type is a **Standard vSwitch**. A vSwitch can route traffic internally between virtual machines and link to external networks.

You can use vSwitches to combine the bandwidth of multiple network adapters and balance communications' traffic among them. You can also configure a vSwitch to handle physical NIC failover. A vSwitch models a physical Ethernet switch.

When the standard vSwitch is created, it has, by default, 120 ports. This parameter is defined at a kernel (hypervisor) layer, and any change to the number of ports in a standard switch requires a reboot of the physical host.

The second type is a **Distributed vSwitch** (**vDS**), which functions as a single virtual switch across all associated hosts. This enables you to set network configurations that span across all member hosts and allows virtual machines to maintain consistent network configuration as they migrate across multiple hosts.

When the distributed vSwitch, also known as a **dvSwitch**, is created, it has, by default, 128 ports. This parameter can be changed dynamically, and does not require a reboot of the physical host to change the number of ports from its original value of 128.

Standard versus distributed switches

Standard vSwitches are not impacted by the loss of a VMware vCenter Server, and are best used by functions such as Service console, vMotion, and storage connectivity, as they can all be easily managed from the command line. However, in large VDI solutions that leverage multiple **Virtual Local Area Networks** (**VLANs**), dozens or hundreds of physical hosts and dvSwitches help to greatly streamline the virtual network management across the virtual infrastructure.

VMware vSphere hosts keep a local cache of dvSwitch, dvPortGroup, and dvPort information to use when the VMware vCenter Server is unavailable. The local cache configuration copies are read-only and cannot be manipulated by the administrator.

Port binding

Port binding is the process of assigning a specific port, also known as a **dvPort**, to a specific **network interface controller** (**NIC**) on a specific virtual machine. Think of this assignment as analogous to taking a patch cable and plugging its one end into the NIC on a physical desktop and the other end into an available switch. dvPorts decide how a virtual machine's network traffic is mapped to a specific distributed portgroup or **dvPortGroup**.

There are three types of port bindings used by dvSwitches; they are as follows:

- Static binding
- Dynamic binding
- Ephemeral binding

Static binding

Static binding assigns an available port on the dvPortGroup of the dvSwitch when a vNIC is added to a virtual machine. For example, if VM009 is a powered-off Windows 2008 virtual machine, and the administrator goes into **Edit Settings** and adds an NIC on dvPortGroup VLAN 71, a dvPort from the VLAN 71 dvPortGroup is assigned to the NIC, assuming one is available. It does not matter if the virtual machine VM009 is powered on or powered off; it is still assigned a dvPort and the dvPort will be unavailable to other virtual machines.

The assigned dvPort is released only when the virtual machine has been removed from the dvPortGroup. Virtual machines using static binding can only be connected to a dvPortGroup through the vCenter Server.

The advantage of static binding is that a virtual machine can be powered on even if the vCenter Server is unavailable. In addition, network statistics are maintained after a vMotion event and after a power cycle of the virtual machine.

The disadvantage of static binding is that the dvPortGroup cannot be overcommitted. In a volatile VDI that uses nonpersistent desktops that are deleted at the time of logoff, it is possible that the solution could run out of available dvPorts on the dvPortGroup. Static binding is strongly discouraged in environments that leverage VMware View Composer.

Dynamic binding

Dynamic binding assigns an available dvPort on the dvPortGroup when a virtual machine is powered on and its NIC is in the connected state. For example, if VM009 is a Windows 2008 virtual machine, and the administrator goes into **Edit Settings** and adds an NIC on dvPortGroup VLAN 71, a dvPort from VLAN 71 dvPortGroup is not yet assigned. Once the virtual machine VM009 is powered on, it is assigned a dvPort on the dvPortGroup, and that specific dvPort will be unavailable to other virtual machines.

The assigned dvPort is released when the virtual machine has been powered off or the NIC is disconnected. Virtual machines that use dynamic binding can only be connected to a dvPortGroup through the vCenter Server.

Dynamic binding is useful in environments where the number of virtual machines is more than the number of available dvPorts on a given dvPortGroup; however, the number of powered-on virtual machines will not exceed the number of available dvPorts on a given dvPortGroup.

The advantage of dynamic binding is that as a virtual machine doesn't occupy a dvPort until it is powered on, it is possible to overcommit the port on a given dvPortGroup. In addition, network statistics are maintained after a vMotion event.

The disadvantage of dynamic binding is that as a virtual machine isn't assigned a dvPort until it is powered on, it must be powered on by the vCenter Server. Therefore, if the vCenter Server is unavailable, the virtual machine will not be able to be powered on. This is not really a problem as much as the nature of the dynamic binding.

Ephemeral binding

Ephemeral binding creates and assigns a dvPort on the dvPortGroup when a virtual machine is powered on and its NIC is connected. For example, if VM009 is a Windows 2008 virtual machine, and the administrator goes into **Edit Settings** and adds an NIC on dvPortGroup VLAN 71, a dvPort from VLAN71 dvPortGroup is not yet assigned. Once the virtual machine VM009 is powered on, a dvPort is first created and then it is assigned a dvPort on the dvPortGroup and that specific dvPort will be unavailable to other virtual machines.

The assigned dvPort is released when the virtual machine has been powered off or the NIC is in the disconnected state. Virtual machines using ephemeral binding can be connected to a dvPortGroup through the vCenter Server or from ESX/ESXi. Therefore, if the vCenter Server is unavailable, the virtual machine network connections can still be managed.

When a virtual machine is vMotion-enabled, the original dvPort is deleted from the source dvPortGroup, and a new dvPort is created on the destination dvPortGroup.

Ephemeral binding is useful in environments of high volatility, for example, in a nonpersistent VDI solution, where virtual machines are created and deleted often. The number of ports on a dvPortGroup is defined and limited by the number of ports available on the dvSwitch.

The advantage of ephemeral binding is that as a virtual machine doesn't occupy a dvPort until it is powered on, it is possible to overcommit the port on a given dvPortGroup.

The disadvantages of ephemeral binding is that network statistics are not maintained after the power cycle of a virtual machine or after a vMotion event as the dvPort is created and assigned at the time of boot or a vMotion event.

Port binding and VMware View Composer

For VDI solutions that leverage View Composer, it is important to recognize that tasks such as Recompose, Rebalance, and Refresh will attempt to use the same port that has been assigned to the replica image.

Therefore, it is recommended that you use dynamic or ephemeral (preferred) binding if VMware View Composer will be leveraged.

Multi-VLAN

In Horizon View 6 (started in Version 5.2), it is possible to configure an automated pool to use multiple VLANS known as network labels. Now, an administrator can assign multiple network labels to a linked-clone pool as well as to an automated pool that contains full virtual machines.

This solves one of the most common problems when implementing large desktop pools prior to the 5.2 release. When creating a desktop pool, each virtual desktop inherits the network label from the parent's image. The network label specifies a portgroup/VLAN/DHCP IP address range. When you created a large pool, it meant thousands of desktops were forced into the same large VLAN, and there had to be enough IP addresses on that subnet for each desktop.

Administrators, on the other hand, either had to accept this limitation or implement some workaround to achieve the industry-standard VLAN size of 256 IP addresses. This meant creating multiple smaller pools, each with their own parent image, and each image had their own unique network label specifying the necessary subnet size. You could also modify (manually in vCenter, or with scripting) the network label for each virtual desktop to overwrite the label from the parent image after provisioning. Another problem was that this would have to be redone after Recompose or Refresh and also any time you modified the pool size.

Now, with this new feature:

- Each pool can be configured with a **network label spec**. This allows the administrator to specify, for each network adapter (NIC) on the parent, a list of selected network labels to automatically assign to each newly-provisioned virtual desktop in the pool.

- Horizon View tracks the per-pool count of virtual desktops and their labels provisioned under the feature, so if the pool size is changed, the configured network label capacity and assignments will be used.

- Each label is given a maximum assignment count. After the system has provisioned, assigned, and exhausted a network label to its assigned capacity for a given NIC, it steps to the next one in the specification list.

- Network labels are treated in the same way as MAC addresses — refresh and recompose operations do not revert the virtual desktop to its parent's network label state.

- Network labels are assigned to desktops upon first provisioning — previously-created desktops are not modified.

This new powerful feature currently does not have an administrative user interface, and can only be configured through Horizon View PowerShell.

This feature is configured using the following steps:

1. Create a network label specification text file using parameters from a Cluster-host and the parent VM.

2. Then, edit the network label specification file to associate any available network labels with the available NICs and add the desired maximum capacity counts.

3. Now, create a new VM pool or update an existing one using the network label specification file created earlier.

For additional information on how to configure and implement multi-VLAN support, refer to the View Integration Horizon 6 guide available at `https://pubs.vmware.com/horizon-view-60/topic/com.vmware.ICbase/PDF/horizon-view-60-integration.pdf`.

Compute considerations

Compute is typically not an area of failure in most VDI projects, but it is still important to understand the computing requirements of an organization before implementing a final design. Programs that can cause unforeseen failure from a compute perspective are as follows:

- Dragon Medical/Dragon NaturallySpeaking
- Defense Connect Online
- AutoCAD
- Eclipse IDE

For VDI solutions that will be based on 32-bit Windows 7 or Vista, one vCPU can likely be used to address most basic computing needs. However, for VDI solutions that leverage Windows 7 (64-bit), or more importantly Windows 8 (all 64-bit), two vCPUs may be necessary to ensure a favorable end user experience.

For the most accurate calculation of CPU requirements, a proper assessment of the environment should be performed. This will help identify potential pitfalls such as some of the applications listed previously, prior to rollout.

While both AMD and Intel-based x86 servers will suffice for VDI solutions, in large-scale and/or demanding environments, Intel-based solutions have consistently outperformed their AMD counterparts from a density (number of vDesktops per core) perspective.

In VDI solutions, there is also the potential for unnecessary CPU load due to tasks such as antivirus scanning, poorly-tuned applications, single-threaded processes, added visual effects, and impacts from video or audio processing.

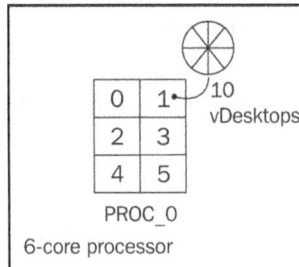

The preceding figure illustrates a single processor with six cores. As a safe baseline, 10 vDesktops (one vCPU) per core is used for design purposes. For basic task workers, this number could be significantly higher, and there are multiple reference architectures that validate 15 to 18 vDesktops per core. The use of the Teradici APEX offload card (see the *Teradici APEX offload card* section in *Chapter 5, The PCoIP Protocol*) could also increase the density of users per core.

We will continue to use the same 10 vDesktops (mentioned earlier) per core as a baseline, and assume that the server has two processors (of six cores each) that nets a total of 12 cores per physical server with 12 cores per server and 10 users per core, which yields 120 users per physical server (*6 cores per processor * 2 processors per server * 10 users per core*). Using 1.5 GB of RAM for each vDesktop (the bare minimum recommendation for 64-bit Windows 7), the same physical server needs 180 GB of RAM (*1.5 GB * 120 users*). That's a relatively sweet spot for memory, as most servers are configurable with 256 GB of RAM from the factory.

The following two tables have been extracted from the *Configuration Maximums, VMware vSphere 5.5* guide at `http://www.vmware.com/pdf/vsphere5/r55/vsphere-55-configuration-maximums.pdf`. The following tables explain compute maximums.

For a host CPU:

Host CPU maximums	Maximum
Logical CPUs per host	320

For a virtual machine:

Virtual machine maximums	Maximum
Virtual machines per host	512
Virtual CPUs per host	4096
Virtual CPUs per core	32

Given the preceding information, we know that the selected processors with significantly more cores per processor (for example, 24 cores per processor or 32 cores per processor) may not help vDesktop density on a given physical server if the number of VDesktops exceeds another limit of the server, for example, memory of the number of VMs.

The following table explains memory maximums:

Host memory maximums	Maximum
RAM per host	4 TB

The reason why increased density may not be realized (or more accurately, maximized) is partly due to memory limitations and also due to existing VMware vSphere limitations. Let's assume, for the sake of argument, that a 32-core physical server was selected as the standard for a given VDI solution, and it was shipped with a maximum supported 2 TB of RAM.

Using the conservative baseline of 10 vDesktops per core would yield 320 vDesktops per host, requiring 640 GB of RAM.

The following table explains cluster maximums:

Cluster maximums	Maximum
Hosts per cluster	32
Virtual machines per cluster	4,000
Virtual machines per host	512

Furthermore, the analysis from the *Configuration Maximum, VMware vSphere 5.5* guide concludes that "if more than one configuration option (such as the number of virtual machines, number of LUNs, number of vDS ports, and so on) is used at their maximum limit, some of the processes running on the host might run out of memory". Therefore, it is advised to avoid reaching the configuration maximums when possible.

As with all portions of a VDI design, it is important to leverage real-world metrics, when possible, to understand how vDesktops will be used, and how they will impact the underlying physical infrastructure.

Given the preceding calculations, it is advisable to conserve capital expenditure on high core count processors and, instead, focus the funding elsewhere. In most environments, six, eight, or twelve core processors will be more than sufficient in terms of performance as well as in ensuring that vSphere maximums are not reached. Also, consider a server failure with 300 desktops that affect many users at once.

Working with VMware vSphere maximums

A strong case can be made that while VMware vSphere is by far the industry-leading hypervisor platform for server virtualization, its current maximums could be limiting in terms of mega-scale VDI environments. The following is a list of vCenter maximums taken from the *Configuration Maximums, VMware vSphere 5.5* guide that are most relevant to a VMware View solution:

vCenter Server scalability	Maximum
Hosts per vCenter Server	1,000
Powered on virtual machines per vCenter Server	10,000
Registered virtual machines per vCenter Server	15,000
Linked vCenter Servers (pod)	10

vCenter Server scalability	Maximum
Hosts in linked vCenter Servers	3,000
Powered on virtual machines in linked vCenter Servers	30,000
Registered virtual machines in linked vCenter Servers	50,000

The preceding limitations will be analyzed with a solution example in the next section.

Solution example – 25,000 seats of VMware View

A VDI architect has been hired by Company, Inc. to design a solution for 25,000 task workers in a single building. In this scenario, the networking and storage will be provided and will meet the necessary requirements of the VDI solution; therefore, the focus is on the physical server specification and the logical design of the VMware vSphere and VMware View environments.

Company, Inc. is looking for the following information:

- **Bill of materials (BOM)** for physical servers
- Logical design of the vSphere infrastructure
- Logical design of the View infrastructure

Taking a quick look at the requirements, the architect has determined the following:

- Powered-on virtual machines per vCenter Server *will be* exceeded (the limit is 10,000)
- Registered virtual machines per vCenter Server *will be* exceeded (the limit is 15,000)
- Powered-on virtual machines in linked vCenter Servers *will not be* exceeded (the limit is 30,000)
- Registered virtual machines in linked vCenter Servers *will not be* exceeded (the limit is 50,000)
- Maximum hosts per vCenter Server *will not be* exceeded (the limit is 1,000)

Solution design – physical server requirements

To support 25,000 task workers running Windows 7 vDesktops, the physical server sizing must be determined. Through initial testing, 10 vDesktops per core was a conservative estimate. As 4-core processors are being phased out, 6-core processors were chosen for their price and availability. Therefore, two 6-core processors per physical host yields 12 cores per host. Using 10 vDesktops per core and 12 cores per host yields 120 vDesktops per host. With 1.5 GB per vDesktop used for the environment, 180 GB of RAM is required for vDesktops. By allocating the maximum supported, 800 MB of RAM to the service console yields 181 GB of RAM required. Therefore, a server with 192 GB of RAM will support the environment nicely. In addition, the following vNetwork maximums exist:

vNetwork Standard and Distributed Switch	Maximum
Total virtual network ports per host	4,096
Maximum active ports per host	1,016
Distributed switches per vCenter	32

Given the preceding maximums, the following physical host design was leveraged:

Description	Value
Cores per processor	6
Processors per host	2
NICs per host	8
Memory per host (GB)	192
Approximate vDesktops per core	10
Approximate vDesktops per host	120
Standard vSwitches	2
Distributed vSwitches	1

The networking configuration is shown as follows:

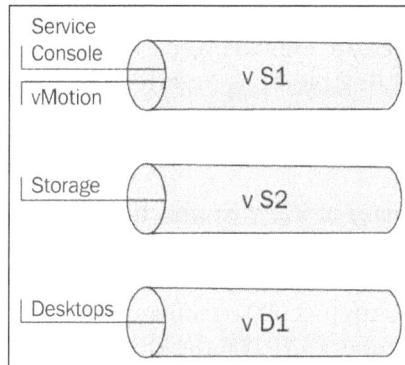

The preceding figure represents two vNetwork standard switches and one vNetwork distributed switch. The first standard vSwitch, vS1, is used for the service console and vMotion. The second standard vSwitch, vS2, is used for network-based storage. The only distributed vSwitch, vD1, is used for virtual machines.

Solution design – the pod concept

The concept of the pod is to give architects a method of creating building blocks to ease the design scalability for large environments. It also provides a conceptual framework for the solution architecture.

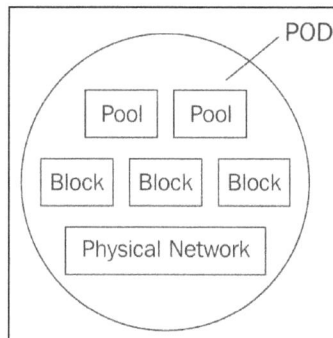

The VMware View pod design

The three main building blocks of the pod design are the **View pod**, **View block**, and **Management block**. All three are logical objects and have some concrete boundaries. The information on the building blocks is described in the following sections:

The View pod

A View pod is a specific cluster of View Connection Servers that replicate the Active Directory Lightweight Directory Services. They also contain the volatile desktop session map, which is replicated in the cluster using a **Java Message Service (JMS)** message bus. The support is up to 2,000 concurrent connections per Connection Server with a maximum number of 10,000 desktops within a View pod.

A large-scale deployment would require your Connection Servers to have at least 10 GB of RAM and no less than 4 vCPUs. Do not exceed the maximum number of concurrent connections on the Connection Servers in the cluster, and take into account Connection Servers that could be offline for maintenance or unexpected downtime.

The View block

VMware View is integrated with VMware vSphere and its vCenter that provisions and controls desktops. For large-scale View designs, it is recommended that you use multiple, separate vCenter instances, and each vCenter instance determines a **View block**. With a large-scale VMware View implementation, there are provisioning and power operations that happen while initially deploying a pool for the virtual desktops. Also, when performing Refresh, Recompose, or Rebalance operations, or when using advanced items such as powering off unused desktops overnight to conserve power consumption of ESXi using Distributed Power Management. When you have multiple vCenter instances, this allows the operations mentioned earlier to occur in parallel as opposed to executing in serial mode. This helps to complete operations with deployments and refit much faster.

The Management block

The Management block is a separate vSphere cluster that contains the server infrastructure that supports the View infrastructure's virtual machines. This consists of the Connection Servers, the vCenter Servers for the View block, and the database servers used by vCenter. It can also include View Security Servers and the Composer servers.

The Management block is a best practice for large-scale solutions. Because server workloads tend to be relatively fixed compared to the highly volatile workloads of the desktops, separating these workloads ensure they do not interfere with each other, which could affect the end user experience. Also, a separate vSphere cluster is a design best practice that encourages you to not manage a vSphere cluster from a virtual vCenter instance that is running on an ESXi host that it manages.

Each View block should be thought of as a resource limit. View desktop pools are confined to a vSphere cluster, and each pool of desktops is restricted to the storage that is visible to the ESXi hosts that contain those virtual desktops. Storage can be dedicated to a View block or shared across multiple View blocks. IOPS (read/write) is the primary constraint, and the second one is the constraint of the total disk space consumed by all desktops in all the pools within the View block.

When running desktops on VMFS datastores, the vSphere cluster size is limited to 8 ESXi hosts per cluster, and when using NFS datastores exclusively, you can go up to 32 ESXi hosts per cluster. Designing for maximum virtual machine density is important.

Scaling desktop pool types

There are different types of desktop image-management solutions for full clones and linked clones. Full clones make up a standalone virtual machine with a monolithic .vmdk file. Linked clones take advantage of the **scalable virtual image** (**SVI**) technology available when using View Composer. Full-clone desktop pools can be quite large. Therefore, they should have a limit of 1,000 desktops per pool. This is not a set limit but should be an operational consideration.

The View Recompose operation is normally applied to an entire pool. During this Recompose action, View deletes the desktop, which includes the linked clone delta disk, and then creates a new one. There is a lot of activity during a Recompose operation, including a lot of provisioning going through vCenter, and also a great deal of disk operations. The larger the pool, the longer it take to recompose the desktops. What this means is that storage performance is a factor in provisioning and recomposing.

The following is the pod design summary:

- **View pod**: This is the cluster of View Connection Servers
- **View block**: This is the View desktop resource limit with a vCenter server as the distinction
- **View Management block**: This is a separate vSphere cluster where the View infrastructure's virtual machines reside

The following is the summary for Connection Servers:

- The maximum supported number of desktops in a View pod is 10,000

- Each Connection Server can support 2,000 concurrent connections

- Multiple vCenter servers provide parallel benefits to power and provisioning operations

The following is the summary for desktop pools and storage:

- Storage systems are shared between View blocks or dedicated to View blocks to increase performance

- Desktop pools are constrained to a vSphere cluster

- vSphere clusters hosting linked clone pools are limited to eight ESXi hosts when using VMFS datastores, or 32 ESXi hosts when using NFS datastores only

The architecture types for pods

This concept of a pod can be carried through with the following architecture types:

- Traditional

- Traditional in a modular form

- Converged virtualization appliances

The **traditional** architecture type involves using servers (rackmount or blade), network switches, storage network switches (if applicable), and storage arrays. A traditional architecture approach is normally sufficient for an initial build-out but may not offer the scale-out capabilities of other approaches. The following figure shows an illustration of a typical traditional architecture approach where disproportionate resources exist:

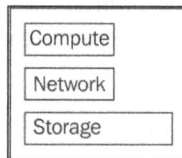

For example, referring to the preceding figure, sufficient compute, network, and storage resources may exist for the initial rollout of 400 VMware View users. In this example, an overabundance of storage capacity exists.

The following figure shows an illustration of a typical traditional architecture scale-out challenge:

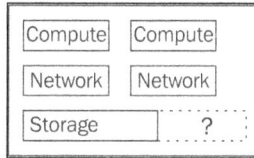

When the organization decides to add an additional 500 VMware View users, it runs into a problem. In the phase 1 rollout, an overabundance of storage capacity exists. However, to add capacity in a modular fashion, compute and network will still require an additional block of storage. Therefore, every addition will have some level of excess, which drives the price per vDesktop up due to architectural inefficiencies.

Most probably, an organization would not want to accept these inefficiencies, so it would redesign its requirements at every step of the way. Designing the scale-out for every additional phase of a VDI solution also drives up the cost through added complexity and man hours.

In addition, every time a scale-out phase is re-architected, the chance of errors occurring becomes greater.

The **traditional in modular form** architecture type involves using servers (rackmount or blade), network switches, storage network switches (if applicable), and storage arrays. While a traditional architecture is normally not able to scale proportionately, a traditional modular form architecture is designed to scale in building blocks. This approach does not need re-engineering for each scale-out phase. Instead, an organization relies on the traditional yet modular architecture for a predictable scale-out design.

The following figure shows an illustration of a typical traditional in modular form architecture approach, where proportionate resources exist:

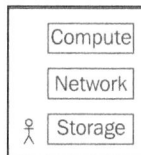

There are typically two ways to implement a traditional in modular form architecture:

- The first is by spending time to architect and test a customer design, where compute (for example, Dell blade) is combined with network switches (for example, Cisco) and a storage array (for example, NetApp). The danger with this approach is that if the person or team that is designing the solution has never designed a VDI solution earlier, they are likely to learn a few lessons through the process that will yield a less-than-optimal solution. This is not to say that this approach is not suitable and should not be taken, but special considerations should be taken to ensure that the architecture is sound and scalable. A seasoned VDI architect can take any off-the-shelf hardware and build a sustainable VDI architecture.

- The second way to implement a traditional modular form architecture is by implementing a branded solution, such as the VCE Vblock (Cisco servers + Cisco switches + EMC storage) or FlexPod (Cisco servers + Cisco switches + NetApp storage). These solutions are proven to be scalable in a predictive manner, and they offer a known architecture for VDI. The drawback of these solutions is that they often have a high barrier to entry in terms of cost and scale-out in large modular blocks (for example, 1,000 users at a time).

The third type of architecture uses **converged virtualization appliances**. Converged virtualization appliances are typically 2U to 6U appliances that comprise of one-to-many ESXi servers with local storage that is often shared among the ESXi servers in the appliance. The storage is typically shared through a virtual storage appliance model, where local storage is represented as either iSCSI or NFS storage to one or more ESXi servers in the appliance. Some converged infrastructures allow enterprises to scale VDI in a linear way that provides a less complex method of deployment.

> Nutanix is an example of a converged infrastructure. It delivers an out-of-the-box infrastructure solution for virtual desktops (http://www.nutanix.com/).

Linked vCenter Servers

As the number of virtual machines per vCenter Server will be exceeded, more than one vCenter Server will be required for this solution.

The following table illustrates the vCenter maximums:

vCenter Server scalability	Maximum
Powered on virtual machines per vCenter Server	10,000
Registered virtual machines per vCenter Server	15,000
Linked vCenter Servers	10
Powered-on virtual machines in linked vCenter Servers	30,000
Registered virtual machines in linked vCenter Servers	50,000

vCenter Linked Mode has a few basic prerequisites. They are as follows:

- Both vCenter Servers must reside in a functional DNS environment, where **fully qualified domain names** (**FQDNs**) of each vCenter Server can be resolved properly

- Any vCenter Server participating in Linked Mode must reside in an Active Directory Domain

- If the vCenter Servers are in separate Active Directory Domains, the respective domains must have two-way trust

- Both vCenter Servers must reside in a functional **Network Time Protocol** (**NTP**) environment, where the difference between the time synchronization of the vCenter Servers is no more than 5 minutes

- The Windows RPC port mapper must be allowed to open the **Remote Procedure Call** (**RPC**) ports for replication; this is covered in detail at `http://support.microsoft.com/kb/154596`

- Both VMware vCenter Servers have the VMware vCenter Standard Edition license (for example, Foundation)

- Separate databases for each VMware vCenter Server

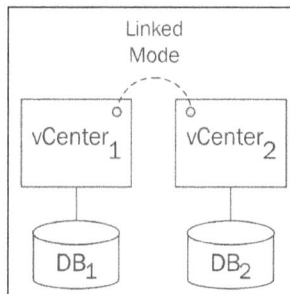

As shown in the preceding figure, VMware vCenter Linked Mode connects two or more vCenter Servers together via ADAM database replication to store information regarding user roles as well as VMware licensing. VMware vCenter Linked Mode does not perform any form of database replication. If VMware vCenter Linked Mode fails for any reason, the two (or more) vCenter Servers will still be viable as standalone instances.

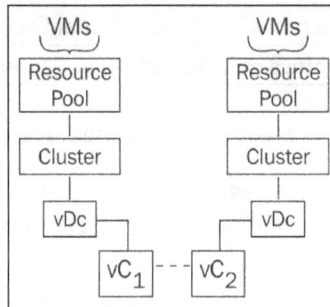

As shown in the preceding figure, where there are two separate vCenter Server instances (vCenter1 and vCenter2), the virtual data centers, clusters, resource pools, and virtual machines are unique to their respective instance of vCenter.

Joining multiple vCenters together with vCenter Linked Mode forms is what is known as a pod. A pod can consist of up to 10 vCenter Servers in Linked Mode.

vCenter Servers

Using calculations from the preceding sections, this solution is expected to have approximately 120 vDesktops per host; this means that 209 physical hosts are needed to support the vDesktop portion of this solution (not taking into account a virtualized vCenter, database, and so on).

Due to the nature of the end user population, the time they log in, and the conservative nature of the original assessment (for example, 10 vDesktops per core), it has been decided that there will be no **High Availability** requirements for the vSphere Servers that support vDesktops.

It has also been determined that the management infrastructure including the View Connection Servers, vCenter Servers, database server, and a few other components require three physical hosts. In order to provide a level of protection, it has been determined to use an $n + 1$ solution and utilize four physical hosts.

By placing the View management components on a management or server-based cluster, you will not need a Windows Datacenter License for the hosts that are just managing virtual desktops.

It was determined previously that any given vCenter can have a maximum of 10,000 powered-on virtual machines at any given time. This solution will need to support more than 25,000 powered-on virtual machines; therefore, this solution will require three vCenter Servers.

To balance the load across the vCenter Servers, the clusters have been as equitably divided as possible.

The naming conventions used for the clusters in this example are as follows:

- vCenter Server: vc-{letter}, for example, vc-b
- Clusters: cl-{letter of vCenter}-{number}, for example, cl-c-6

The vCenter Servers are named vc-a, vc-b, and vc-c respectively. Their details along with the figures are as follows:

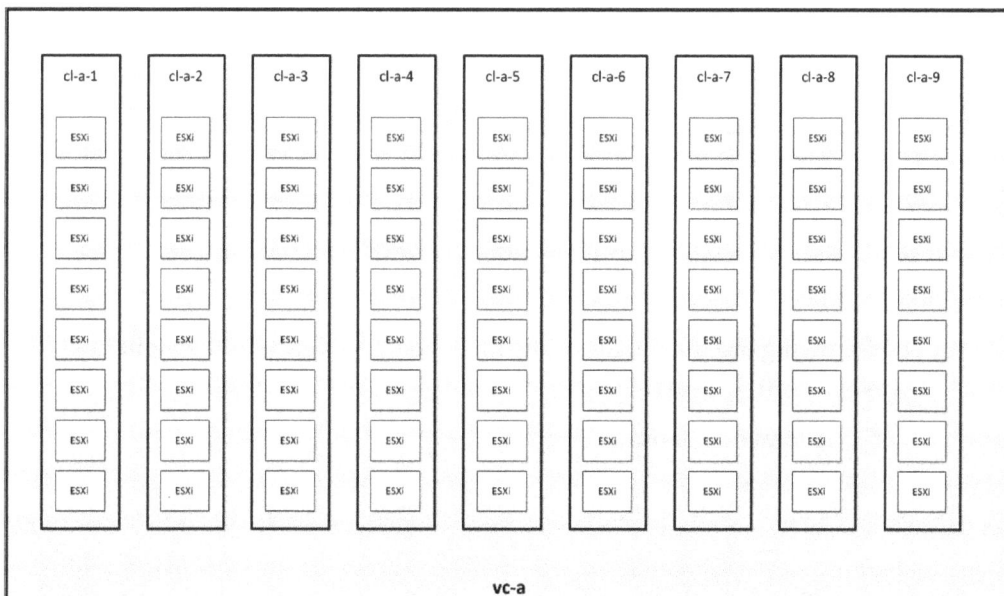

The preceding figure explains the vCenter Server vc-a. The following list gives the details about vc-a:

- The following are the details of the nine clusters of each of the eight hosts (cl-a-1, cl-a-2,..., cl-a-9):

  ○ A total of 72 hosts

  ○ A total of 8,640 vDesktops (120 vDesktops per host multiplied by 72 hosts)

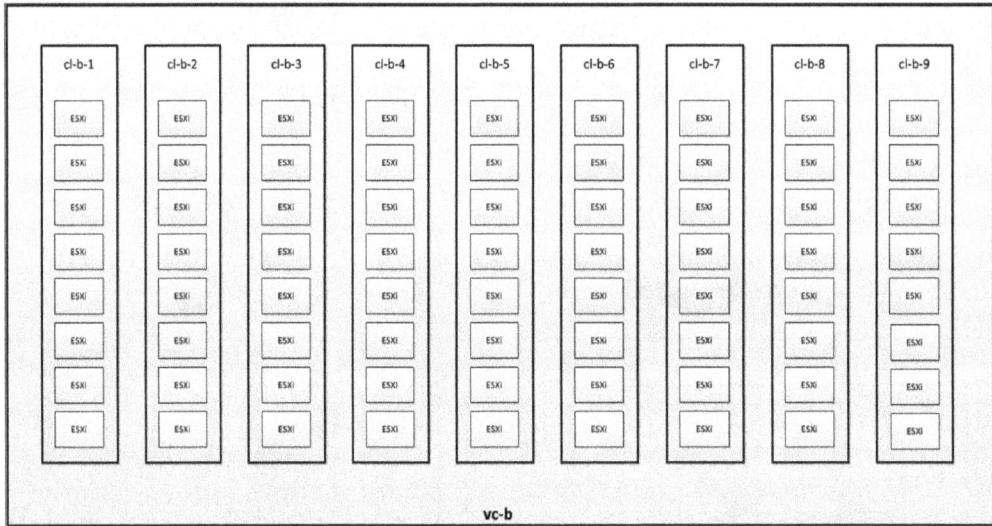

The preceding figure explains the vCenter Server vc-b. The following list gives the details about vc-b:

- The following are the details of the nine clusters of each of the eight hosts (cl-b-1, cl-b-2, ..., cl-b-9):

  ○ A total of 72 hosts

      °   A total of 8,640 vDesktops (120 vDesktops per host multiplied by 72 hosts)

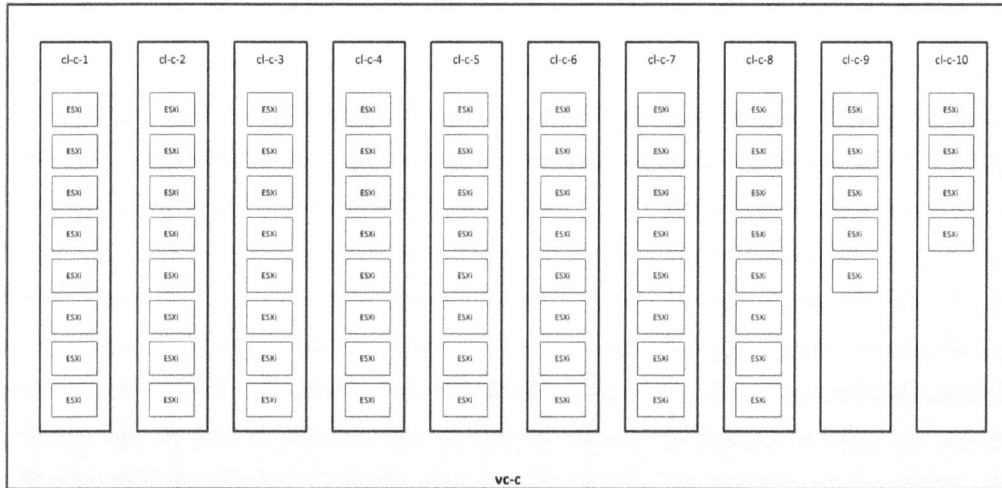

The preceding figure explains the vCenter Server vc-c. The following list gives the details about vc-c:

- Seven clusters, each with eight hosts
- One cluster of five hosts
- One cluster of four hosts
- One cluster of four hosts dedicated to management. The following are the details:

      °   A total of 69 hosts

      °   A total of 7,800 vDesktops and approximately 30 vServers (View Connection Server, database server, vCenter server, and so on)

vCenter `vc-c` has a cluster (`cl-c-10`) dedicated for hosting the infrastructure virtual machines, as shown in the following figure. These virtual machines include:

- Three VMware vCenter Servers (`vc-a`, `vc-b`, and `vc-c`)
- 15 View Connection Servers
- Supporting infrastructure (if needed), such as database servers, Liquidware Labs TM, and so on

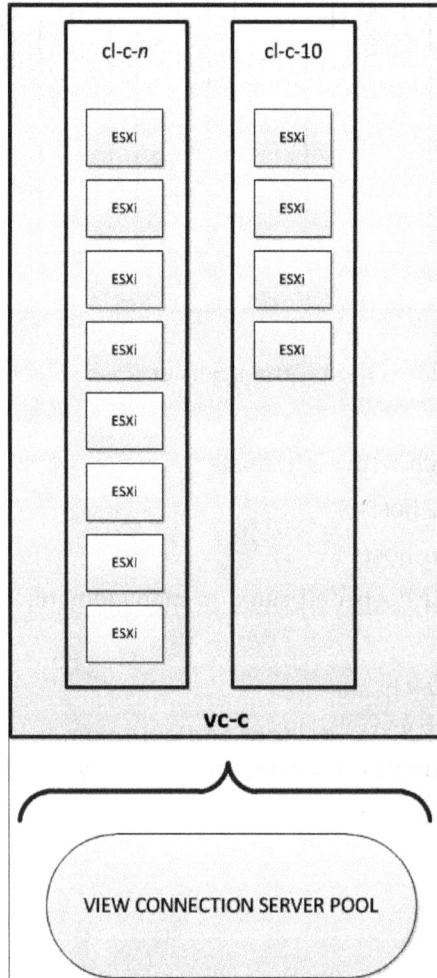

VMware Update Manager Servers

VMware Update Manager is a solution that automates the application of patches to both vSphere Servers and virtual machines. It's most often used to patch vSphere Servers in large environments as it handles the task of placing a host in the maintenance mode, and migrating virtual machines, patch application, reboots, and normalization with a minimal amount of user interaction.

VMware Update Manager Servers can only be paired with one VMware vCenter Server instance at a time. Therefore, in this solution, three VMware Update Manager Servers will be required (one per vCenter Server instance), as shown in the following figure:

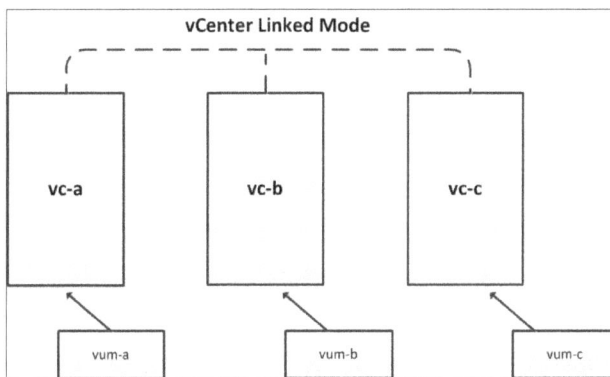

Solution design – pools

Here, we will cover View Connection Servers.

View Connection Servers

The VMware View infrastructure introduces its own maximums in addition to those already imposed by the VMware vSphere infrastructure. The View Connection maximums are given in the following table:

Connection Servers per deployment	Maximum
1 Connection Server that supports direct RDP or PCoIP	2,000
7 Connection Servers (5 hot + 2 spare) that support direct RDP or PCoIP	10,000
Maximum hosts in a cluster when not using View Composer	32
Maximum hosts in a cluster when using View Composer	8

If a solution such as Unidesk TM is used in lieu of View Composer, the end design can support more hosts per cluster.

For the solution example, whereby 10,000 vDesktops must be supported, it's important to understand how many end users will be logging in at any given time. A VMware View Connection Server can support 2,000 direct PCoIP connections at any given time. In this example, all 10,000 end users could potentially log in at the same time. Therefore, a minimum of five View Connection Servers are required (*2,000 * 5 = 10,000* simultaneous direct PCoIP connections supported).

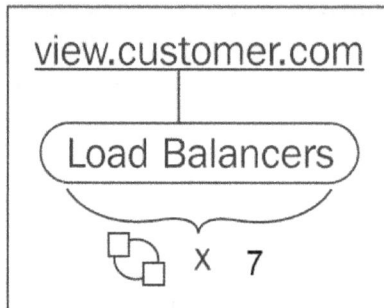

In order to provide a level of redundancy in case of a View Connection Server outage, it is advised to add in $n + 2$ (or more) solutions. For example, increasing the required number of View Connection Servers, that is, 13 to a total of 15 View Connection Servers, provides the ability to support a maximum of 30,000 simultaneous PCoIP connections. Therefore, even if two View Connection Servers fail, all 25,000 users would be able to log in to the VDI without incident.

The 15 View Connection Servers should be placed behind a redundant load balancing solution and should be configured to check that the View Connection Server is online via a simple ping (if **Internet Control Message Protocol (ICMP)** is allowed) and HTTP GET on the View Connection Server's URL. The entire pool of View Connection Servers should be accessible by a single name, such as `view.customer.com`, as shown in the preceding figure, whereby end users would use `https://view.customer.com` to access the View environment.

By leveraging the HTTP GET to verify functionality of a View Connection Server, a server whose applicable services have stopped will not successfully reply to the `GET` command and therefore will be removed from the load balancing pool.

Solution design – the formulas

The following are some formulas to calculate the minimum number of vCenter Servers, Connection Servers, and pods:

- Minimum number of vCenter Servers = Number of desktops / 10,000

- Minimum number of View Connection Servers = Number of simultaneous connections / 2,000

- Minimum number of vCenter pods = Number of vCenter Servers / 10

Summary

As detailed in this chapter, there are many design considerations such as DHCP lease time, the minimum number of vCenters, and the number of cores to buy in a server platform. For large environments of thousands of vDesktops, it may be easiest to start with the vSphere maximums and work down. For small environments or **Proof of Concepts (PoCs)** that don't require a massive virtual infrastructure, the concepts covered in this chapter are still relevant as a successful PoC can grow rapidly in adoption. Finally, the concept of a pod architecture, or a collection of vCenter Servers, is typically new to those familiar only with designing virtual server solutions on the VMware vSphere platform. They can take some time to understand the new concepts and working up against the vSphere and vCenter maximums.

The next chapter shows how it's important to understand all of the possible failure points within the VDI solution and how redundancy can be built in to mitigate those failures. Failing to build proper redundancy could render the VDI solution completely unreachable. The next chapter will cover the physical failure points to consider, such as network switches, power supplies, and hard drives.

7
Building Redundancy into the VDI Solution

When building a proper VDI, it's imperative to understand all of the possible failure points within the solution, so redundancy can be built in to mitigate any failures. While sizing a VDI incorrectly will cause a slow response time or poor end user experience, failing to build proper redundancy could render the solution unreachable. In a VDI solution, there are physical failure points to consider, such as network switches, power supplies, and hard drives. There are also software failure points such as the VMware vCenter Server, VMware View Connection Server, and the database server(s) to take into consideration.

This chapter analyzes the following potential points of failure within a VDI and offers up suggestions to provide redundancy for each component:

- Physical host failure
- Lack of sufficient resources on the host
- vCenter failure
- VMware View Connection Server failure
- User profiles

Physical infrastructure

This book will focus on developing a highly available solution for the VDI environment. While providing a solution for the entire virtual infrastructure is outside the scope of this book, Horizon View uses vSphere components, and understanding and utilizing the following VMware vSphere features are important to implement a robust VDI.

VMware High Availability

VMware High Availability (HA) can be used to monitor and protect against physical host failures and can also be used to monitor and protect vDesktops themselves. VMware HA works by monitoring physical hosts in a given cluster. If a host is unable to communicate to the specific default gateway on a service console interface for 15 continuous seconds, an HA failover event is triggered. vSphere 5 also introduced **datastore heartbeating**, which is used when a network heartbeat failure has occurred. Datastore heartbeats provide an additional level of host isolation verification.

> For more information on VMware HA, please refer to the *HA Deepdive* article by Duncan Epping at `http://www.yellow-bricks.com/ vmware-high-availability-deepdiv/`. You can also check it out in his book *vSphere 5 Clustering Technical Deepdive*.

A host is determined to be isolated when a host has stopped receiving heartbeats from other hosts in the cluster and the specified isolation address cannot be pinged.

If the **Isolation Response** for the HA cluster is set to **Leave Power On**, the vDesktops and other virtual machines on the host will remain powered on. Just because a host has lost network connectivity on its service console interface, it does not necessarily mean that the vDesktops have lost network connectivity.

If the Isolation Response for the HA cluster is set to **Power Off**, the vDesktops and other virtual machines on the host will be powered off. This setting avoids the possibility of a split-brain scenario.

The split-brain scenario would occur when you have:

- **Host Isolation Response** set to **Leave VM Powered On**
- Network storage (iSCSI / NFS storage)

When one of the hosts is completely isolated, including the storage network, the following will happen. HA will restart the virtual machine as it appears to HA that the host has completely failed. The reasons are as follows:

- There will be no heartbeats from the datastore
- There are no network heartbeats that come from the host

- The file locks on the virtual machines are released by the isolated host because it cannot access storage any longer
- The host's management address cannot be pinged
- The isolated host cannot inform the master it is isolated because it can't write to the datastore

The isolated host will also take no action because the **Leave Powered On** option was set. This means that the virtual machines that run on the isolated host will continue to run. However, the master thinks the host has failed and will initiate a restart of the VMs on the non-affected hosts. Remember, the iSCSI/NFS network is also isolated, and the lock that is on the VMDK will time out. This will allow the remaining non-affected hosts to boot up the VMs.

When the isolated host returns, you will then have two instances of the same VM on the network. However, only one of the instances has disk access. The one without disk access will automatically be killed by the host that it is running on. This feature was introduced in vSphere 4 U2 and is still applicable today.

To prevent this entire scenario, it is recommended that you change the **Isolation response** to **Power off**.

With the advancements in vSphere 5, the host isolation events are highly verified and accurate and very likely indicate an actual host problem. Therefore, in VMware View solutions, it's preferred to set the Isolation Response to **Power Off**.

If a specific host that contains vDesktops has been isolated from the cluster, it will perform the following:

- All virtual machines and vDesktops will be powered off
- Users with active connections will be disconnected from their vDesktops:
  - If the vDesktop is part of a persistent desktop pool, the user will be able to log back in once their specific vDesktop has been powered up and is online. The estimated outage time is 2 minutes.
  - If the vDesktop is part of a nonpersistent desktop pool, the user will be able to log back in immediately to a vDesktop assuming that there is an available vDesktop in the pool on a host that is currently online. The estimated outage time is less than or equal to 30 seconds.

Using VMware HA

VMware HA provides a level of protection for host failures, where vDesktops that reside on a host that has failed will automatically be powered up without intervention from the virtual infrastructure administrator, as shown in the following figure:

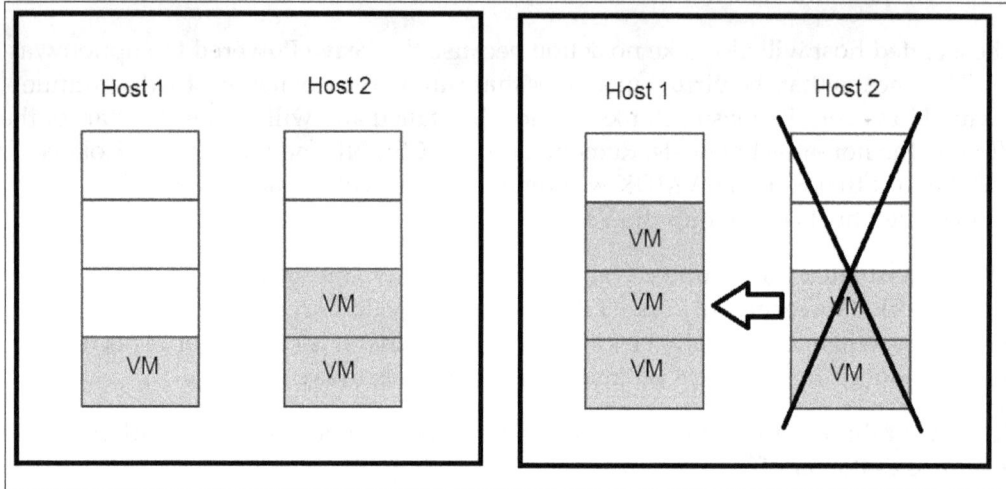

If **Admission Control** is set to **Strict**, the vDesktops will only be powered on if there are available resources on another host in the cluster.

VMware HA works by determining the slot size or the minimum amount of CPU and memory required to support a failover of the most intensive virtual machine (or vDesktop).

For example, if vDesktop_A has 4 GHz of CPU and 2 GB of RAM while vDesktop_B has 1 GHz of CPU and 6 GB of RAM, the slot size will be 4 GHz of CPU and 6 GB of RAM (with additional calculations taken into consideration for memory overhead).

In VMware View environments, there will likely be many vDesktops with identical specifications (for example, a Windows 7 vDesktop with 2 GHz of CPU and 2 GB of RAM); therefore, a concept known as **slot fragmentation**, as shown in the following figure, is primarily avoided. Slot fragmentation occurs when the collective availability of sufficient resources in a cluster supports the virtual machines being powered on during a HA event, but there is a lack sufficient resources on an individual physical host to support a virtual machine's requirements. For instance, a VM needs resources equal to four slots. There are six slots available across three hosts, but there is not one host that has the four slots required to start the VM.

> For more information on slot fragmentation, please see Duncan Epping's detailed article at the same URL: http://www.yellow-bricks.com/vmware-high-availability-deepdiv/, as mentioned earlier.

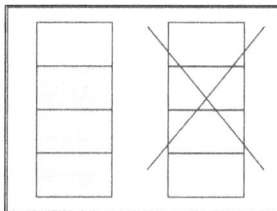

As for vSphere 4.1, HA also works in conjunction with DRS to free resource slots, should slot fragmentation occur within a cluster. This will involve a failed server that has to wait for virtual machines to have vMotion across hosts in the cluster until resources exist to power on necessary virtual machine(s).

Using HA with persistent vDesktops

With a VMware View solution based on persistent vDesktops, HA should be used.

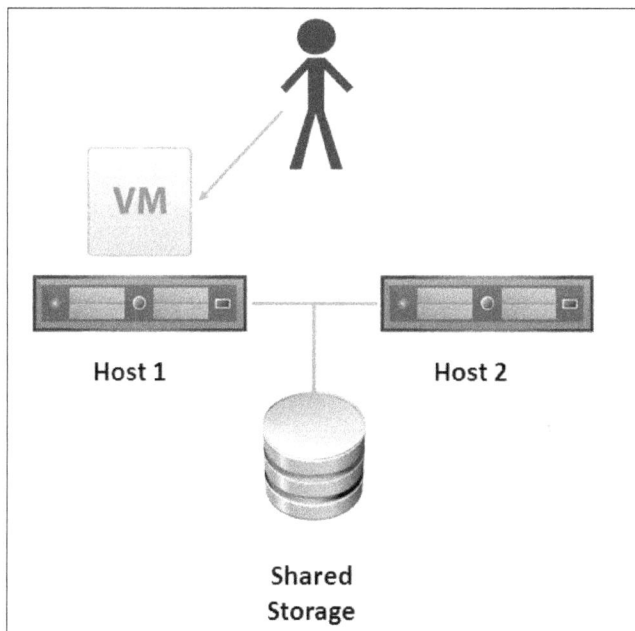

In the preceding figure, the end user is connected to a vDesktop on Host 1. Both Host 1 and Host 2 are part of the same cluster and can use the same shared storage. As illustrated in the figure, the actual virtual disk files for the vDesktop reside on the shared storage and not on the local storage within Host 1.

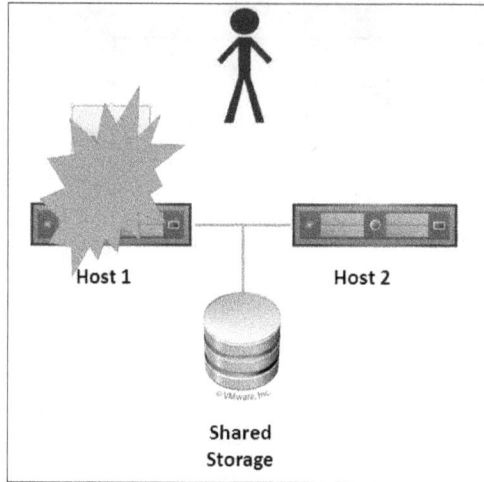

As illustrated in the preceding figure, when Host 1 fails, the end user is disconnected from the vDesktop. In a persistent vDesktop solution, the end user is assigned to a specific vDesktop. In this case, the vDesktop is unavailable as it resides on Host 1, which has just failed.

The end user will be unable to work until the vDesktop is back online or the end user is manually assigned to another (available) vDesktop resource.

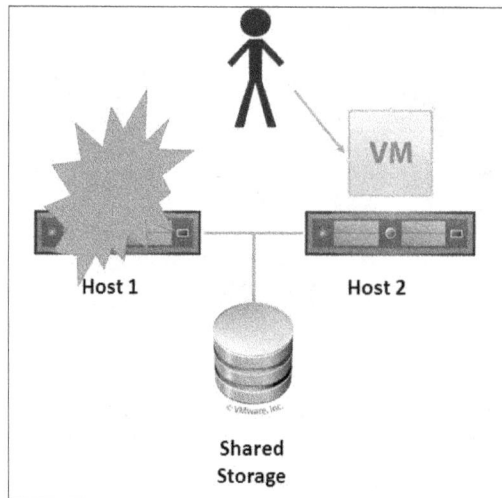

As illustrated in the preceding figure, VMware HA has powered up the end user's vDesktop on Host 2, an available host in the cluster. By default, the end user is not notified that their vDesktop is now available, so the end user will need to repeatedly try for the time it takes for a vDesktop to come online on Host 2. This typically takes 1 to 3 minutes.

> An advanced solution concept for persistent vDesktop environments is to monitor the individual vDesktop outages. If a user's persistent vDesktop is determined to be offline, an e-mail can be sent to the end user (who would likely receive it on their mobile device) letting them know that their vDesktop is currently unavailable but that the resolution is in progress. The same concept can then be used to detect when the vDesktop is back online and available (for example, by adding a 2-minute wait when a vDesktop enters the VMware Tool's OK state), and then notify the user that their vDesktop is now available.

Solutions with nonpersistent vDesktops

For solutions that use nonpersistent vDesktops, the use of VMware HA is a topic of great debate. While nonpersistent solutions rely on a pool of vDesktops spread across multiple hosts in a cluster, end users are not assigned to an individual vDesktop, as illustrated in the following figure:

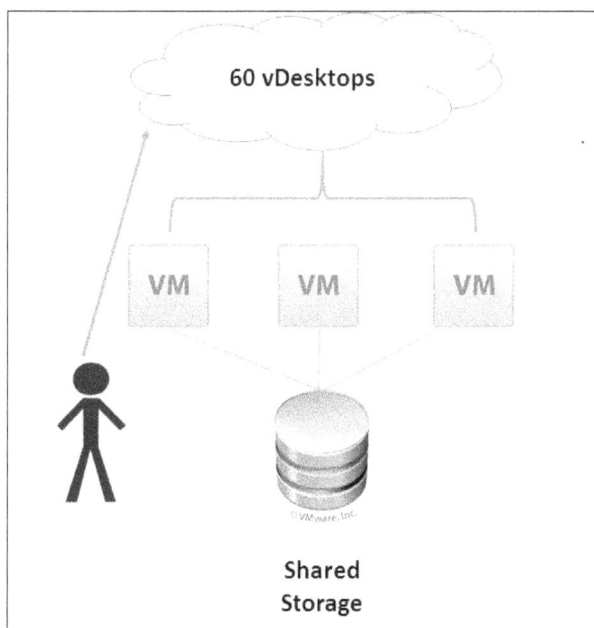

When a host fails in a nonpersistent solution, any end users connected to vDesktops on that specific host lose their connectivity. The end users can then reconnect to the VMware View environment, and as long as another vDesktop is available, that user will successfully connect to a resource. This is because vDesktop assignment is done randomly at the time of login when using nonpersistent vDesktops.

In this example, Company_A has 60 end users and has created a nonpersistent vDesktop pool with the following settings:

- Numbers of end users: 60
- Desktop pool size (maximum number of desktops): 60
- Number of spare (powered-on) desktops: 0
- Power setting: **Always On**
- Provisioning all desktops up front

With these settings, when the pool is initially built, it will automatically provision 60 vDesktops and power them on.

The count is authoritatively held by VMware View in the **ADAM database**. If the pool's power settings are set to **Always On**, VMware View will create a pool of 60 vDesktops and immediately power all of them on. No matter what load exists from the end user community, 60 vDesktops will always be powered on. If 61 end users try to log in concurrently, one end user will be unable to access a resource.

Imagine a scenario where Host 1 hosts 30 vDesktops and Host 2 hosts 30 vDesktops. The desktop pool is configured to host 60 vDesktops.

In this environment, if Host 1 suddenly fails, the 30 vDesktops being hosted on Host 1 enter an "Agent Unreachable" state. While the VMware View Connection Server has recognized that there are now 30 vDesktops that are unreachable, it does not provision 30 new vDesktops on the available hosts in the cluster (for example, Host 2).

Therefore, without using HA to restart the vDesktops on another host, the pool's total number of vDesktops will be reduced. By using VMware HA, the pool's total number of vDesktops will not be reduced, although there could be a decrease in overall performance (if the ability to exceed available resources is allowed).

There are two design paths for nonpersistent vDesktop solutions:

- The first is to simply use VMware HA to ensure that any vDesktops that reside on a failed host are restarted on another available host in the cluster. This is most likely to be the easiest configuration and results in 5 to 10 minutes of downtime (as vDesktops power up and enter a useable state).

- The second design path is to design the desktop pool(s) with enough vDesktops to sustain a host failure. The following figure shows that one of the VMs has failed, yet there is still a pool of available VMs for the user to connect to. It is important to ensure that the number of used vDesktops does not exceed the legally-licensed amount from VMware. However, by building a desktop pool with additional capacity (for example, 30 extra vDesktops), outage of one host has minimal impact on the end user environment. For those users that were connected to a vDesktop on the failed host, they simply log back into the VMware View environment and connect to one of the already provisioned, already available, extra vDesktops.

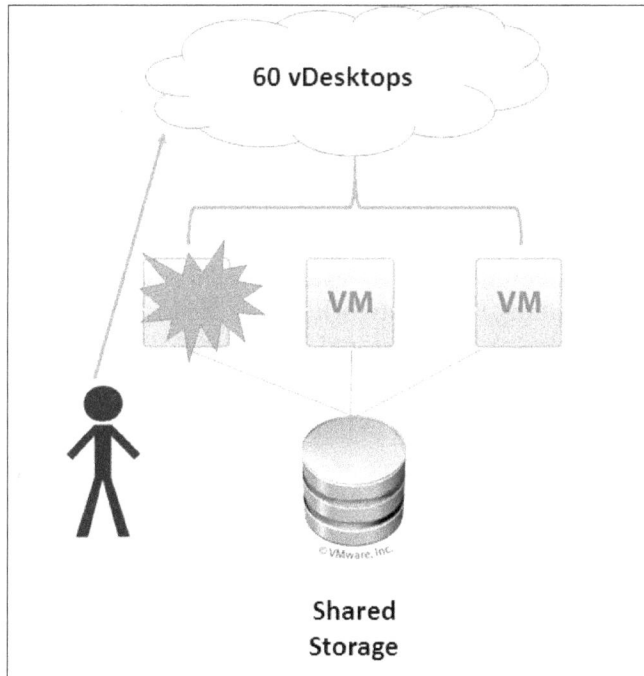

Using local storage

We have added a note about using local storage in this section. As it will be covered later in this book, local storage is a viable option for certain VDI solutions. If the end user's vDesktop resides on the local storage of Host 1, during a host failure, VMware HA would not be able to bring the vDesktop up on another host (for example, Host 2) as other hosts would not have access to the virtual disk files that reside on the local storage on Host 1.

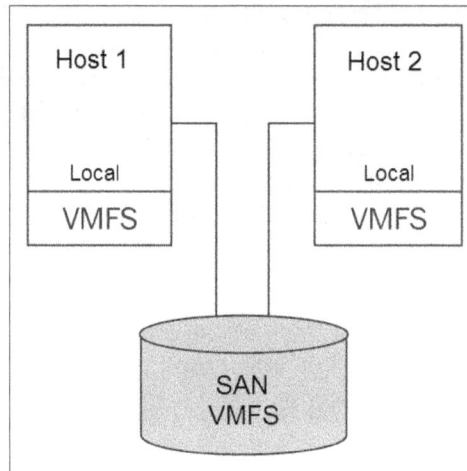

As illustrated in the preceding figure, both Host 1 and Host 2 have a local **Virtual Machine File System** (**VMFS**) datastore as well as access to a shared VMFS datastore on the **storage area network** (**SAN**). If Host 1 has an outage, any vDesktops or templates that were stored on the local VMFS datastore on Host 1 would be unavailable.

If a persistent solution was in use and vDesktops were placed on the local VMFS datastore, the end users would not have access to their vDesktops during a host outage. VMware HA would not matter as the vDesktops were not on shared storage, but were instead on the local VMFS datastore of the host.

Therefore, it is imperative to use a nonpersistent solution when placing core virtual disks of a vDesktop on the local storage as the end users are not specifically assigned to a unique vDesktop. If the physical servers that host vDesktop_17 (a persistent vDesktop assigned to the employee User_LL) were to fail, User_LL would not be able to connect to a desktop resource.

Now, with that said about local storage, Horizon View 6 can use VSAN for local storage, and it provides the flexibility that local storage alone cannot. This is covered in more detail in *Chapter 12, Exciting New Features in Horizon View 6*. VSAN uses the host's local disk drives (you need both SSD and HDD) to aggregate them to appear as a cluster-wide storage pool shared across all hosts. It creates a highly available scale-out clustered storage solution to host your VMs, but you need at least three hosts to install VSAN. The implementation of VSAN is illustrated in the following figure:

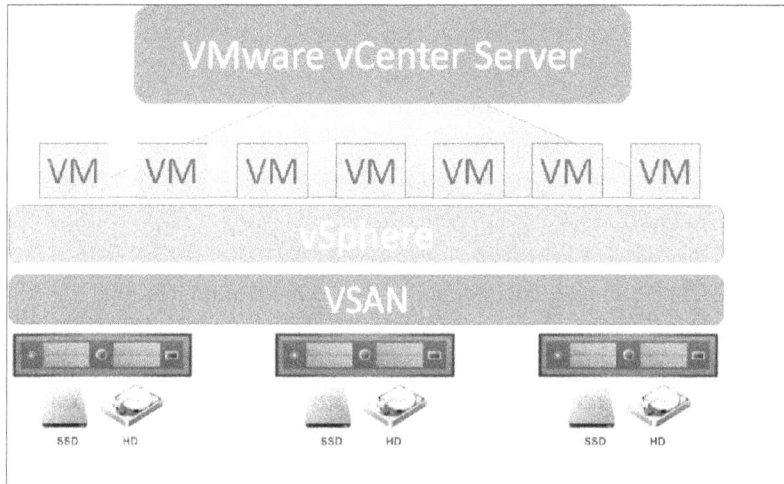

VMware Distributed Resource Scheduling

While **VMware Distributed Resource Scheduling (DRS)** does not provide resilience, it does minimize the potential impact during an unpredicted physical host failure. By balancing the processing load across all of the available hosts in a cluster, a host failure will have the minimum impact possible. This is true for both virtual machines running a server OS and vDesktops. In a VMware View solution with virtualized VMware vCenter Server(s) and/or VMware View Connection Server(s), it is prudent to use VMware DRS to balance the load in the cluster and minimize the impact. For additional considerations, please refer to the *Anti-affinity* section explained next.

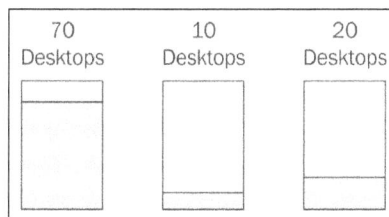

In the example given in the preceding figure, there are three hosts in a cluster that do not have VMware DRS enabled in them. On the first host in the cluster, there are 70 vDesktops. On the second one, there are 10 vDesktops, and on the third host, there are 20 vDesktops. As VMware DRS is not enabled, the load (and therefore the number of vDesktops) is not balanced across all of the available hosts in the cluster.

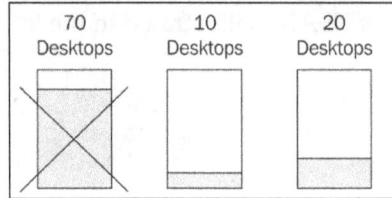

Continuing with the example, as shown in the following figure, if the first host were to have an unpredicted outage, 70 vDesktops would be impacted. If DRS was enabled and all vDesktops had roughly the same CPU consumption, approximately 34 vDesktops would be placed on each host. This will drastically reduce the number of end users that would experience an outage, should a physical host fail.

Anti-affinity

Affinity and **Anti-affinity** are settings within VMware DRS that determine how virtual machines in a given cluster react to one another.

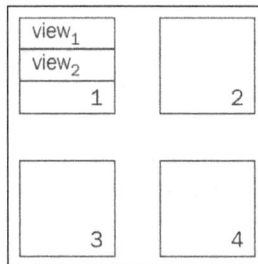

In the preceding figure, DRS is enabled for the four-host cluster, and is set to **Automatic**. There are no affinity or anti-affinity rules set. The VMware View solution requires two View Connection Servers, both of which have been virtualized and placed in the previously mentioned cluster.

Through normal DRS activities, both the View Connection Servers find themselves on Host 1. If Host 1 were to have an outage, no new connections would be permitted in the VDI.

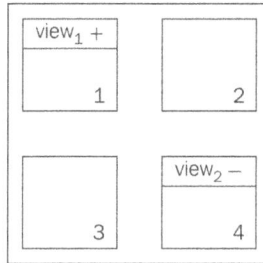

In the previous figure, the two View Connection Servers, View1 and View2, have been placed in an anti-affinity rule, and they have opposing polarity. This rule states that the two View Connection Servers are never to reside on the same host as long as there are available hosts in the cluster.

With anti-affinity in place, a single host outage would not have the potential to bring down the entire VMware View Connection Server environment.

VMware vCenter Server

Horizon View uses VMware vCenter for all provisioning tasks, and without a functioning VMware vCenter Server, it is impossible to create, refresh, recompose, rebalance, or delete vDesktops. Therefore, utmost importance must be placed on protecting the VMware vCenter Server(s) used in the solution.

There are two primary components to the VMware vCenter Server service. They are as follows:

- The VMware vCenter Server service
- The backend database

The VMware vCenter Server service should be protected in a way that minimizes downtime or provides a **recovery time objective** (**RTO**) that meets the organization policies. The host and virtual desktops continue to operate when vCenter Server is down. However, the absence of vCenter Server will greatly impact the management and operation of the View environment. For an extremely active VDI, prolonged downtime can result in an inability to provide desktop resources to the requesting end users.

As vCenter needs a minimum of 2 vCPUs, the **VMware Fault Tolerance (FT)** option cannot be used to protect the vCenter virtual machine.

In the following sections we will discuss a few options for you to consider.

VMware Data Protection

VMware Data Protection (VDP) utilizes storage-based snapshots to provide disk-level backup and restore capabilities.

With the 5.5 release, VDP now provides the option of host-level backup. VDP can be used to back up the vCenter Server environment and provides the ability to restore as necessary to a specified vSphere host.

vSphere High Availability

You can employ vSphere **High Availability (HA)** to enable recovery of vCenter Server virtual machines. vSphere HA monitors virtual machines with heartbeats from the VMware Tools, and it can be configured to initiate a reboot of the vCenter virtual machine when the heartbeat is no longer received. Although vSphere HA requires vCenter Server to enable and configure the recovery options for your virtual machine, it will execute a virtual machine restart without a dependency on the vCenter Server. This type of protection is fairly easy and free with vSphere. In the case of an HA event, your vCenter will be unavailable during the restart period. Note that HA does not protect you against OS-level corruption.

Database High Availability

The database for vCenter is a very important component—the vCenter Server will not function without it. Therefore, providing a solution that can blend your protection levels for the database with the vCenter Server is essential. Depending on the database vendor that you use for your vCenter installation, there are different methods of database mirroring and clustering to achieve a high level of availability. Not all vendor solutions will be supported by VMware, and you should check to verify the support statement for the option you choose.

Cold/Standby vCenter

This option probably should not be used for production, but if you had a **Proof-of-Concept (PoC)** or a small development environment, you could use the Standby option, especially if the vCenter is a physical server; therefore, you cannot use vSphere HA.

The architecture of this deployment would also require a remote database for vCenter. You configure two servers with the same version of vCenter, and if the first one goes down, you power on the second (standby) server, which then connects to the same database. This method works but requires human intervention. This means if your vCenter goes down in the middle of the night, the recovery would not begin until you realize this in the morning.

View Connection Server

The View Connection Server is responsible for processing incoming requests for vDesktops; interacting with VMware vCenter Server to provision, recompose, and delete vDesktops; as well as a variety of other tasks necessary for a properly functioning VDI.

Installing the Replica Connection Server

When installing the VMware View Connection Server, there are three installation types. They are as follows:

- Standard
- Replica
- Security

> With the release of Horizon View 6, the transfer server is no longer used.

For the first VMware View Connection Server instance in a View Connection Server pool, the standard installation should be selected. However, to eliminate the View Connection Server as a single point of failure, a second (and additional) View Connection Server can be installed. Once a View Connection Server exists in the infrastructure, additional View Connection Servers (up to 7) can be joined to the original, forming a View Connection Server pool. To join a new View Connection Server to an existing View Connection Server or View Connection Server pool, select the replica installation mode.

When a replica View Connection Server instance is created, it copies the VMware View LDAP configuration from the existing View Connection Server instance.

Load balancing

VMware View Connection Servers are responsible for brokering the connection between an authorized end user and a vDesktop in the VDI. Therefore, if there are no available VMware View Connection Servers, no new connections can be made in the VDI. However, the existing connections will not be affected if there are no available VMware View Connection Servers. Also, remember that Horizon View has the ability to enable a View Client to connect directly to a View desktop without going through the View Connection Server. Once a connection has been successfully authenticated, the View Client directly connects to the View Agent within the vDesktop; this is referred to as a direct connection. For direct connections, a failure of the View Connection Server does not impact the existing connections.

Therefore, it is important to protect the available View Connection Server(s) in the VDI. The best practice is to have a minimum of two VMware View Connection Servers. The easiest way to accomplish resilience for the VMware View Connection Servers is to use a load balancing solution. There are various load balancing solutions available, including **Microsoft Network Load Balancer** (**NLB**) and hardware appliances from other third-party companies.

A load balancing solution will create a virtual IP address that will be used by the end users to connect to the VDI, as shown in the following figure:

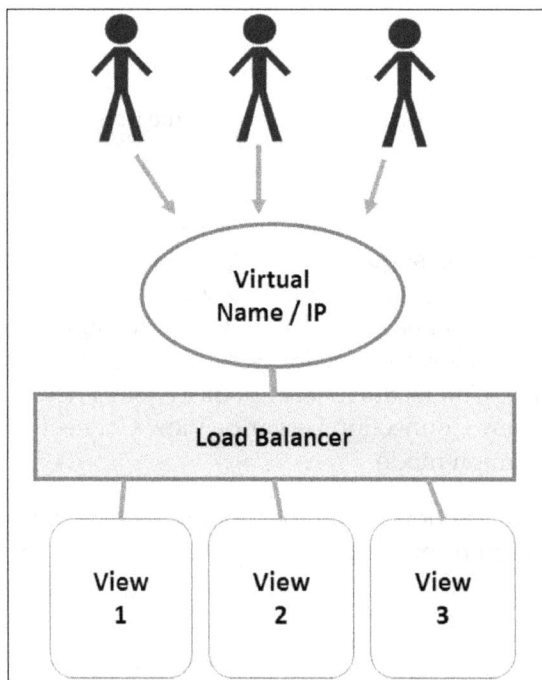

Parent vDesktop and templates

Virtual machine templates are used by VMware View when deploying vDesktops with the full virtual machine option selected.

Standard virtual machines (not templates) are used by VMware View when deploying vDesktops with the View Composer linked clones option selected. However, for a linked clone to be created by View Composer, it must have at least one snapshot. View Composer deploys all linked clone vDesktops in the pool from the selected snapshot.

It is important to understand that if the parent vDesktop (for linked clone pools) or the gold vDesktop template (for full desktop pools) are not available, then new vDesktops cannot be provisioned.

Templates

Virtual machine templates are a bit confusing to protect. When creating a virtual machine template or adding a virtual machine template in the inventory, the administrator must select a specific host within a cluster. According to the **graphical user interface** (**GUI**), choose a specific host within the cluster. On high-availability clusters and fully-manual dynamic workload management clusters, each template must be assigned to a specific host.

Therefore, if the gold template for vDesktops resides on Host 1, and if Host 1 experiences a failure, VMware HA will not recover this template. Instead, the original template will be shown as unavailable within vCenter. From this point, the original inventory entry in vCenter for the template can be removed and then, the template can be re-added. This is possible because while the host is unavailable, the virtual machine template actually resides on shared storage (assuming that the best practice was followed).

When assisting an organization with operational readiness, the preceding recovery process should be listed in a standard operating procedure (SOP) manual.

Parent vDesktops with snapshots

To protect the parent vDesktop and its snapshot, a simple clone virtual machine task will not suffice. This is because the clone task consolidates the snapshot tree (SNAP 1, SNAP 2, and SNAP 3) and thus removes all snapshots associated with the base virtual machine. The following figure shows the results of cloning, which is a new base with all the snapshots consolidated within.

This is not the desired result of protecting the parent vDesktop.

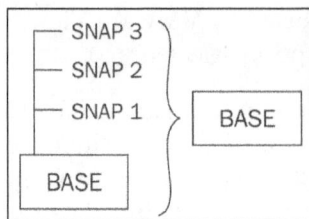

Therefore, it is imperative that VMware HA should be used to protect the parent vDesktop used to create linked clones. Remember, the parent vDesktop is simply a virtual machine with snapshots (as opposed to a virtual machine template in the preceding scenario used to create full clones) and the snapshots associated with the vDesktop must be protected too. VMware HA will restart the parent vDesktop (with the snapshots) to an available host in the cluster during a host outage.

User personas

For environments that leverage a user persona solution, such as Liquidware Labs ProfileUnity, placing the user personas on a highly available network share is critical to ensure end user data is always available. By using the **Distributed File System (DFS)** service or **Distributed File System Replication (DFS-R)** service, a user persona that stores file shares will still be available in the event of a file server failure. In addition, with DFS-R, user personas can be replicated to other servers in the same site or other sites. DFS-R enables a VDI to provide **Continuity of Operations (COOP)** by ensuring that the file share that contains the user personas has its data replicated offsite.

Microsoft DFS also leverages Active Directory sites to ensure that an end user is retrieving their persona from the nearest server that is participating in the DFS/DFS-R group. In addition, site costing can be used to state the least expensive target selection for the end users that attempt to retrieve their user persona from a network share. There are other solutions such as **Microsoft Clustering, Scale-out File Server**, and **Unified Storage Solution** with vendors such as NetApp or EMC VNX, which will also protect the file servers. Check with the vendors of your choice for more details.

The following table shows a summary of the types of failures for the components:

Component	Type of failure	Protected by	Downtime	Notes
vCenter Server	Underlying physical host	VMware HA	Approximately 10 minutes	During the outage, vDesktop tasks such as provision, recompose, and so on, are unavailable. vCenter may take longer to start (as opposed to View Connection Server) because of the database actions that are performed during an initial service start.
vCenter Server	Underlying physical host	Cold/Standby	This is a manual process and requires admin intervention	This requires a remote database for vCenter, and is not recommended for a production environment.
vCenter Database	Any	Clustering solution	Less than 1 minute	This requires two database servers.
vCenter Database	Database corruption	Backup/ restore/ snapshots (VDP)	Varies	The time to restore depends on the solution used, speed of media, and throughput available.
View Connection Server	Underlying physical host	VMware HA	Approximately 5 minutes	This requires multiple View Connection Servers behind a load balancer to mitigate impact to the end users.

Component	Type of failure	Protected by	Downtime	Notes
View Connection Server	Underlying physical host	Load balancer	0 minutes	This requires multiple View Connection Servers behind a load balancer to mitigate impact to the end users. Without VMware HA, the total number of inbound connections may be impacted.
View Connection Server	View Connection Server service	Load balancer	0 minutes	This requires multiple View Connection Servers behind a load balancer to mitigate impact to the end users.
View Connection Server	Operating system (blue screen of death)	VM monitoring with VMware HA	Approximately 5 minutes	It requires multiple View Connection Servers behind a load balancer to mitigate impact to the end users.
View Composer	Underlying physical host	VMware HA	Approximately 10 minutes	During the outage, vDesktop tasks such as provision, recompose, and so on, are unavailable. vCenter may take longer to start (as opposed to View Connection Server) because of the database actions that are performed during an initial service start.

Component	Type of failure	Protected by	Downtime	Notes
Template (full clones)	Underlying physical host	Manual procedure	Depends on intervention by the admin	Remove the original template from vCenter and re-add it (template must be on shared storage).
Parent with snapshots (linked clones)	Underlying physical host	VMware HA	Approximately 5 minutes	HA will restart the parent vDesktop to an available host in the cluster.
User persona	File server failure	Persona Management Solution combined with Distributed File System (DFS)	Varies	DFS allows user personas to be replicated to other servers in the same site or other sites.

Summary

Thus, some of the most important design considerations (for example, persistent or nonpersistent) have been addressed, as well as proper sizing of the overall VDI. A VDI without redundancy can result in unexpected outages and downtime. Designing a VMware View solution that is highly resilient from insufficient resources or from the failure of the host, vCenter, or the connection server is paramount to a production-quality solution.

In the next chapter, the last major hurdle, storage design, will be discussed. A VDI with improperly designed storage can not only result in poor end user experience but also significantly add to the overall cost of the VDI solution. As storage is often one of the most expensive components of a VDI solution, judicious sizing that will still meet the requirements is the key.

8
Sizing the Storage

The storage layer is perhaps one of the most critical components in a VMware View design. For many VDI professionals, this is likely to be the major issue when called in for a performance troubleshooting exercise. Commonly, the storage layer is the root cause of the performance issue. Why is storage so critical? To answer this question, we first need to understand how Intel-based desktops work and interact with Windows operating systems before diving into the world of storage for VDI.

Physical desktops have always had dedicated hard disks to rely upon and only a single Windows kernel had access to the disk causing a single I/O stream. Despite being dedicated to the desktop, the Windows device also faced disk contention. This contention could have been generated due to an excessive amount of disk I/O operations or I/O block sizes. The important thing is that no matter what type of operation causes the contention, the end result is slow response time, also known as **latency**.

Recent disk technology advancements such as **solid state drives** (**SSDs**) drastically reduced the latency implications, and thus improved the end user experience. The most advanced SSD can ingest and deliver an enormous amount of I/O and throughput.

With the ability to use faster disks, users came to expect enhanced performance. However, microprocessors and RAM technology also evolved in such a fast fashion that technologies such as Intel Core i7 and DDR3 quickly made even the fastest SSD become the performance bottleneck once again.

With a few exceptions, VDI implementations do not utilize a single dedicated disk. Instead, VDI uses a pool of disks to provide storage capacity, I/O, and throughput to vDesktops.

Most VDI implementations require shared storage to provide datastores to multiple servers. Shared storage is also a key enabler for VMware vSphere features such as vMotion, DRS, and fault tolerance. Implementations that utilize a combination of floating pools and roaming profiles may opt for storage appliance solutions, where no persistent data is stored on those appliances.

Local disks, **Dedicated Attached Storage (DAS)**, and even diskless solutions can be employed in VDI deployments. It is important to understand the use cases and implications behind each of the approaches.

Storage architecture decisions made during the VDI design phase will have a deep impact on how the infrastructure will perform and operate. The type of storage and transport protocol chosen will determine how VMware View and vSphere will operate. Yet, the type of storage and protocol will also dictate how datastores should be designed or how many desktops per datastore should be used.

In this chapter, we will cover the following topics:

- VMware View Composer
- VMware vSphere files
- VMware View specific files
- Tiered storage
- Storage overcommit
- Storage protocols
- Maximums and limits
- Storage I/O profile
- Read/write I/O ratio
- Storage tiering and I/O distribution
- Disk types
- VMware VSAN
- Capacity sizing exercises
- vSphere 5.0 video swap

VMware View Composer

The VMware View infrastructure includes VMware View Composer as an optional component. View Composer runs as a Windows service on the vCenter Server(s) or on a standalone server (cannot run on the View server) and enables View Manager to rapidly clone and deploy multiple virtual desktops from a single centralized standard base image. View Composer was originally designed to reduce the total storage required in VDI deployments; however, today View Composer also provides essential management features such as the Refresh and Recompose operations.

View Composer uses linked clone technology. Unlike a traditional virtual machine model wherein each VM exists as an independent entity with dedicated virtual disks, View Composer creates dependent VMs all linked to a master VM. This master VM is called the **parent VM** in VMware terminology.

The parent VM is used as a base image; a snapshot and copy are taken from the parent VM to create the replica image, which will serve as the master VM disk for all linked clones in a desktop pool, as shown in the following figure:

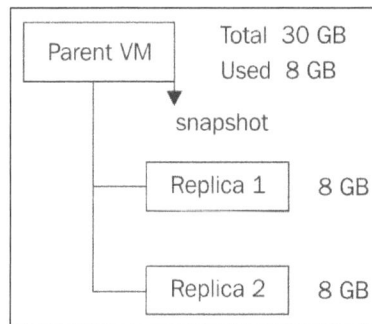

The replica disk is created as a read-only thin provisioned entity from the parent VM to ensure that any subsequent changes to the parent VM do not impact the linked clone desktops. As mentioned previously, the replica is thin provisioned, which means that only the data contained within the parent VM is copied to the replica. As an example, if the parent VM was created with a 40 GB disk but only 20 GB appears on the guest's Windows NTFS volume, then the replica will be 20 GB.

The replica image is a protected entity in vCenter Server via a **VM LockStatus** parameter added to the VM annotations, as shown in the following screenshot:

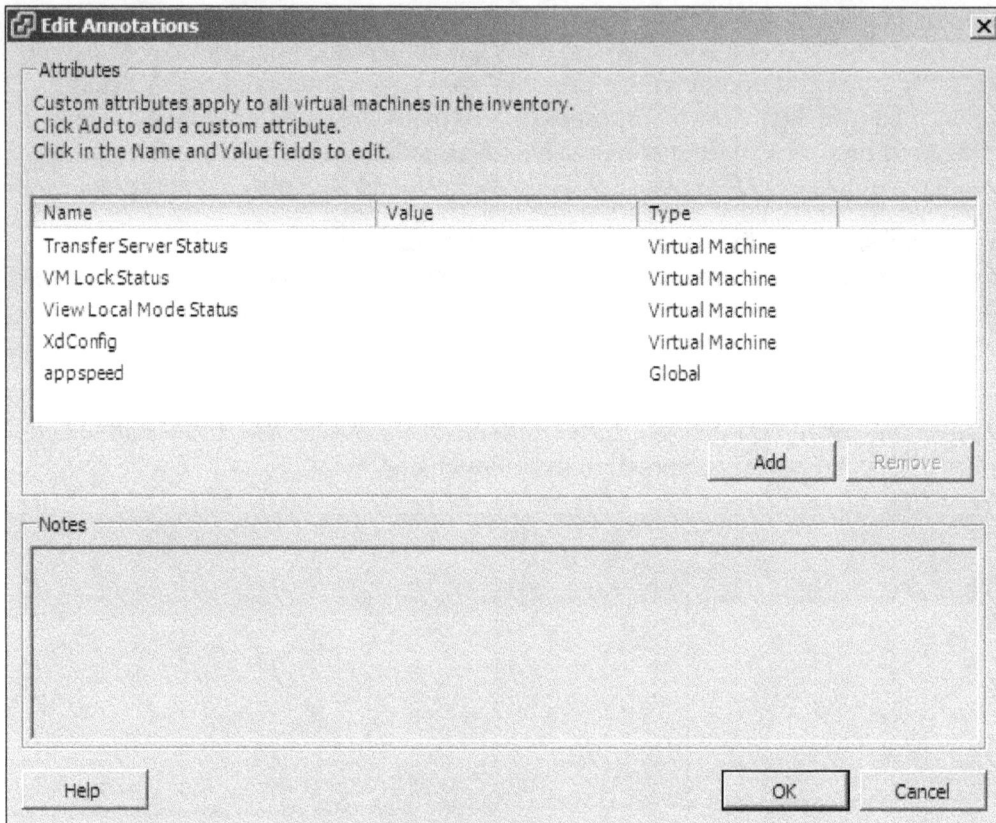

> If a replica needs to be deleted for any reason, the process outlined in *KB1008704* must be followed. The process is given at http://kb.vmware.com/selfservice/microsites/search.do?language=en_US&cmd=displayKC&externalId=1008704.

Snapshots

A parent VM may contain several snapshots that represent changes introduced to the base image. These differences may be due to fixes, patches, and upgrades required by the Windows Guest OS. The deployment of new applications to the base image, application upgrades, or even Windows configuration changes can be added to the snapshots.

After each modification, the parent VM must be shut down by the administrator and a new snapshot should be taken.

The snapshot to be used in a desktop pool is selected during the desktop pool configuration. A single snapshot is assigned to the entire desktop pool. However, it is possible to individually recompose virtual desktops using different snapshots from the same or different parent VM.

The following screenshot shows VMware vCenter Server Snapshot Manager with a few snapshots already taken. It is a recommended practice to annotate the changes made to the parent VM in the **Description** field:

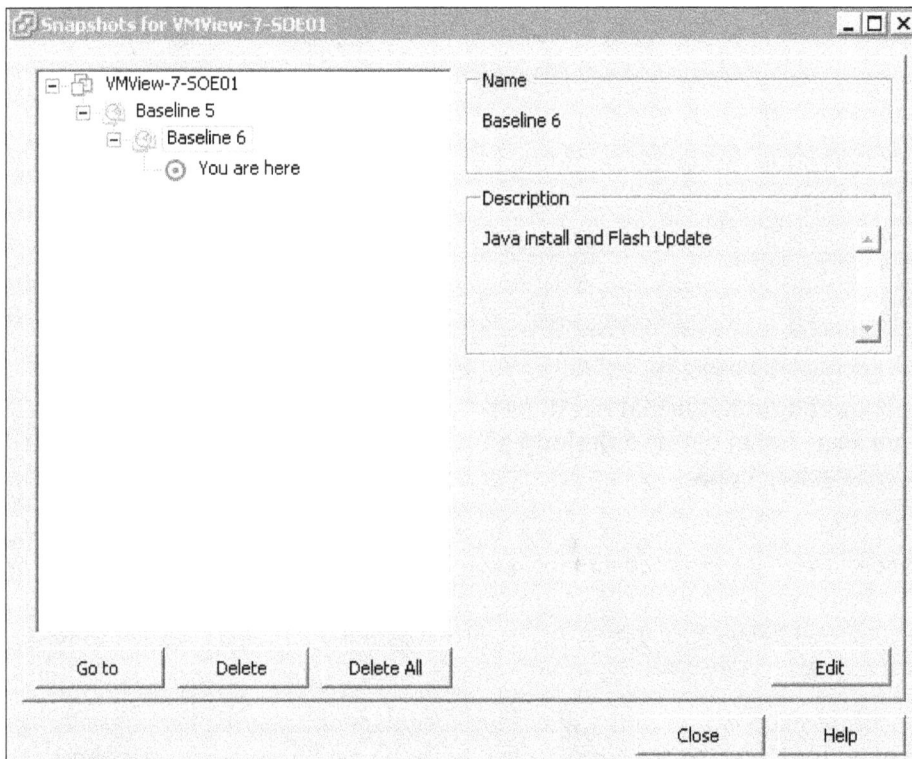

The VMware View snapshot selection during the desktop pool configuration process can be seen in the following screenshot, which shows snapshot selection in the View Admin console:

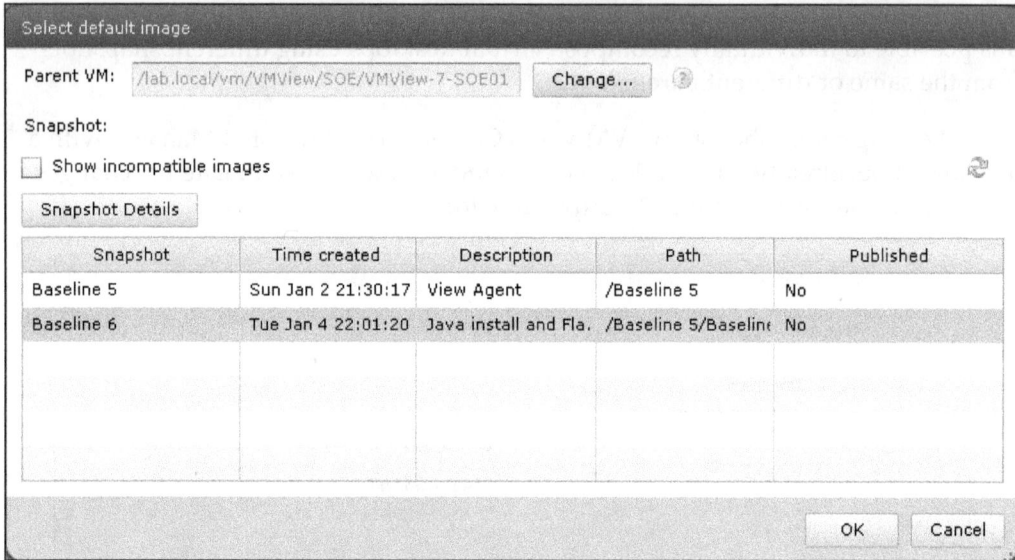

Snapshot	Time created	Description	Path	Published
Baseline 5	Sun Jan 2 21:30:17	View Agent	/Baseline 5	No
Baseline 6	Tue Jan 4 22:01:20	Java install and Fla.	/Baseline 5/Baselin(	No

Select default image

Parent VM: /lab.local/vm/VMView/SOE/VMView-7-SOE01 Change...

Snapshot:

Show incompatible images

Snapshot Details

OK   Cancel

In releases prior to VMware View 4.5, a unique replica disk was created in each datastore hosting virtual desktops for a desktop pool. Additionally, for each different snapshot in use by a desktop pool, a new replica disk used to be created for each datastore in use.

Only a single snapshot can be assigned to the desktop pool at any time. However, you can choose to change the snapshot for the desktop pool and then execute a Recompose action. The Recompose action creates a second replica disk representing the new snapshot on each datastore in use by the virtual desktops. In this case, each datastore may contain two replicas for the desktop pool.

In a Recompose operation, the original replica image is only deleted after all desktops in the datastore are recomposed with the new base replica disk and the old replica is not required anymore. Therefore, it is important to ensure that there is ample space available on the datastore(s) dedicated to storing replicas.

This scenario is still applicable in VMware View 6.0 when the administrator does not select the optional **Dedicated Replica Datastore** feature during the datastore selection.

VMware View 4.5 and later implemented the ability to specify a unique datastore to host replica disks for an entire desktop pool. This piece is part of the VMWare View **tiered storage** feature.

The following screenshot shows datastore selection in the View Admin console:

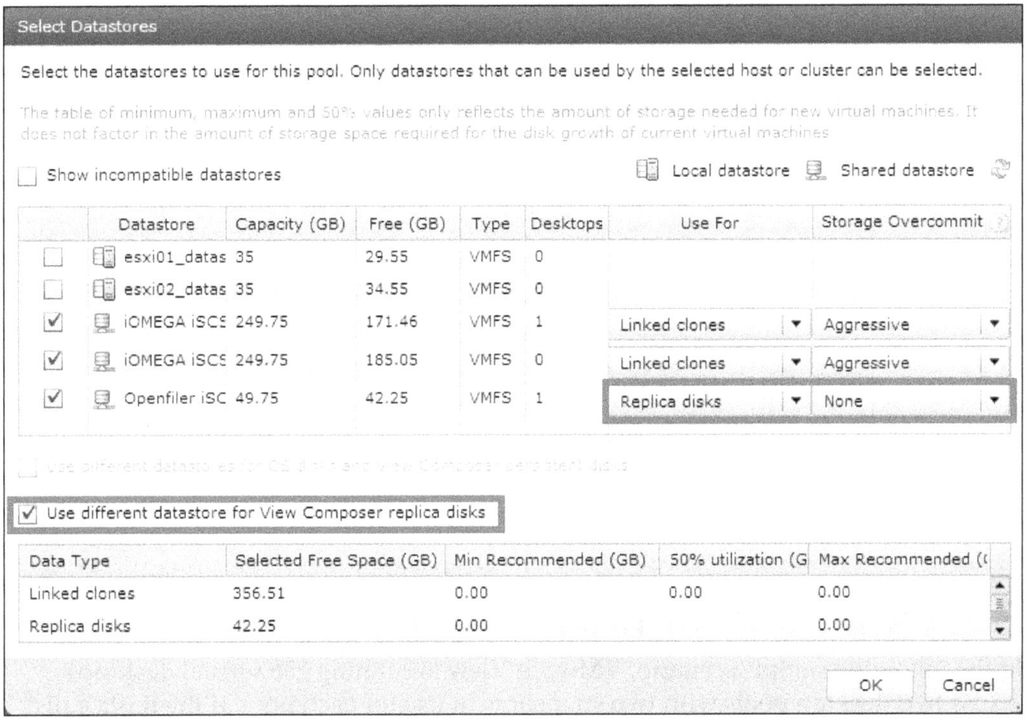

If the desktop pool is large and eventually uses the entire vSphere cluster resources, it is possible to end up with a single replica disk for the entire cluster. For VMware View 6.0, the maximum number of virtual desktops supported in a single desktop pool is 1,000. While it is possible to go further than 1,000 desktops, it is neither recommended nor supported.

In some cases where multiple snapshots are in use, multiple replicas will be created in the single datastore selected during the pool configuration. The following figure shows the differences between not using and using the **Dedicated Replica Datastore** option in VMware View 4.5 and above:

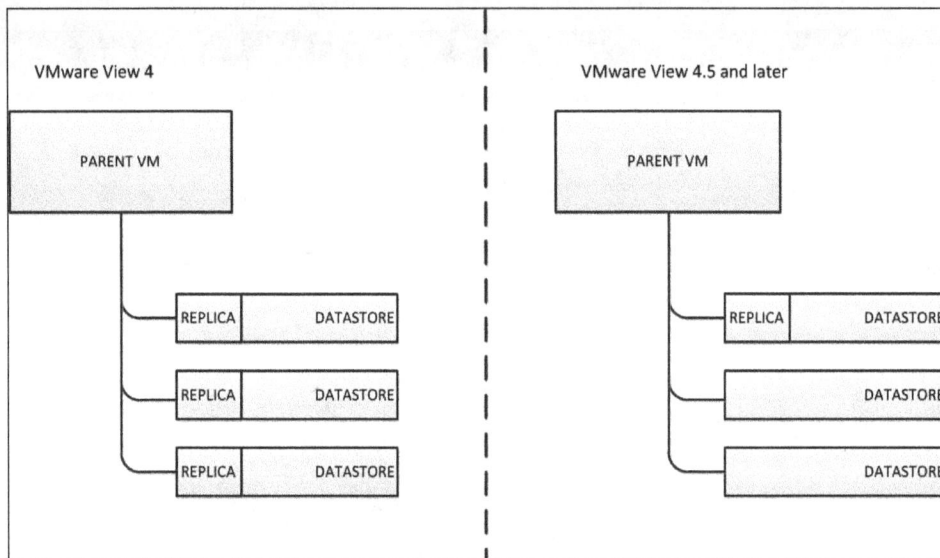

Snapshot and replica usage

In the following sample scenario, VMware View is running 256 virtual desktops across two desktop pools with two snapshots in use for each pool. If the replica disk size is 20 GB, the total storage allocation for the replica disks would be 320 GB, that is, 80 GB per datastore, as shown: *Number of desktop pools * replicas in use * number of data stores * replica size = 2 * 2 * 4 * 20 GB = 160 GB.*

Using the same sample scenario with the **Dedicated Replica Datastore** option, the total storage allocation for the replica disks would be 80 GB in a single datastore, as shown: *Number of desktop pools * replicas in use * replica size = 2 * 2 * 20 GB = 80 GB.*

The following figure shows both scenarios. It is an illustration showing the difference between the replica disk placement when using multiple snapshots and **Dedicated Replica Disk Datastore** in View 4.5 and above:

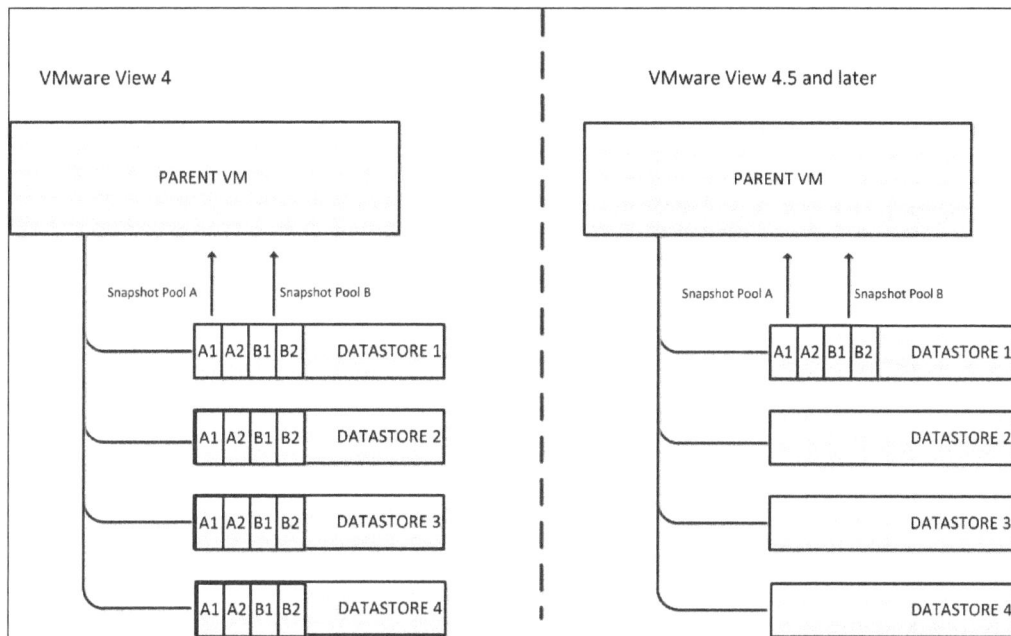

Running the same calculations for the preceding scenario with 2,000 virtual desktops, the storage savings provided by the View Composer technology could be as large as 6.3 TB. The more the number of virtual machines and desktop pools in the environment, the bigger the number of replicas per datastore when the **Dedicated Replica Datastore** option is not selected.

It is possible to break down the amount of replica disks and storage consumption if all datastores are not selected for each desktop pool, therefore, limiting the placement of virtual desktops across datastores.

The number of datastores and datastore sizes must provide the capacity and performance requirements for the provisioning of the required number of desktops. This concept assumes that the administrator will carefully manage and select the datastores in use by the desktop pool, not allowing all datastores to be used by all desktop pools.

The following screenshot shows a solution where the **Dedicated Replica Datastore** option is not used:

Select Datastores

Select the datastores to use for this pool. Only datastores that can be used by the selected host or cluster can be selected.

The table of minimum, maximum and 50% values only reflects the amount of storage needed for new virtual machines. It does not factor in the amount of storage space required for the disk growth of current virtual machines

☐ Show incompatible datastores   🖥 Local datastore 🖳 Shared datastore 🔄

	Datastore	Capacity (GB)	Free (GB)	Type	Desktops	Storage Overcommit ⑦
☐	🖽 esxi01_datastore1	35	29.55	VMFS	0	
☐	🖽 esxi02_datastore1	35	34.55	VMFS	0	
☑	🖳 iOMEGA iSCSI Disk0	249.75	171.46	VMFS	1	Moderate ▼
☐	🖳 iOMEGA iSCSI Disk1	249.75	185.05	VMFS	0	
☑	🖳 Openfiler iSCSIi Disk0	49.75	42.25	VMFS	1	Moderate ▼

☐ Use different datastores for OS disks and View Composer persistent disks

☐ Use different datastore for View Composer replica disks

Data Type	Selected Free Space (GB)	Min Recommended (GB)	50% utilization (G	Max Recommended (G
Linked clones	213.71	0.00	0.00	0.00

OK   Cancel

Linked clone disk

A linked clone disk is also called a **delta disk** because it accumulates delta changes. After the replica disk is created, View Composer starts to create the linked clone virtual desktops. Each linked clone has a unique delta disk and is linked to the replica disk.

Delta disks contain only the differences from the original read-only replica disk that are unique to the cloned virtual desktop, resulting in significant storage savings. Linked clone disks will grow over time according to the blocked write changes requested by the Guest OS, and they may grow up to the maximum size of the parent VM.

As an example, if the parent VM was originally configured by the administrator with a 30 GB flat disk, this will be the maximum size of the delta disk.

View Composer allows for great storage savings; however, there will be dozens or hundreds of linked clone virtual desktops using the same datastore to read that single existing replica disk. If the **Dedicated Replica Datastore** option is not in use, the replica is only used by the desktops hosted in the same datastore.

All virtual desktops accessing the replica disk will cause I/O stress on LUNs, the RAID group, and disks, and may create I/O contention. The I/O contention is caused by multiple virtual desktops and users accessing the same datastore, all at the same time.

Each datastore is normally backed by a LUN if **Fibre Channel Protocol (FCP)** is in use or by an Export operation if NFS is in use. Both LUN and Export are backed by a RAID group configuration that encompasses a pool of disks configured to support the workload. Those disks and LUNs together must be able to meet the required performance specifications for the replica disk. These specifications are **Input/Output Operations Per Second (IOPS)** and throughput.

If a decision to use a dedicated replica datastore is made during the design phase, it is recommended to allocate Tier 1 storage, for example, SDD to host the replica disk.

The following figure shows a typical virtual disk to drive type associations:

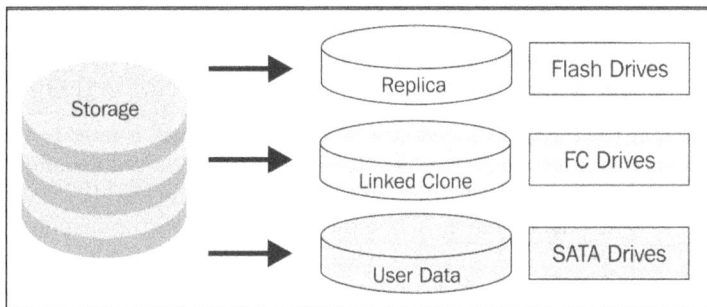

Storage vendors have different solutions and architectures to solve response time and latency issues. Some of the solutions available are automated storage tiering, storage pools, diskless environments, inline I/O deduplication, and local host caching.

VMware vSphere files

The following table contains the files and disks created for the virtual desktop provisioned through VMware View and are the standard files for any virtual machine created on a vSphere hypervisor. Normally, you would not have to interact with these files, but understanding their functions can help when you are experiencing problems with your environment:

File type	Description
.vmx	This file is the primary configuration file for a virtual machine. It contains information such as the operating system, disk sizes, networking, and so on.
.vmsd	This contains information and metadata about snapshots.
.vmxf	This contains supplemental configurations file for virtual machines that are in a team. Note that the .vmxf file remains if a virtual machine is removed from the team.
.vswp	This file is a swap file created for each virtual machine to allow VM memory over commitment on an ESXi host. This file is created when a VM is powered on and will be equal in size to the unreserved memory configured for the VM. When VMs are created, the default memory reservation is 0 MB, so the size of the .vswp file is equal to the amount of memory allocated to the VM. If a VM is configured with a 1024 MB memory reservation, the size of the .vswp file will be equal to the amount of memory allocated to the VM minus the 1024 MB reservation.
.vmss	This file is created when a VM is suspended and is used to save the suspended state. In essence, this is a copy of the VM's memory and will always have the size of the total amount of allocated RAM. Note that a .vmss file is created when the machine enters the suspended state; however, it's not removed when the VM is removed from the suspended state. The .vmss file is only removed when the VM is powered off. If a VM is configured with 2048 MB memory, the size of the .vmss file will be 2048 MB.
.nvram	This is the file that stores the state of the virtual machine's BIOS.
.vmsn	This is a snapshot state file that stores the running state of a virtual machine at the time you take the snapshot.
-flat.vmdk	This file is a raw disk file that is created for each virtual disk allocated to a given VM and will be of the same size as the virtual disks added to the VM at the time of creation. It's a preallocated disk file only available with full clone VMs.
.log	VM logfiles are relatively small.

VMware View specific files

The following table contains the files and disks created for virtual desktops provisioned through VMware View. Some of the disks are only created by View Composer or when assigning a persistent or disposable disk to the desktop pool. Having knowledge of the files that are used in the View environment could help when troubleshooting an event:

File type	Composer	Description
`replica-GUID.vmdk`	Yes	Replica VM is used to spin-up linked clone VMs.
`-internal.vmdk`	Yes	This contains data configuration for QuickPrep/Sysprep.
`VM-s000[n].vmdk`	Yes	This is created when a virtual machine has snapshot(s). This file stores changes made to a virtual disk while the virtual machine is running. There may be more than one such file. The three-digit number after the letter (`000` after `s` in this case) indicates a unique suffix added automatically to avoid duplicate filenames.
`VDM-disposable-GUID.vmdk`	Yes	This contains redirected the Windows operating system page file and temporary files.
`.log`	No	This contains VM logfiles.

Tiered storage

VMware View 4.5 and above allow administrators to select different datastores to host different types of virtual disks (replica, linked clone, and persistent). Data performance classification is an important part of storage tiering implementation and allows administrators to select datastores that provide the most appropriate storage tier with regards to performance, cost, and capacity for each type of disk in use.

> Do not confuse the storage tiering feature provided by VMware View with auto storage tiering or subLUN tiering offered by storage vendors. The solution provided by VMware View is static and does not automatically move data around to achieve best performance. The solutions are complementary to each other.

With the introduction of storage tiering and the ability to segment workloads across datastores and types of disks, it is important to understand what type of disks and data are created for each virtual desktop. The type of disks created may differ for each implementation. Desktop pools that utilize linked clone technology may have additional virtual disks that are not created when using traditional full clone provisioning.

The following figure shows the multiple types of virtual disks in use by VMware View:

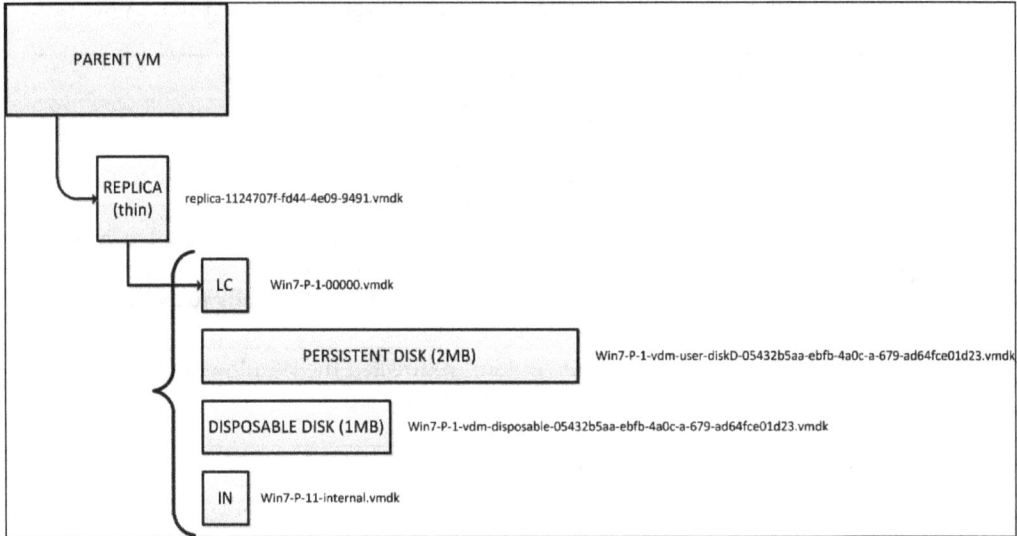

Replica disk

The `replica-GUID.vmdk` folder contains all files required to run the virtual machine; however, it will be exclusively used as read-only and as the base for linked clone virtual desktops. The following screenshot shows the folder and files created to host a replica disk:

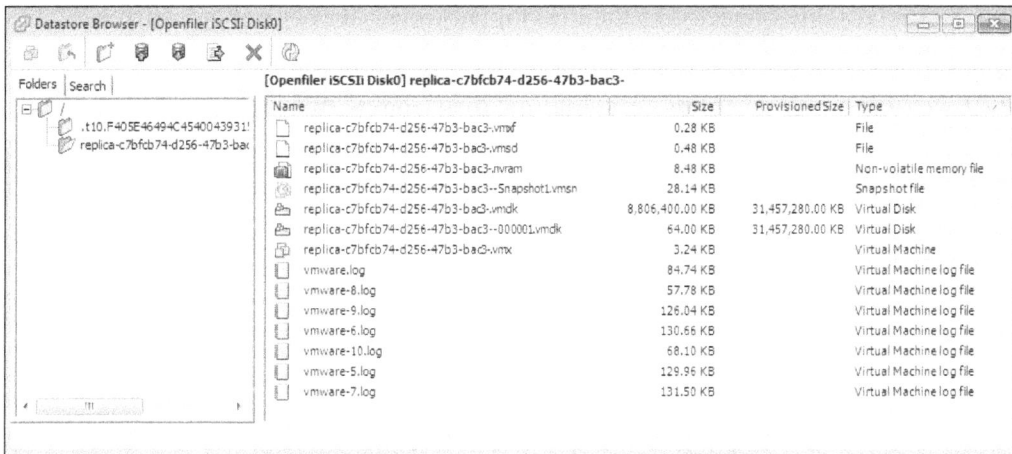

Despite the fact that the provisioned size of the disk is set to 30 GB (31,457,280 KB) in the previous example, only 8 GB is actually used. The reason for this is that View Composer makes use of vSphere VMFS thin provisioning technology to create replica disks. This is an automatic setting that cannot be changed via View Manager UI and will work independently of the parent VM being thin or thick provisioned. For NFS deployments, this is also the only provisioning mechanism.

Internal disk

The `internal.vmdk` disk is a small disk and contains the configuration data for QuickPrep/Sysprep. QuickPrep/Sysprep personalizes each desktop created from the master image. In previous VMware View releases, operations such as Refresh would incur a full desktop deletion, followed by provision and customization of a new virtual desktop. This process takes a long time to complete and would normally draw a high number of compute and storage resources. VMware View 4.5 and later started implementing a different technique to refresh virtual desktops that make use of the vSphere snapshot technology.

A Refresh operation is simply a snapshot revert-back operation. The internal disk is created to store the Active Directory computer account password changes that Windows performs so often, as per the default AD policy setting. The computer account password is encrypted before being stored on the internal disk.

Whenever the domain computer account password is changed, VMware View Agent stores another encrypted copy of the password in the disk. This ensures that domain connectivity is maintained when a desktop is refreshed.

The internal disk is connected to the desktop; however, it does not get a drive letter assigned to it.

The following screenshot shows the internal disk from within a guest vDesktop:

Name ^	Date modified	Type	Size
$RECYCLE.BIN	27/03/2011 12:59 PM	File folder	
System Volume Information	27/03/2011 9:02 AM	File folder	
domstate.dat	31/03/2011 10:53 AM	DAT File	1 KB
sim.dat	27/03/2011 8:50 AM	DAT File	1 KB
simvol.dat	27/03/2011 8:50 AM	DAT File	1 KB

The internal disk is the only disk created by VMware View that is not thin provisioned. Its size is so small that being thick provisioned doesn't change the capacity requirements in the solution. This disk is typically around 20 MB in size.

Delta/differential disk

The following screenshot shows folders and files created in the VM folder to host a linked clone desktop. In the following example, the delta disk is `VMView-7-D-01-000001.vmdk`:

Datastore Browser - [iOMEGA iSCSI Disk0]

Folders | Search

[iOMEGA iSCSI Disk0] VMView-7-D-01

VMView-7-D-01

Name	Size	Provisioned Size	Type
vmware-7.log	131.50 KB		Virtual Machine log file
VMView-7-D-01.nvram	8.48 KB		Non-volatile memory file
vmware-11.log	84.74 KB		Virtual Machine log file
vmware-8.log	57.78 KB		Virtual Machine log file
vmware-9.log	126.04 KB		Virtual Machine log file
VMView-7-D-01-000001.vmdk	558,080.00 KB	31,457,280.00 KB	Virtual Disk
vmware-10.log	68.10 KB		Virtual Machine log file
VMView-7-D-01_21-internal.vmdk	20,480.00 KB		Virtual Disk
VMView-7-D-01.vmx	5.10 KB		Virtual Machine
VMView-7-D-01.vmxf	0.26 KB		File
VMView-7-D-01.vmsd	0.68 KB		File
VMView-7-D-01.vmdk	33,792.00 KB	31,457,280.00 KB	Virtual Disk
vmware-12.log	229.40 KB		Virtual Machine log file
VMView-7-D-01-Snapshot1.vmsn	29.97 KB		Snapshot file
vmware.log	134.28 KB		Virtual Machine log file
VMView-7-D-01-96552ddd.vswp	2,097,152.00 KB		File

After the customization process is complete, the VM is shut down and View Composer takes a snapshot of the linked clone.

After the snapshot is taken, data is no longer written to the base `.vmdk` file. Instead, changes are written to the delta disk. A delta disk will be created every time a snapshot is taken. It is important that any requirements to use snapshots are considered when defining the datastore size requirements.

Disposable disk

VMware View allows for the creation of an optional fixed-size nonpersistent disk for each virtual desktop. When disposable disks are assigned to a desktop pool, VMware View redirects temporary Windows system files and folders to a disposable disk.

Disposable disks are automatically deleted when the virtual desktop is powered off, refreshed, or recomposed, which means that temporary files are also deleted during these operations. Disposable disks are also thin provisioned and will grow over time to the maximum size set during the desktop pool configuration.

The following screenshot shows the **Disposable File Redirection** configuration within the View Admin console:

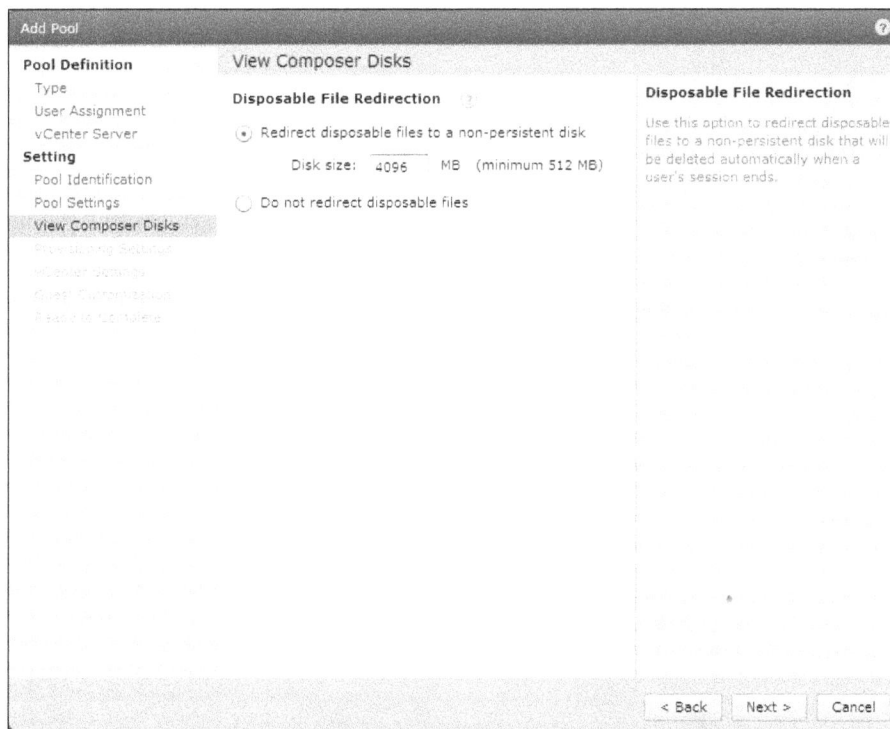

The disposable disk is hardcoded to register itself as the first available drive on the Windows desktop. This behavior may cause some implications while trying to map network drives in Windows virtual desktops. Even when the CD-ROM is not in use, the first available drive letter would be E:, because C: is taken by the OS and D: is taken by the disposable disk.

The files that are commonly offloaded to disposable disks are Windows paging files, VMware logfiles, and temporary Internet files.

Windows paging files

When Windows is constantly running out of physical memory, it will start to page memory to disk. This paging process will incur in block writes that will increase the size of the disposable disk. As a recommended approach, administrators should make sure that virtual desktops have enough virtual memory available to avoid disk paging. Disk paging has a negative impact on performance.

Temporary Internet files

User temporary files are kept on the system or persistent data disk, and this may include files written to %USERPROFILE%\AppData\Local\Temp and Temporary Internet Files. These are the temporary files that can grow very fast and consume disk space.

As the temporary files are offloaded to the disposable disk, the steady growth of the delta file is reduced. Instead of utilizing delta disks that will grow according to block changes, View Composer utilizes the disposable disk. However, it is important to size the disposable disks according to the virtual desktop and workload requirements. Once assigned to a virtual desktop pool, this setting cannot be changed through the View Manager.

The following screenshot shows a disposable disk with Windows temporary files:

Name ▲	Date modified	Type	Size
$RECYCLE.BIN	7/09/2010 1:03 AM	File folder	
System Volume Information	6/09/2010 12:51 AM	File folder	
TEMP	7/09/2010 9:13 AM	File folder	
pagefile.sys	6/09/2010 1:52 PM	System file	1,048,576 KB
simvol.dat	4/09/2010 4:50 PM	DAT File	1 KB

When configuring a linked clone pool, make sure that the disposable disk is larger than the Windows paging file size plus overhead for temporary files.

Persistent disk

Persistent data disk is the new name for what used to be called a **user data disk** (**UDD**) in previous releases of VMware View and maintains similar characteristics to the UDD. Persistent disks were created to maintain a one-to-one relationship between users and virtual desktops.

When selected during the desktop pool configuration, the persistent disk is created and VMware View Agent makes modifications to the Windows Guest OS to allow the user profile to be redirected to this disk.

In VMware View 4.5 and later, persistent disks can be managed. The disk can be detached and reattached to virtual desktops. Note that this will only work if the disks are created in VMware View 4.5 or later. If a VMware View environment has been upgraded from earlier releases, these operations will not be available.

Just like disposable disks, persistent disks cannot be disabled or enabled once they are configured for the desktop pool. It is also not possible to change the size through the View Manager graphical user interface after the initial configuration. However, it is possible to change the persistent disk's size for virtual desktops being newly provisioned in the desktop pool if the administrator changes the pool settings.

When configuring persistent disks, you should make sure that the size of the disk is adequate for your users. If Active Directory Folder Redirection or VMware View Persona Management is not in use, the user profile size could be several gigabytes in size.

As a general rule, if you are using persona management or Windows roaming profiles, make sure the disk is large enough to cater to the user's roaming profiles, or apply quotas to roaming profiles.

The following screenshot shows the **Persistent Disk** selection screen during the desktop pool configuration. It shows the configuration of persistent disks within the View Admin console:

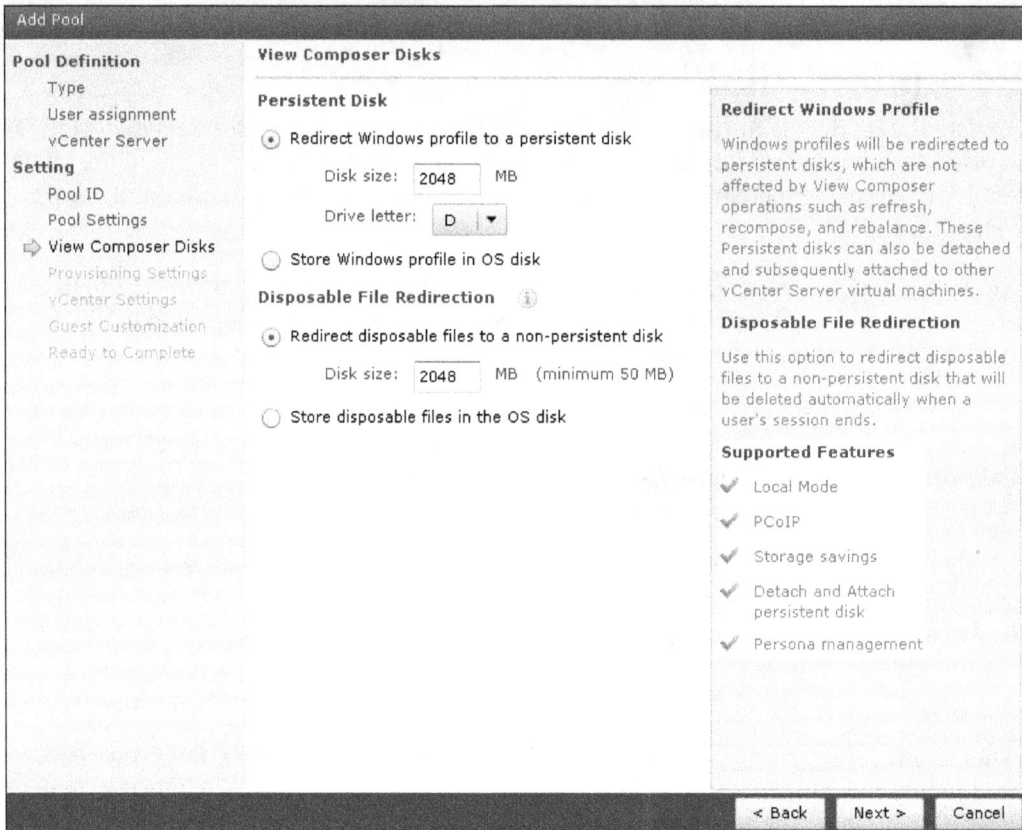

Add Pool

Pool Definition
Type
User assignment
vCenter Server
Setting
Pool ID
Pool Settings
⇨ View Composer Disks
Provisioning Settings
vCenter Settings
Guest Customization
Ready to Complete

View Composer Disks

Persistent Disk

(•) Redirect Windows profile to a persistent disk

Disk size: [2048] MB

Drive letter: [D ▼]

( ) Store Windows profile in OS disk

Disposable File Redirection (i)

(•) Redirect disposable files to a non-persistent disk

Disk size: [2048] MB (minimum 50 MB)

( ) Store disposable files in the OS disk

Redirect Windows Profile

Windows profiles will be redirected to persistent disks, which are not affected by View Composer operations such as refresh, recompose, and rebalance. These Persistent disks can also be detached and subsequently attached to other vCenter Server virtual machines.

Disposable File Redirection

Use this option to redirect disposable files to a non-persistent disk that will be deleted automatically when a user's session ends.

Supported Features

✔ Local Mode

✔ PCoIP

✔ Storage savings

✔ Detach and Attach persistent disk

✔ Persona management

[< Back] [Next >] [Cancel]

In the Windows operating system, the persistent disk and the disposable disk can be seen in Windows Explorer. Important folders will be locked and users cannot delete them. However, through the use of Windows Group Policy, it is possible to hide the drives while still making them available for use.

The following screenshot shows the various disks within the guest vDesktop:

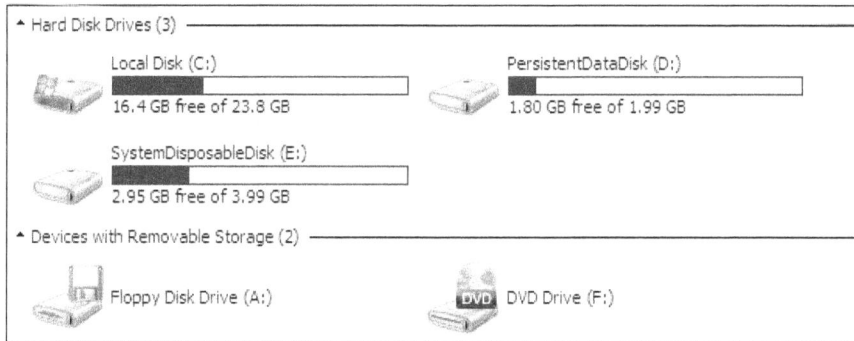

The persistent disk's drive letter is selected during the desktop pool configuration process and the content is similar to what's shown in the following screenshot. In the **Users** folder, the profile folders and settings are found.

Name ▲	Date modified	Type	Size
personality	1/04/2011 1:01 PM	File folder	
personality.bak	1/04/2011 12:17 PM	File folder	
Users	1/04/2011 10:41 AM	File folder	

Storage overcommit

With the introduction of linked clone technology and the ability to specify when each virtual desktop is refreshed or recomposed, there is an opportunity to specify how much storage should be overcommitted to help reduce storage consumption.

Let's assume that not every virtual desktop will utilize the full provisioned storage at the same time, thereby leaving a gap for storage utilization and overallocation (overcommit).

During the desktop pool provisioning process, the administrator has the option to select **Refresh OS Disk after logoff** with one of the following options:

- **Never**: If this option is selected, then virtual desktops will never execute the delta disk Refresh operation. The delta disk will grow with every block change up to the limit of the disk itself. If the disk size defined for the virtual desktop is 40 GB, this is the limit. When 40 GB is reached, then vSphere VMFS starts reutilizing the blocks just like it does with full clones. You will not run out of disk space in this case.

- **Always**: If this option is in use, then virtual desktops will be refreshed every time a user logs off from the desktop. Assuming that only a few gigabytes have been added to the delta disk during use, they will then be recuperated when the virtual desktop is refreshed.

- **Every x number of days**: If this option is selected, then virtual desktops will be refreshed on the number of days defined, independent of the utilization of the delta disk. Delta files grow over time based on a number of factors that include Windows and application utilization. Therefore, while selecting this option, it is important to understand how big the delta can get during that period so that you are able to size datastores accordingly.

- **At y percent of disk utilization**: If this option is selected and y is set to 50 percent, then the virtual desktop will be refreshed when half of the total provisioned storage is utilized by the delta. This calculation does not include additional disks such as persistent or disposable. If a virtual desktop has been created with a total disk size of 40 GB, the Refresh operation would take place when the user logs off and the delta disk utilization is more than or equal to 20 GB.

An important point to remember is that linked clones start at a fraction of their full provisioned size. The storage capacity savings provided by VMware View Composer through the Refresh operation allow administrators to decide how the available storage capacity should be utilized until the storage is fully occupied. As an example, the administrator who selected the **Always** option knows that delta files, on average, will grow up to 300 MB while the desktop is in use during business hours.

Based on the storage utilization, it is possible to enforce the placement of more virtual desktops per datastore than would be possible with full clone virtual desktops. This is called the **storage overcommit level**.

> VMware View does not allow administrators to configure the maximum number of linked clones per datastore and the limitation on the number of desktops comes from the datastore size. It is critical to size datastores appropriately to support the required number of desktops, yet be compliant with VMware View and View Composer limits specified at `http://kb.vmware.com/selfservice/microsites/search.do?language=en_US&cmd=displayKC&externalId=2080467`.

Typically, the overcommit level is defined based on how virtual desktops are used. If a desktop pool with floating assignment has desktops that have **Always Refresh** option after logoff, storage consumption will be low and you may set the overcommit to **Aggressive**. However, if virtual desktops are not frequently refreshed, you may prefer to set it to **Conservative**.

Storage overcommit level options

It is possible to define different overcommit levels among different types of datastores to address different levels of capacity, performance, or availability provided. For example, a NAS datastore may have a different overcommit level than a SAN datastore; in the same way, an SSD datastore can have a different overcommit level than an FC datastore. The following table explores the overcommit options and the level of storage overcommit:

Option	Storage overcommit level
None	Storage is not overcommitted.
Conservative	This is four times the size of the datastore. This is the default level.
Moderate	This is seven times the size of the datastore.
Aggressive	This is 15 times the size of the datastore.
Unbound	View Manager does not limit the number of linked clone desktops that it creates based on the physical capacity of the datastore. It's up to you to calculate the space and determine the number of VMs you want to place and that can be supported by the datastore.

> It is recommended practice to always match vSphere datastores with LUNs or Exports on a one-by-one basis. Administrators should avoid using large storage LUNs backed by multiple datastores.

The number of linked clones per datastore defined by the storage overcommit level is based on the size of the parent VM. Based on a 30 GB VM and a 200 GB datastore, VMware View would be able to fit approximately six full clone virtual desktops. However, if using overcommit level 7 (Moderate), VMware View would be able to fit approximately 42 desktops. The following table shows the effect of the overcommit level you choose:

VM size (GB)	Datastore size (GB)	Overcommit level	Number of full clone VMs	Number of linked clone VMs
30	200	4	6	24
30	200	7	6	42
30	200	15	6	90

> It's possible to run out of storage capacity. When the storage available in a datastore is not sufficient, VMware View will not provide new desktops; however, the existing linked clone desktops will keep growing and eventually fill up the datastore. This situation is more common with the overcommit level set to **Aggressive**.

To make sure that linked clones do not run out of disk space, administrators should periodically refresh or rebalance desktop pools to reduce the linked clone footprint to its original size.

The following screenshot shows the selection of storage overcommit during the desktop pool provisioning or configuration process:

Select Datastores

Select the datastores to use for this pool. Only datastores that can be used by the selected host or cluster can be selected.

The table of minimum, maximum and 50% values only reflects the amount of storage needed for new virtual machines. It does not factor in the amount of storage space required for the disk growth of current virtual machines

☐ Show incompatible datastores   Local datastore   Shared datastore ⟳

	Datastore	Capacity (GB)	Free (GB)	Type	Desktops	Use For	Storage Overcommit ?
☐	esxi01_datas	35	29.55	VMFS	0		
☐	esxi02_datas	35	34.55	VMFS	0		
☑	iOMEGA iSCS	249.75	182.25	VMFS	0	Linked clones ▼	Aggressive ▼
☑	iOMEGA iSCS	249.75	184.48	VMFS	1	Linked clones ▼	Moderate ▼
☑	Openfiler iSC	49.75	41.39	VMFS	1	Replica disks ▼	None
							Conservative
							Moderate
							Aggressive

☐ Use different datastores for OS disks and View Composer persistent disks

☑ Use different datastore for View Composer replica disks

Data Type	Selected Free Space (GB)	Min Recommended (GB)	50% utilization (G	Max Recommended ((
Linked clones	366.73	0.00	0.00	0.00
Replica disks	41.39	0.00	0.00	0.00

OK   Cancel

Storage protocols

VMware View is supported by the VMware vSphere, and therefore supports multiple storage protocols for storing data. VMware vSphere is capable of using fiber channel, iSCSI, **Fiber Channel over Ethernet (FCoE)**, and NFS.

The main considerations for protocol choice for VMware View are maximum throughput, VMDK behavior, and the cost of reusing existing versus acquiring new storage infrastructure. These considerations affect network design and performance.

The intention of this section is not to cover each protocol or how they perform in a VDI environment. The numbers in the following table are based on VMware View 5.3 and vSphere 5 and are intended to help with the decision on the storage protocol to be used:

	Fiber channel	**iSCSI**	**FCoE**	**NFS**
Type	Block	Block	Block	File
VAAI	Yes	Yes	Yes	Yes
Transmission rate	4, 8, or 16 Gbps	Multiple 10 Gbps	Multiple 10 Gbps	Multiple 10 Gbps
Maximum number of hosts	32	32	32	32
LUNs/Exports per host	256	256	256	256
Clones per datastore	64 to 140	64 to 140	64 to 140	Not validated

Maximums and limits

Designing a large-scale VMware View solution is a complex task. The challenges faced in large deployments may be faced in small deployments if VMware-validated maximums and limits are not observed.

> It is recommended that you use a conservative approach when sizing the VDI environment.

There are tools to help administrators understand requirements and constraints from graphics, CPU, memory, and storage perspectives. Other tools help to calculate the infrastructure size based on the number of virtual desktops, average IOPS, memory size, percentage of shared memory, percentage of used memory, percentage of read/write IOPS, and so on.

No matter what results these tools provide, the VDI architect should always ensure that the numbers are within VMware vSphere and VMware View limits.

Linked clones per datastore

For FC arrays with support for **vStorage APIs for Array Integration (VAAI)**, the maximum number of linked clones per datastore is 140. The VAAI primitives that augment the number of virtual desktops per datastore are called **hardware-assisted locking** or **Atomic Test and Set (ATS)**.

The vSphere VMkernel has to update VMFS metadata for operations involving the virtual desktops stored in the VMFS. Updates to metadata occur as a result of powering on/off virtual desktops, suspending/resuming virtual desktops, and various other operations.

In a VDI environment, that would mean the VMkernel may have to update metadata for many hundreds of virtual desktops, and would therefore have to lock the entire VMFS in order to update its metadata just to power on a single virtual desktop. That operation takes no more than a few milliseconds, but does become problematic when powering on many virtual desktops simultaneously.

Hardware-assisted locking, available with vSphere 4.1 and compatible vendor array code, allows the VMkernel to lock metadata at the block level within the VMFS stored on the array and allow multiple operations to occur simultaneously within the VMFS, which in turn allows many desktop VMs to be powered on at the same time.

For datastores backed by **Network File System (NFS)**, there is no limitation on the number of virtual desktops per datastore because NFS doesn't present the same SCSI reservation problems. NFS is a file-based storage system and with **View Composer for Array Integration (VCAI)** support, there are many storage vendors adopting NFS, which is becoming a common choice Horizon deployment. NFS doesn't have any limitations on maximum linked clones per NFS datastore, although as a best practice the suggestion would be 180-250 as a balanced maximum.

Full clone desktops per datastore

Can you only have 32 VMs per VMFS? The origins of the very conservative numbers were from storage vendors, but that was to protect the user from themselves in some cases. The limitation is also based on server workloads, SCSI reservations, and storage administrators not doing a good job at sizing the infrastructure.

For you to understand how to make effective use of your storage and determine how many virtual machines can share the same LUN, you need to research:

- How SCSI reservations affect shared storage performance in ESX
- How many LUNs and VMFS filesystems can be configured on a single ESX host

Also, you have to understand things such as the effects of I/O queuing at the various layers in the virtual infrastructure as you increase the number of VMs sharing the same storage. There are effects of SCSI reservations on VM I/O performance and other factors that are out of the scope of this book. There is an excellent white paper that explains all this and more in great detail, found at `http://www.vmware.com/files/pdf/scalable_storage_performance.pdf`.

32 hosts per vSphere cluster with View Composer

VMware View will stop the provision of new virtual desktops if the number of hosts in a cluster with View Composer surpasses 32. The behavior is hardcoded into View Composer. However, the source of the limitation lies in the VMFS layer.

The VMFS structure now allows for a maximum of 32 hosts to access to read or write a single VMDK file. In a linked clone implementation, all hosts in a cluster may have virtual desktops reading storage blocks from the same replica disk.

1,000 clones per replica

The number of clones per replica also determines the number of linked clones that may coexist in a single desktop pool. This number is resulting from VMware's QA validation labs; however, this is a soft limit and it can be increased (although this is not recommended).

In previous releases, the VMware View validated limit was 512 virtual desktops per replica or desktop pool. This limit was a result from a maximum of 64 linked clones per datastore multiplied by 8 hosts per vSphere cluster (*64 * 8 = 512*).

Storage I/O profile

The I/O storage profile produced by each virtual desktop is entirely dependent on which type of Windows operating system is in use, the applications deployed, and even how each user individually interacts with the environment.

IOPS (pronounced as **eye-ops**) is a common performance measurement used to benchmark computer storage devices such as **hard disk drives (HDDs)**, **solid state drives (SSDs)**, and **storage area networks (SANs)**. As with any benchmark, IOPS numbers published by storage device manufacturers do not guarantee real-world application performance.

According to Wikipedia, predictions of what the average virtual desktop I/O profile will likely be is one of the most difficult tasks when designing a VDI solution. The reason for that is the lack of information about the workload that will be running in each one of the virtual desktops at the design time.

It is possible to use pre-trended numbers as a baseline; however, despite the indication of what the workload would likely be, it could be a point out of the curve in some cases.

In an ideal scenario, a VDI pilot project has been operational for a little while and data can be collected and trended appropriately.

A few metrics must be taken into consideration to size storage correctly. They are as follows:

- **Storage size**: How much storage capacity is required?
- **LUN size**: How many LUNs and/or datastores are required?
- **Tier type**: What type of disk is required and what is the disk placement?
- **IOPS (cmd/s)**: What is the number of I/O commands per second?
- **Read/write ratio**: What is the read and write ratio?

The first three items in the list may be calculated without major understanding of the I/O workload; however, it would require knowledge about the virtual desktop storage capacity utilization.

The real problem lies with the I/O per second and the read/write I/O pattern. Without these values, storage architects/administrators will probably not be able to provide storage with the performance that the virtual desktop infrastructure requires.

IOPS, also known as the **disk I/O profile**, will differ for each type of Windows operating system. The profile is also dependent upon the type and number of applications deployed, including services running in the OS. The I/O profile is also dependent on how users interact with their virtual desktops. VMware and partners have validated I/O profiles that can be used as a baseline. It is highly recommended that you find out the correct I/O profile for your particular VDI environment.

The VMware View documentation establishes some I/O baselines:

- **Light (5 IOPS)**: Light users typically use e-mail (Outlook), Excel, Word, and a web browser (Internet Explorer or Firefox) during the normal workday. These workers are usually data entry operators or clerical staff.

- **Heavy (15 IOPS)**: Heavy users are full knowledge workers using all the tools of the light worker (Outlook, Excel, Word, Internet Explorer, and Firefox) and also working with large PowerPoint presentations and performing other large file manipulations. These workers include business managers, executives, and members of the marketing staff.

The preceding information and other sizing guidelines can be found at `http://www.vmware.com/files/pdf/view/Server-Storage-Sizing-Guide-Windows-7-TN.pdf`.

Another study performed by PQR Consultants (Herco van Brug) shows I/O profiles as follows:

	Windows XP	**Windows 7**
Light	3 to 4	4 to 5
Medium	6 to 8	8 to 10
Heavy	12 to 16	14 to 20

> The *VDI & Storage – Deep Impact v1-25 hot!* article can be found at `http://pqr.com/deep-impact-vdi-storage`.

It is common to talk about average IOPS per virtual desktop; however, when sizing the VDI solutions, it is crucial that the peaks are also catered for. Otherwise, the storage infrastructure will be under heavy stress and will not be able to deliver the required IOPS and throughput.

Common scenarios where high performance and high throughput are required are during boot and login storms. As an example, a Windows 7 desktop can generate up to 700 IOPS during boot time. Another good example is if the **Refresh on logoff** option is used in conjunction with floating pools, it is common to see utilization peaks at the end of the work shift when business users start to log off.

Now, we have an existing paradigm where, from a cost perspective, the storage infrastructure should be sized for the average performance requirements over time, but from a performance perspective it should be sized for those peaks. For this reason, storage vendors have implemented their own proprietary caching solutions to optimize storage arrays to deal with the high peaks yet volatile VDI I/O requirements.

Most architecture documents or white papers published will show some divergences on these numbers. If you want to run your own I/O benchmarking during the pilot phase, use storage array admin tools, VMware vCenter client, or tools (for example, **vscsiStats**) that will provide you with a much more granular overview.

Read/write I/O ratio

The read/write I/O ratio will determine how many disks are required to support the VDI workload in a RAID configuration. Now, we will learn how critical it is to understand the read and write I/O ratio to allow administrators to properly size storage arrays from a frontend (storage processors) and backend (disks) standpoint.

In the previous topic, we talked about the total number of IOPS that a virtual desktop produces during boot, login, and steady state utilization. IOPS may be read or written. Every time a disk block is read, we have a read I/O and every time a block is written, we have a write I/O.

The Windows operating systems are, by nature, very I/O-intensive, and most of those I/Os are write I/Os. This is actually a very interesting subject. During workload simulations, it is possible to identify that Windows is constantly issuing more write than read I/Os. However, the most interesting fact is that even when Windows is idle, it still produces more write than read I/Os.

The same study performed by PQR Consultants (Herco van Brug) says that:

> "*The amount of IOPS a client produces is very much dependent on the users and their applications. But on average, the IOPS required amount to eight to ten per client in a read/write ratio of between 40/60 percent and 20/80 percent. For XP the average is closer to eight, for Windows 7 it is closer to ten, assuming the base image is optimized to do as little as possible by itself and all I/Os come from the applications, not the OS.*"

During an experiment conducted by Andre Leibovici and published in his blog at `http://myvirtualcloud.net/?p=2138`, it was possible to clearly identify the intensive write I/O pattern in contrast to the read I/Os during login VSI workload generation.

The following screenshot shows I/O testing performed at `http://myvirtualcloud.net/`. It shows the write I/O pattern (darker) compare to the read I/O (lighter) and the actual numbers of the results under the chart.

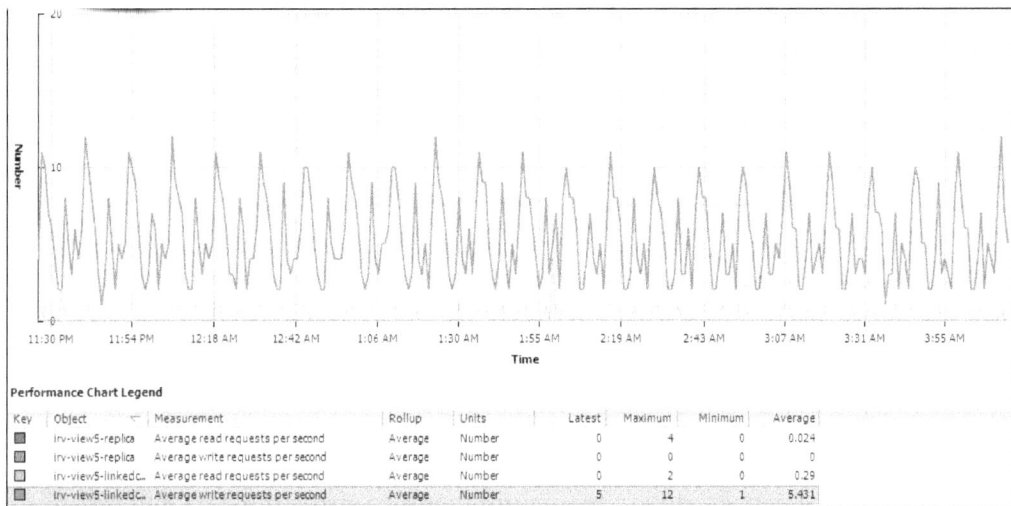

Key	Object	Measurement	Rollup	Units	Latest	Maximum	Minimum	Average
■	irv-view5-replica	Average read requests per second	Average	Number	0	4	0	0.024
■	irv-view5-replica	Average write requests per second	Average	Number	0	0	0	0
☐	irv-view5-linkedc..	Average read requests per second	Average	Number	0	2	0	0.29
■	irv-view5-linkedc..	Average write requests per second	Average	Number	5	12	1	5.431

The VMware View Reference Architecture documentation points us to read and write ratios with the following magnitudes: 70/30, 60/40, and 50/50. However, it's not uncommon to see VDI workloads with 10 percent reads and 90 percent writes.

The following figure shows an illustration of the read/write ratio from real production data:

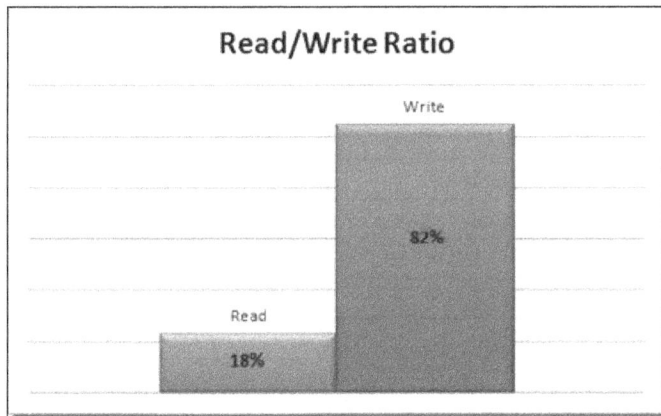

The reason we are focusing so much on the I/O pattern is because it determines how many drives are required to support the VDI workload. There are numerous proprietary technologies that reduce the impact of the I/Os on the physical drives. However, the methodology to calculate the number of I/O per second required will not change.

In many cases, architects will be asked to design a solution without knowing what the I/O profile will look like. For most of those cases, there is an ongoing pilot. It's very common for organizations to try to understand costs before actually going to a pilot and that's what makes it a difficult task to guess the IOPS. If all organizations went first for a small pilot and then decided to buy the whole infrastructure to support the VDI solution, we would be living in an ideal world.

If you are designing VDI architecture without a knowledge of the I/O profile, you should be extremely conservative to avoid undersizing the storage solution. If this is the case, you should use the heavy I/O profile for all virtual desktops with read and write ratios of 20 reads and 80 writes. Hopefully, you will not be in this situation.

The RAID type selected will determine the performance and number of hard drives required to support the workload based on the amount of IOPS and read/write ratio. When sizing the storage infrastructure, the RAID group selected will add a write performance penalty due to the requirements to stripe the data and record the parity across disk drives. The read I/Os do not suffer a penalty for different types of RAID groups.

The most common RAID types utilized with VDI workloads are RAID 5, 6, and 10:

- RAID 10 adds a write penalty of 2
- RAID 5 adds a write penalty of 4
- RAID 6 adds a write penalty of 6

The preceding numbers can be tabulated as follows:

	I/O impact	
RAID level	Read	Write
RAID 0	1	1
RAID 1 (and 10)	1	2
RAID 5	1	4
RAID 6	1	6

It could be argued that for RAID 10, the read impact is 0.5 as the Windows operating system is able to read the same block off two disks at the same time, or read half of one disk and half of the other. Therefore, we get twice the read performance.

The formula commonly used to calculate these penalties is as follows: *VM I/O = VM Read I/O + (VM Write I/O * RAID Penalty).*

Other important information for architecting a VDI solution is that Windows operating systems predominantly have random I/Os. Jim Moyle, in his paper *Windows 7 IOPS for VDI: Deep Dive* (`http://jimmoyle.com/wordpress/wp-content/uploads/downloads/2011/05/Windows_7_IOPS_for_VDI_a_Deep_Dive_1_0.pdf`), defines the nature of Windows to generate small I/Os:

> *"This is due to how Windows memory works, memory pages are 4 K in size, as such windows will load files into memory in 4 K blocks, this means that most of the read and write activity has a 4 K block size. Windows 7 does try and aggregate sequential writes to a larger block size to make writing a more efficient process. It will try and aggregate the writes to up to 1 MB in size. The reason for this is that again Windows is expecting a local, dedicated spindle and spinning disks are very good at writing large blocks."*

Windows operating systems constantly read and write information in blocks with different disk placement, and the native user interaction is another reason for the behavior. Random access with small blocks is a time-consuming task for mechanic disk drives and the number of operations per second (IOPS) for each drive is limited. For this reason, it is important to utilize RAID groups to achieve the required I/O throughput.

SSDs provide excellent read performance, but also have limitation for small, random write I/Os. Nonetheless, they provide better performance over disk drives, at a much higher cost.

The following figure shows the difference between sequential access and random access:

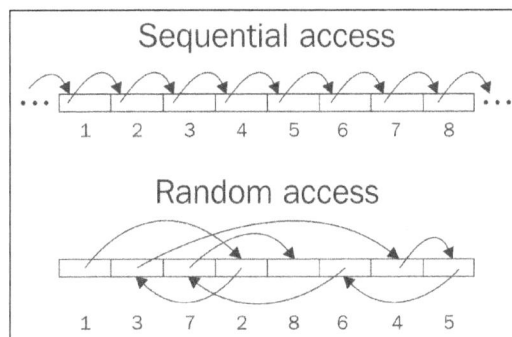

Storage tiering and I/O distribution

Earlier in this chapter, we discussed VMware View tiered storage and the ability to assign different datastores or exports to different types of disks. Now, we will discuss how those tiers interact with the storage infrastructure from an I/O perspective.

VMware View 4.5 introduced the ability to select a dedicated datastore, where replica disks are stored. The VMware View Architecture Guide recommends that this datastore should be served by a pool of SSDs. SSDs generally provide a larger amount of IOPS and throughput.

As mentioned earlier, common scenarios where high performance and high throughput are required occur during boot and login storms and during large scale application deployment to users or AV updates. As an example, Windows 7 can generate up to 700 IOPS during boot time. Another good example is if the **Refresh on logoff** option is used in conjunction with floating pools, it is common to see utilization peaks at the end of the work shift, when business users start to log off.

The total number of IOPS generated by a virtual desktop is the sum of the number of read I/Os in the replica disk and the read and write I/Os on all other disks. During the different utilization phases, the virtual desktop performs differently and requires a different number of I/Os and a different read/write I/O pattern for each individual tier.

The best way to understand how many I/Os are required for power on, customization, and first boot is to find out the averaged maximum I/O per datastore. The reason for this is that each storage tier will have different performance requirements.

The following figure shows the IOPS breakdown. It shows the number of IOPS generated by a virtual desktop from the first power on operation to its first boot. The operations involved are as follows:

- Power on
- Customization
- First boot

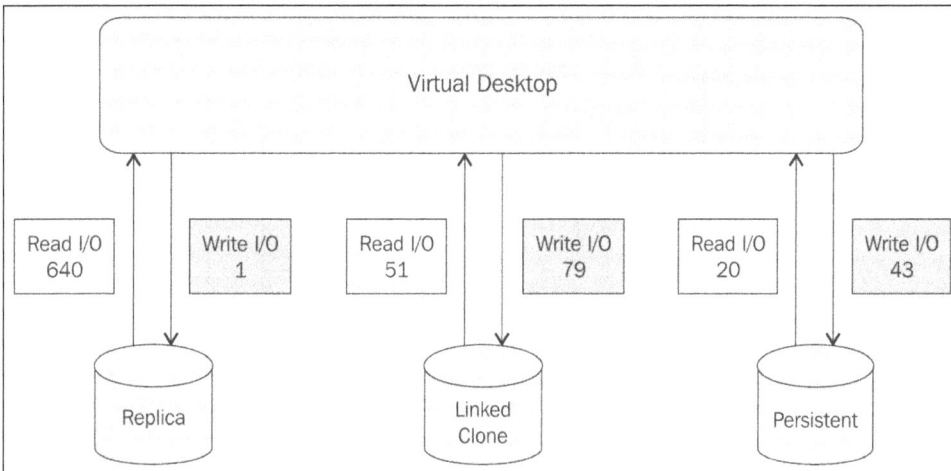

The same numbers from the preceding figure can be shown in a percent style per storage tier. The following screenshot shows a table that provides great visibility of what is happening with the virtual desktop during its creation process:

Replica		Linked Clone		Persistent Disk	
641 IOps		130 IOps		63 IOps	
Read	Write	Read	Write	Read	Write
99.8%	0.2%	39%	61%	32%	68%
640	1	51	79	20	43

Please remember that those numbers may be completely different in your VDI environment.

Understanding how many virtual desktops will be booting, logging on, or working simultaneously is critical to correctly design the tier supporting replica disks. If the **Dedicated Replica Datastore** option is selected, it is even more critical that this single disk tier supporting the replica disks can efficiently deliver the performance required. This is important due to the fact that up to 1,000 virtual desktops may be using that single replica disk simultaneously.

The following figure shows the use of a **Dedicated Replica Datastore** option:

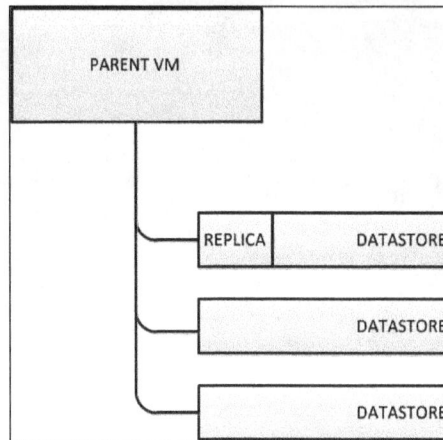

Getting to the exact number of IOPS required for each tier of the storage solutions can be a tireless task. To provide you with an insight into how complex this can get, imagine a linked clone virtual desktop making use of a disposable disk and persistent disk. Assume that the replica disk is hosted in the dedicated replica datastore, the linked clone and the disposable disk on a different datastore, and the persistent disk on yet another datastore. The following figure shows this scenario, and displays the breakdown of I/O when using the various virtual disks of VMware View:

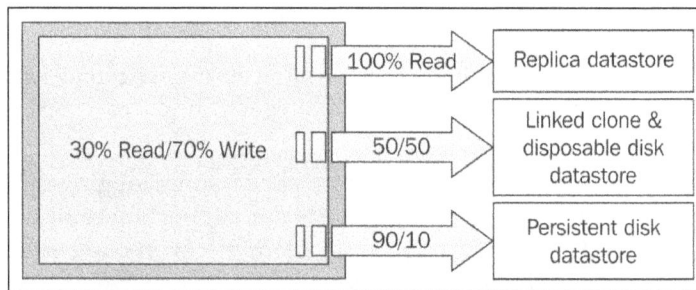

As can be observed in the preceding figure, in this scenario the virtual desktop is generating 30 percent read I/O and 70 percent write I/O. Let's assume that the total I/O for the virtual desktop is 20; then we have six read I/Os and 14 write I/Os.

We know replicas are 100 percent read; however, unless we scrutinize the replica disk it's not possible to know how many of the 14 read I/Os are actually being issued against the disk. Read I/Os could also be issued to the linked clone, disposable, or persistent disk.

For the tier supporting linked clones and disposable disks and for the tier supporting the persistent disk, we will also have a different number of read and write I/Os that are a small percentage of the six read I/Os and 14 write I/Os produced by the virtual desktop.

As you can see, the total number of operations produced by a virtual desktop will often be split across multiple tiers and datastores. The best time to gather those numbers is during the VDI pilot. VMware has the ideal tools for the job — **esxtop** and **vscsiStats**.

The truth is that there is no magic formula to help you get to the exact I/O profile other than analyzing an existing environment's usage patterns. Plan your storage for performance and utilize real workload data to calculate the environment, whenever possible. Pre-trended data from white papers and reference architecture guides may give you a baseline; however, they may not apply to your workload and you may end up with an undersized or oversized infrastructure.

The most common formulas for IOPS calculation are as follows:

- *Replica tier (read I/O only) = (Concurrent Boot VMs * Peak Boot IOPS) + (Concurrent VMs - Concurrent Boot VMs) * (Replica Steady State IOPS)*

- *All other tiers = (VM Read I/O + (VM Write I/O * RAID Penalty) * concurrent VMs*

> Paul Wilson from Citrix has created an attention-grabbing, complex model based on peak IOPS, steady state IOPS, and estimated boot IOPS that takes into consideration the launch rate and desktop login time. His article can be found at http://blogs.citrix.com/2010/10/31/finding-a-better-way-to-estimate-iops-for-vdi.

Disk types

A common question is related to the type of disk that should be utilized for each storage tier. That's a complex discussion that you will need to have with your storage administrator or vendor. Most intelligent storage arrays provide some type of acceleration or caching mechanism that will potentially reduce the storage backend requirements. With the reduction of the requirements, disks with higher capacity and lower performance may be used.

The following figure shows the virtual disk-to-disk type relationship typically used by storage providers:

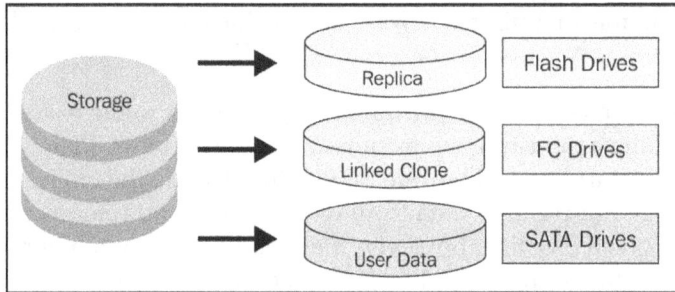

The most common type of disks used for VMware View deployments are as follows:

- **SSDs**: They provide the best throughput performance and may be leveraged for the replica tier requiring bursting capabilities during boot and login storms.

> As always, there are some trade-offs with technology and which of the two types of flash SSD you select. The **multi-level cell (MLC)** flash is more common and is found in consumer-grade products, but can be present in some enterprise storage products. MLC flash's main characteristic is its low price, but it suffers from lower write performance and higher wear rates when compared with the **single-level cell (SLC)** technology. SLC is faster and more reliable and is normally featured in the best-performing storage arrays. But this comes at a price and SLC is more expensive.

- **Fibre Channel and SAS**: They provide the best relationship between costs and performance. Nowadays, Fibre Channel and SAS disks are probably the most common type of disks in an enterprise environment and may be leveraged to host linked clone disks.

- **Serial Advanced Technology Attachment (SATA)**: They provide the highest capacity and lowest cost, but with lowest performance. A common use for SATA disks is for persistent or user profile disk placement.

It's important to note that these are just conventional recommendations and your environment may pose different challenges or features. As an example, some scale-out NAS appliances may use very large pools of SATA disks and perform as well as Fibre Channel disks when the matter is throughput.

Also, consider that to get performance out of the NAS system, the disk spindles are still important. Hard drives may grow in size but their access time isn't proportionally improving. What this could mean is for a given solution, you may need to overprovision storage by increasing the number of spindles to improve performance. However, as your storage your performance requirements continue to increase, it could be a better solution to add SSDs to your existing environment instead of increasing the number of disks.

VMware Virtual SAN

The new release of Horizon 6 View fully supports VMware **virtual SAN (VSAN)** storage policies. VMware VSAN is a storage feature integrated in the vSphere 5.5 kernel that pools internal disk drives across multiple ESXi hosts. You will need a minimum of 3, as shown in the following screenshot:

The distributed architecture of this software-defined storage feature enables the parameters of the storage policy to be enforced despite any changes in workload demands of the virtual machine, along with hardware or network failures. Administrators will define storage requirements, such as performance and availability, for the virtual machines running on a VSAN cluster. Administration of a cluster and implementation of storage policies is issued using the vSphere 5.5 Web Client.

Each host in the VSAN cluster requires at least one solid-state drive that is used for caching the reads and also buffering writes, along with at least one hard disk drive. The hard drive is for the actual data storage. You can expand the storage by adding hard drives to ESXi hosts and then the storage is added to the pool.

The new View release delivers an excellent level of integration with Virtual SAN by taking advantage of the key benefits VSAN has to offer:

- Simple management and configuration
- Policy base management framework
- Scalable capabilities (both up and/or out)
- Performance and capacity along with a resilient foundation

By using vSphere's policy-driven control plane with the storage policy-based management framework, Horizon 6.0 View will guarantee performance and services levels to the virtual desktops. This guarantee happens by using **VM Storage Policies** defined for the virtual desktop based on their needs of storage capacity, performance, and availability.

Horizon 6.0 will automatically deploy the set of VM storage policies for the virtual desktops into vCenter Server. The policies are individually and automatically assigned per disk (the VSAN objects) and maintained for the entire life cycle of the virtual desktop. The policies and their assigned performance, capacity, and availability feature are as follows:

- **VM_HOME**: This sets the number of disk stripes per VM_HOME to 1 and the number of failures to 1. This is the default policy of Virtual SAN.
- **OS_Disk**: Again, the number of disk stripes per OS_DISK is set to 1 and the number of failures is set to 1. This is also the default policy.
- **REPLICA_DISK**: For this, the number of disk stripes per REPLICA_DISK is 1 and the number of failures to 1, but also **Flash Read Cache Reservation** is set to 10 percent. This policy assigns some of the flash capacity (SSD) to the replica disk. This is to provide greater caching for the higher level of reads that this disk experiences.
- **Persistent Disk**: Here, the number of disk stripes per persistent disk is 1 and number of failures is 1. The persistent disk space reservation is set at 100 percent. This policy ensures this type of disk is guaranteed all the space that is required.

When you combine the lower cost of the server-based storage with the benefits of a shared datastore and then on top of that add the performance increase from the SSD-based storage, VSAN produces tremendous cost savings with the overall implementation of your VDI solution. This also gives you the scale-out model along with predictive performance and a repeatable infrastructure, which also simplifies your operations. This proves to be a big win for Horizon 6 View.

Capacity-sizing exercises

Sizing the storage infrastructure correctly might be the difference between succeeding or failing in a VDI rollout. Many deployments that have excellent performance during the pilot and initial production quickly start to run into storage contention issues because of the lack of understanding of the storage layer.

In the next section, we will discuss a few sizing exercises for different VMware View implementations.

Sizing full clones

Let's see two scenarios for sizing full clones.

Scenario 1

The following are the parameters:

- Desktops: 1,000
- Pool type: Dedicated (full clones)
- Guest OS: Windows 7
- RAM: 2 GB
- Disk size: 40 GB
- Disk consumption: 22 GB
- Overhead: 10 percent

Parent VM

The parent VM may be thin or thick provisioned and is usually powered off. If the parent VM is thick provisioned, its size is similar to the creation of the disk plus logfiles. For example, if the parent VM disk size is set to 40 GB, this will be the approximate size of the parent VM.

If the parent VM is created using thin provisioning, its size is equal to the amount of storage utilized by the Windows operating system at the NTFS plus logfiles. For example, if the parent VM disk size is set to 40 GB but only 10 GB is used, the total size of the parent VM will be approximately 10 GB plus logfiles.

There is no considerable performance improvement using thick provisioning over thin provisioning for the parent VM, given that these are master images and won't be used unless a new replica disk is required.

Overhead

The VMware recommendation on storage overhead per datastore is at least 10 percent.

The following table explains the features and requirements:

Feature	Requirement	Reason	
VMs per datastore	32 VMFS	Recommended limit of full clones per datastore	
VM datastore size		Size based on the following calculations:	
		Raw file size	40,960 MB
		Logfile size	100 MB
		Swap file size	2,048 MB
		Free space allocation	10 percent overhead
		*Minimum allocated datastore size = (VMs * (raw + swap + log) + overhead) = (32 * (40,960 MB + 2,048 MB + 100 MB) + 137 GB) = 1.44 TB*	
Number of datastores	One per 32 virtual desktops	*Number of VMs/VMs per datastore = 1,000/32 = 32*	
Total storage		*Number of datastores * datastore size = 32 * 1.44 TB = 46 TB*	

As a safe number, it's an assumption that all full clone raw files will eventually achieve the full size (40 GB). Some administrators may prefer to use a fraction of the full utilization size to cut storage costs during calculation. In addition to the storage allocation required to support all full clone virtual desktops, it is important to set aside at least another one datastore per VMware View cluster to host the parent VM and ISO images.

Scenario 2

Here are the parameters:

- Desktops: 2,000
- Pool type: Dedicated (full clones)
- Guest OS: Windows 7
- RAM: 2 GB
- Disk size: 32 GB
- Disk consumed: 22 GB
- VM memory reservation: 50 percent (1,024 MB)
- Overhead: 10 percent

The following table shows the features and requirements:

Feature	Requirement	Reason	
VMs per datastore	32 VMFS	Recommended limit of full clones per datastore	
VM datastore size		Size based on the following calculations:	
		Raw file size	32,768 MB
		Log file size	100 MB
		Swap file size	1,024 MB
		Free space allocation	10 percent overhead
		Minimum allocated datastore size = (VMs * (raw + swap + log) + overhead) = (32 * (40,960 MB + 1,024 MB + 100 MB) + 108 GB) = 1.13 TB	
Number of datastores	1 per 32 virtual desktops	*Number of VMs/VMs per datastore = 2,000/32 = 33*	
Total storage		*Number of datastores * datastore size = 32 * 1.12 TB = 36 TB*	

The disk size for this scenario has been changed to 32 GB, reducing the overall storage footprint required. It's important to size virtual desktops appropriately for what the users require, not adding extra fat to the infrastructure. This scenario also introduces 50 percent VM memory reservation, reducing the size of the .vswp file to half of the virtual desktop memory. In this scenario, the .vswp file is 1,024 MB.

Sizing linked clones

Sizing linked clone virtual desktops is, to a certain extent, more complex than sizing full clones due to the number of variables involved in the calculation. As mentioned earlier in this chapter, linked clone virtual desktops introduce new files and may work differently when the **Dedicated Replica Datastore** option is selected.

Parent VM

The parent VM used with linked clones is similar to the one used with full clones; however, it includes VM snapshots that are used by View Composer to determine what baseline image is used to create replica disks.

Replica

Replica disks are created as thin provisioned clones derived from the parent VM. If the parent VM is set to a 40 GB disk size, the replica is equal to the amount of storage utilized by the Windows operating system at the NTFS plus the snapshot selected. For example, if the parent VM disk size is set to 40 GB but only 10 GB is used, the total size of the replica is approximately 10 GB.

Without making use of the **Dedicated Replica Datastore** option, for any desktop pool, a unique replica is created in each datastore assigned to the pool. If multiple snapshots are in use in a desktop pool, multiple replicas per datastore may be created if VMware View decides to use the datastore. It is common to have two or more snapshots in use at the same time in a single datastore, especially during the Recompose operations:

- *Desktop pools * snapshots * datastores = number of replicas*
- *2 * 1 * 32 = 64 replicas (2 per datastore)*
- *2 * 2 * 32 = 128 replicas (4 per datastore)*

If the **Dedicated Replica Datastore** option is in use, VMware View uses a single datastore to create all replicas for the desktop pool. The calculation of the number of replicas is also subject to the number of snapshots concurrently in use:

- *Desktop pools * snapshots * datastores = number of replicas*
- *2 * 1 * 1 = 2 replicas*
- *2 * 2 * 1 = 4 replicas*

Scenario 1

Here are the parameters:

- Desktops: 5,000
- Pool type: Floating (linked clones)
- Guest OS: Windows 7
- RAM: 2 GB
- Disk size: 32 GB
- Disk consumption: 22 GB
- Refresh on logoff: 10 percent
- Overhead: 10 percent
- VAAI: Enabled

The following table explains the features and requirements:

Feature	Requirement	Reason	
VMs per datastore	140 VMFS (VAAI)	Recommended limit of full clones per datastore	
VM datastore size		Size based on the following calculations:	
		Raw file size	3,277 MB
		Log file size	100 MB
		Swap file size	1,024 MB
		Free space allocation	10 percent overhead
		*Minimum allocated datastore size = (VMs * (raw + swap + log) + overhead) = (140 * (3,277 MB + 1,024 MB + 100 MB) + 60 GB) = 661 GB*	
Number of datastores	One per 140 virtual desktops	*Number of VMs/VMs per datastore = 5,000/140 = 36*	
Total storage		*Number of datastores * datastore size = 36 * 661 GB = 23 TB*	

The desktop pool type is floating and that means that whenever the user has logged off, the virtual desktop will be refreshed. The important information here is to know for how long, on an average, the users will remain connected to the virtual desktop and how much data they will generate on the delta disk during their usage. If the desktops are designated to classes that will last 45 minutes, the chances are that the delta disk will present marginal growth. However, if the virtual desktop is used for a whole day, the chances are that the delta will grow a few hundred megabytes.

For this exercise, we are assuming that the delta disk will grow to a maximum size of 10 percent of the parent VM, which is 3,277 MB.

VAAI is enabled in this scenario, enabling higher virtual desktop consolidation per datastore. The maximum number of virtual desktops per datastore supported with VAAI is 140.

Scenario 2

The following are the parameters:

- Desktops: 10,000
- Pool type: Persistent (linked clones)
- Guest OS: Windows 7 (64 bit)
- RAM: 4 GB
- Disk size: 32 GB
- Disk consumption: 22 GB
- Refresh: Never
- Overhead: 10 percent

The following table explains the features and requirements:

Feature	Requirement	Reason
VMs per datastore	100 VMFS	Recommended limit of full clones per datastore

Feature	Requirement	Reason	
VM datastore size		Size based on the following calculations:	
		Raw file size	32,768 MB
		Logfile size	100 MB
		Swap file size	4,096 MB
		Free space allocation	10 percent overhead
		Minimum allocated datastore size = (VMs * (raw + swap + log) + overhead) = (100 * (32,768 MB + 4,096 MB + 100 MB) + 360 GB) = 3.9 TB	
Number of datastores	One per 100 virtual desktops	*Number of VMs/VMs per datastore = 10,000/100 = 100*	
Total storage		*Number of datastores * datastore size = 100 * 3.9 TB = 390 TB*	

This scenario explores the idea of using linked clones but not having an internal policy to refresh virtual desktops so often. The result is similar to implementing full clones as the delta disks will grow to its full capacity, 32 GB in this case.

With 64-bit Windows 7 and 4 GB RAM without any VM memory reservation, the swap file is responsible for consuming 4 GB of storage capacity per virtual desktop. In total, the .vswap file will be consuming 40 TB; however, with only 20 percent memory reservation, this total would go down to approximately 31 TB of used storage space.

vSphere 5.0 video swap

VMware View has always automatically calculated video RAM based on resolution and color depth. Up to VMware View 4.6, only 24-bit color depth was supported and VMware published the vRAM overhead that each resolution type would require. vRAM overhead is part of the VM memory overhead in virtual machines running on ESXi. The other part of the overhead comes from the number of vCPUs and amount of RAM.

VMware View 5.0 introduces a 32-bit color depth and makes it the default option. On top of that, to allow 3D support, VMware introduced a new feature in View 5.0 that allows administrators to select how much video RAM should be assigned to virtual desktops.

The following screenshot shows the configuration of vRAM for vDesktops requiring 3D capabilities:

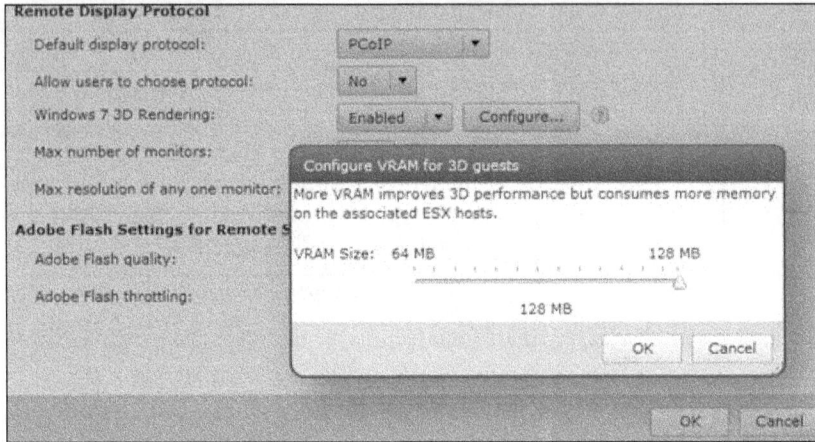

The VMware View explanation of how to configure vRAM for 3D support is not very helpful and essentially says that more the vRAM, the more the 3D performance available to vDesktop(s).

To support the new 3D option, vSphere 5.0 implements a second `.vswp` file for every virtual desktop created either using hardware version 7 or 8. This second `.vswp` file is dedicated to video memory overhead and will be used when the virtual desktop is under video resource constraint.

The following screenshot shows the second `.vswp` file; this is used for video memory:

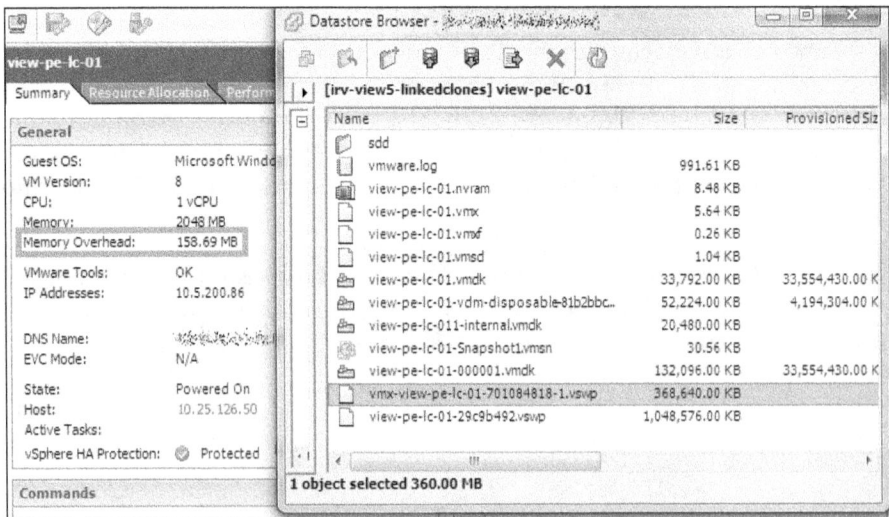

The total memory overhead is defined by the following factors:

- Number of virtual CPUs
- Amount of RAM
- Amount of vRAM (defined by number of displays, screen resolution, and color depth)
- 3D support

Memory overhead is nothing new to VMware administrators, as they are used to calculate overhead based on vCPU, RAM, and vRAM. However, with the introduction of a video memory calculator, vSphere Client 5.0 provides an easy way to define the amount of vRAM required for a given video configuration.

The following screenshot shows the advanced **Video Memory Calculator** window:

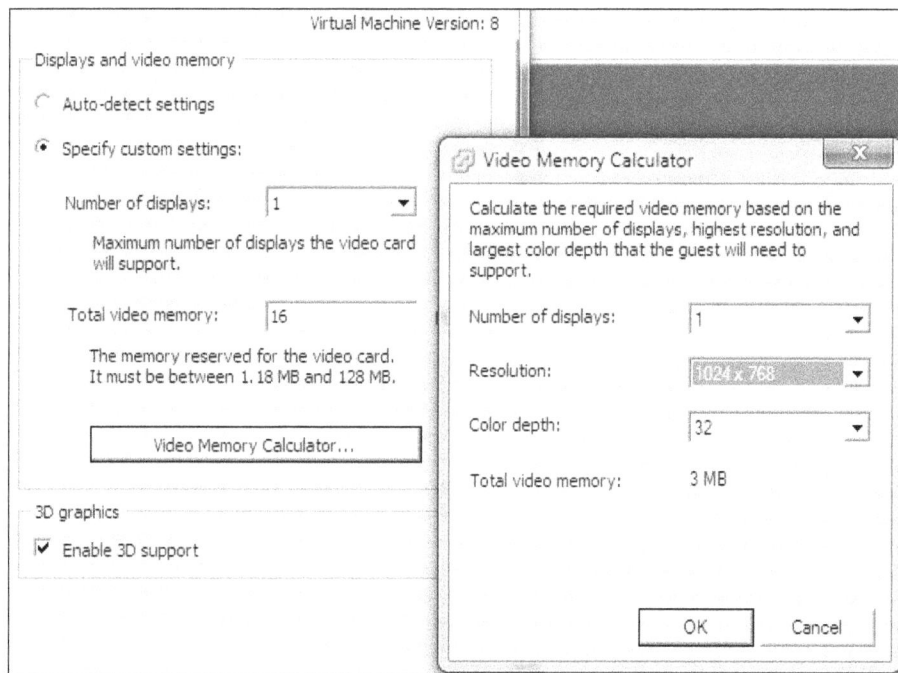

The new video overhead .vswp file will affect storage footprint and datastore sizing. In order to understand the real impact, we have reverse-engineered the new video support option. The **swap (MB)** column shows the total storage utilized by the video swap file, and the **overhead (MB)** column shows the amount of RAM overhead utilized for each combination of vCPU, vRAM, and color depth:

vCPU	vRAM	video	overhead (MB)	swap (MB)
1vCPU	1GB	8	71.24	49.00
1vCPU	1GB	16	79.35	57.00
1vCPU	1GB	64	128.00	104.00
1vCPU	1GB	128	192.88	104.00
1vCPU	2GB	8	90.34	49.00
1vCPU	2GB	16	98.45	57.00
1vCPU	2GB	64	147.10	104.00
1vCPU	2GB	128	211.98	104.00
1vCPU	4GB	8	128.52	49.00
1vCPU	4GB	16	136.63	57.00
1vCPU	4GB	64	185.29	104.00
1vCPU	4GB	128	250.16	104.00
2vCPU	1GB	8	107.62	50.00
2vCPU	1GB	16	115.79	58.00
2vCPU	1GB	64	164.82	105.00
2vCPU	1GB	128	230.20	105.00
2vCPU	2GB	8	137.75	50.00
2vCPU	2GB	16	145.92	58.00
2vCPU	2GB	64	194.95	105.00
2vCPU	2GB	128	260.33	105.00
2vCPU	4GB	8	197.99	50.00
2vCPU	4GB	16	206.16	58.00
2vCPU	4GB	64	255.20	105.00
2vCPU	4GB	128	320.57	105.00

When 3D support is enabled, a 256 MB overhead is added to the secondary .vswp file. Therefore, if you are planning to use 3D, you should size datastores appropriately to accommodate this difference. This additional 256 MB will help virtual desktops to not run into video performance issues when executing 3D display operations. The 256 MB overhead is independent of how much vRAM you assigned to the virtual desktop in VMware View 6.0.

A datastore with 100 desktops will require additional 25 GB with 3D support enabled: *100 VMs * 256 MB = 25 GB*.

The following screenshot shows a table that has the `.vswp` file (swap) resulting from the 3D support enabled:

vCPU	vRAM	video	overhead (MB)	swap (MB)
1vCPU	1GB	8	71.24	305.00
1vCPU	1GB	16	79.35	313.00
1vCPU	1GB	64	128.00	360.00
1vCPU	1GB	128	192.88	360.00

When sizing for 3D support, you will need to ensure that datastores are appropriately sized for the amount of virtual desktops that will reside in the datastore, plus any additional 3D swap overhead.

Summary

Storage for virtualized server environments already offers significant complexity from a design perspective. By adding VDI on top of a classic server virtualization solution, the additional storage technologies were (for example, View Composer) potentially utilized—making the storage design exponentially more complex. This chapter covered both the high-level aspects of storage design for VMware View solutions as well as the subtle intricacies that can often make or break a solution. Storage design, especially for solutions that are intended to scale over time, can require significant effort. It is important to not only understand fundamental storage principles before embarking on a VMware View storage design, but also understand the various types of virtual disks, as well as how the underlying guest uses its disk.

Now that all of the major design concepts have been covered, the next chapter will focus on backup and recovery. While a robust VMware View solution should be able to mitigate most outage scenarios, there may be times where a recovery action needs to be taken, such as understanding the points of interest from a backup perspective as well as the recovery process is important as a design is implemented and handed over to an operations team.

9
Security

Whether deployed at a hospital, college, corporation, federal agency, or a nonprofit organization, security of the end device has become a critical component of any organization's data loss prevention and information assurance policies. With data loss events, for example, WikiLeaks or stolen laptops with social security numbers from organizations such as the U.S. Census Bureau, Ireland Department of Social and Family Affairs, or Anheuser-Busch, ensuring that sensitive data stays within the confines of the corporate infrastructure has gained much visibility.

In a traditional physical desktop model, end users are issued desktops or laptops that contain writeable media (hard drives). These end devices store data such as the user's profile, copies of data from file shares, browser cache, plain text documents, images, spreadsheets, and other business and personal data.

Even with encryption of the hard drive on the end device, sensitive data can still reside on the laptop. With the availability of high-powered compute instances with processing power ideal for password cracking algorithms, such as Amazon EC2 GPU instances, cracking passwords and encryption algorithms can be offloaded to a public cloud. Therefore, the safest end device is a device that does not store any sensitive information, whether encrypted or not. For this reason, PCoIP zero clients (end devices that have a PCoIP chip from Teradici) are arguably more secure than thin clients (with a locked down operating system). Both are exponentially more secure than thick clients (traditional laptop or desktop).

This chapter will cover the security items related to:

- Firewalls, zones, and antivirus
- Virtual enclaves
- USB redirection and filtering

- Smart card authentication
- Preventing copy and paste functions
- View Connection Server tags
- Forensics

The inherent security of VDI

With a properly designed VDI solution, all of the sensitive data resides in a secured data center versus living on hard drives in devices such as laptops and desktops. While it is possible to copy data within the vDesktop to, for example, a USB thumb drive plugged into the end device, it is also possible to prevent USB redirection of such devices.

In secure VDI implementations, the only data that is typically transmitted is the visual and audio stream to deliver the desktop experience to the end device. This means that if an end user is using Microsoft Word to manipulate a document while connected to their vDesktop, the document does not reside on his or her end device (for example, a laptop). Instead, it completely resides within the vDesktop running, ideally, within the data center. The visual representation of the desktop, including the visual display of Microsoft Word and the document are streamed down to the end device via the secured PCoIP protocol.

In a properly designed VDI solution, if an end device is broken, stolen, lost, or misplaced, the end user simply needs a new end device to connect back to their vDesktop. For example, if Lily has a PCoIP zero client that is no longer working, she can be issued a new zero client and can immediately resume working in the VDI. There is no reimaging process for zero clients and Lily can quickly return to productive tasks.

Without VDI, she may have to wait for days for an end device to be repurposed, procured, or provisioned before she can return to productivity.

In addition, there are no data salvage actions that need to be performed because no data exists on the end device. In environments that employ the use of **hot desking** (http://en.wikipedia.org/wiki/Hot_desking) or the practice of providing unassigned workspaces without reservations in an office environment, Lily could simply walk to an available workspace, log in, and reconnect to the VDI. Again, all of Lily's data resides in the data center.

Firewalls, zones, and antivirus

The basic fundamentals of securing a VMware View environment involve only allowing the specific ports and protocols absolutely necessary for a functioning VDI. In addition, it also involves the use of **Secure Sockets Layer** (**SSL**) (as opposed to unencrypted traffic over port 80 and other ports) when available. In addition, requiring the use of PCoIP, as opposed to also allowing **Remote Desktop Protocol** (**RDP**) connections, can further increase security in the environment.

Within a given VDI solution, there are potentially several firewalls that come into effect. These firewalls include:

- **Windows OS firewall**: This firewall is used to restrict inbound and outbound traffic at the operating system layer
- **Network firewall** (**internal**): This firewall is used to restrict traffic within the internal LAN environment
- **Network firewall** (**external/DMZ**): This firewall is used to restrict traffic (typically) generated from the Internet
- **Virtual firewall**: This firewall is used to restrict traffic across virtual port groups and switches within the virtual infrastructure

The calculated use of firewalls helps create physical and virtual security enclaves known as **zones**.

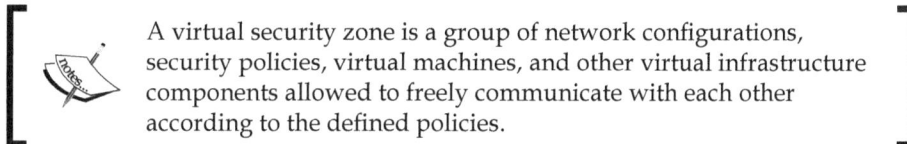

> A virtual security zone is a group of network configurations, security policies, virtual machines, and other virtual infrastructure components allowed to freely communicate with each other according to the defined policies.

Virtual security zones have the following possibilities for cross-zone communication:

- **Permitted**: Virtual machines in Zone_A and Zone_B are able to freely communicate with each other based on a mutual trust relationship (not to be confused with technologies such as Active Directory trusts and relationships)
- **Restricted**: Virtual machines in Zone_A and Zone_B are able to communicate with each other along predefined ports and protocols only
- **Prohibited**: Virtual machines in Zone_A and Zone_B are not permitted to communicate with each other

One of the final pieces of the security matrix is an antivirus protection for vDesktops. Antivirus protection ensures that malware does not penetrate and proliferate the physical and/or virtual desktop environment.

Firewall rules

For a more detailed list of ports and protocols, please see Christoph Harding's excellent article *Firewall settings for a VMware View environment* at `http://ThatsMyView.net` found at `http://www.thatsmyview.net/2011/04/24/firewall-settings-for-a-vmware-view-environment/` or the official knowledge base (KB) article found at `http://kb.vmware.com/kb/2061913`.

Source IP	Direction	Destination IP	Transport protocol	Port	Application protocol	Description
End user device	Inbound	View Security Server	TCP	443	HTTPS	Authentication and other communications
End user device	Both	View Security Server	TCP and UDP	4172	PCoIP	PCoIP handshake and data transfer
View Security Server	Inbound	View Connection Server	TCP	8009	AJP13	AJP-data traffic
View Security Server	Inbound	View Connection Server	TCP	4001	JMS	Java
View Security Server	Inbound	View Transfer Server	TCP	443	HTTPS	Communication with View Transfer Server
View Security Server	Both	View Agent	TCP and UDP	4172	PCoIP	PCoIP handshake and data transfer
View Security Server	Both	View Agent	TCP	32111		USB Redirection (if applicable)
View Connection Server	Outbound	Active Directory	TCP and UDP	389	LDAP	Active Directory Authentication and ADAM
View Connection Server	Both	View Connection Server	TCP	4100	JMSIR	Internal View Connection Server communication
View Connection Server	Both	View Connection Server	TCP	636	LDAPS	AD LDS
View Connection Server	Both	View Connection Server	TCP	1515		Microsoft Endpoint Mapper

Source IP	Direction	Destination IP	Transport protocol	Port	Application protocol	Description
View Connection Server	Both	View Connection Server	TCP	4001	JMS	Java
View Connection Server	Both	View Connection Server	TCP	8009	AJP13	AJP-data Traffic
View Connection Server	Both	View Transfer Server	TCP	8009	AJP13	AJP-data Traffic
View Connection Server	Outbound	View Transfer Server	TCP	443	HTTPS	Communication with View Transfer Server
View Connection Server	Outbound	View Transfer Server	TCP	4001	JMS	Java
View Connection Server	Outbound	View Transfer Server	TCP	4100	JMSIR	Internal communication
View Connection Server	Outbound	vCenter Server	TCP	18443	SOAP	View Composer communication
View Connection Server	Outbound	vCenter Server	TCP	443	HTTPS	vCenter communication
View Connection Server	Both	View Agent	TCP	4001	JMS	Java
End user device	Outbound	View Connection Server	TCP	443	SSL	Communication with View Connection Server for authentication and other activities
View Security Server	Inbound	View Connection Server	TCP	8009	AJP13	AJP-data Traffic
View Security Server	Inbound	View Connection Server	TCP	4001	JMS	Java
End user device	Inbound	View Transfer Server	TCP	443	HTTPS	Communication with View Transfer Server

Source IP	Direction	Destination IP	Transport protocol	Port	Application protocol	Description
View Security Server	Inbound	View Transfer Server	TCP	443	HTTPS	Communication with View Transfer Server
View Security Server	Inbound	View Transfer Server	TCP	8009	AJP13	AJP-data Traffic
View Security Server	Inbound	View Transfer Server	TCP	4100	JMSIR	Internal communication
View Security Server	Inbound	View Transfer Server	TCP	4001	JMS	Java
View Connection Server	Inbound	View Transfer Server	TCP	8009	AJP13	AJP-data traffic
End user device	Both	View Agent	TCP and UDP	4172	PCoIP	PCoIP connection and data
End user device	Both	View Agent	TCP	32111		USB redirection (if applicable)
View Agent	Outbound	View Connection Server	TCP	4001	JMS	Java
End user device	Both	View Agent	TCP and UDP	4172	PCoIP	PCoIP connection and data
End user device	Inbound	View Agent	TCP	32111		USB redirection (if applicable)
End user device	Inbound	View Connection Server	TCP	443	HTTPS	
End user device	Inbound	View Connection Server	TCP	443	HTTPS	
End user device	Both	View Connection Server	TCP and UPD	4172	PCoIP	PCoIP connection and data
End user device	Both	View Connection Server	TCP	8443	Blast	Client connections to the Blast Secure Gateway
Security Server	Both	Virtual Desktop	TCP	22443	HTML	HTML Access

Source IP	Direction	Destination IP	Transport protocol	Port	Application protocol	Description
Horizon Client	Both	Virtual Desktop	TCP	3389	RDP	Microsoft RDP traffic to View desktops if direct connections are used instead of tunnel connections
Security Server	Both	Virtual Desktop	TCP	3389		Microsoft RDP traffic to View desktops
Web Browser	Both	Security Server	TCP	8443	HTML	HTML Access
Connection Server	Both	Virtual Desktops	TCP	3389	RDP	Microsoft RDP traffic to View desktops if tunnel connections via the View Connection Server are used

Virtual enclaves

A **virtual enclave** is a defined group of virtual machines, virtual port groups, resources (if using resource pools), and potentially underlying datastores. The notion of a virtual enclave is to provide segmentation within the VDI, separating one group from another.

The following figure is an illustration showing three separate enclaves:

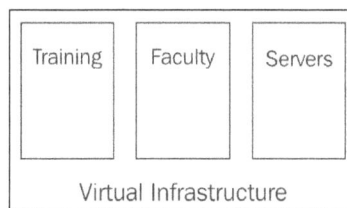

In the preceding figure, three classifications of vDesktops exist within the overall virtual infrastructure. These classifications are composed of desktop pools of the same name. They are as follows:

- **Training**: This enclave is used by training rooms to provide vDesktops for training purposes
- **Faculty**: This enclave is used by faculty members at the organization for their primary vDesktop
- **Servers**: This enclave is used by all of the virtual machines running a server-based operating system

From within the virtual infrastructure, there are ways to isolate the three enclaves:

- VLAN tagging
- Separate vSwitch/vDSwitch uplinks
- Enabling vSwitch/vDSwitch security settings
- Using resource pools to isolate compute consumption
- Using separate datastores to isolate data and I/O
- Using separate clusters

All of the preceding methods are available with VMware vSphere without additional software components.

However, with solutions such as VMware vShield TM, Reflex Systems vTrust TM with vmTagging TM, and other security products, it's possible to provide virtual air gaps from within the virtual infrastructure.

The following figure shows different segmentation options with VMware virtual networking:

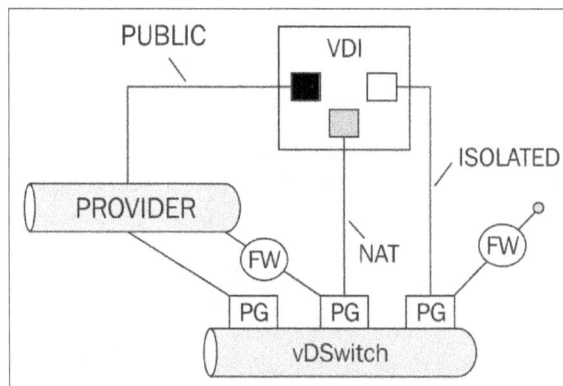

The preceding figure showcases several virtual networking technologies:

- A **virtual distributed switch** (**vDSwitch**)
- Three separate virtual distributed **portgroups** (**PG**)
- Two separate software firewalls (provided through VMware vShield technology or Reflex Systems vTrust technology) (**FW**)
- A provider network connection; this connection has direct access to the Internet (in this example)
- Three separate vDesktop groups (black, gray, and white)

The black enclave contains vDesktops that provide support within a given organization that require direct access to the Internet for functions that support external clients.

This enclave's vDesktops are connected to the provider port group, which has direct access to the Internet from within the virtual infrastructure. However, the connection could be filtered further upstream at the physical layer.

The gray enclave contains vDesktops used by the majority of the work staff within a given organization.

This enclave's vDesktops are connected to a portgroup that has access to the provider network; however, instead of direct access to the provider network, it uses **network address translation** (**NAT**) to mask the actual IP addresses of vDesktops within the blue enclave.

The white enclave contains vDesktops used by the training rooms within a given organization.

This enclave's vDesktops are connected to a portgroup that does not have access to the provider network (note the fact that the connection terminates as it exits the firewall). Its virtual enclave provides access for the vDesktops and resources within the white enclave to communicate freely. However, there is no mechanism for virtual machines within the white enclave to communicate with resources outside of the enclave. This enclave is described as being isolated.

In addition to performing network segmentation, both the VMware vShield and Reflex Systems solutions can provide software-based firewall protection between the various enclaves.

For example, vDesktops in the gray enclave may only be allowed to communicate with vDesktops in the white enclave over port 443 (HTTPS).

The jailbreak scenario

The **jailbreak scenario**, pulled from a real-world solution, involves preventing communications between vDesktops within the same desktop pool. Desktop pools are used to define several key settings of all of their vDesktops; one of these settings is the specific portgroup (standard or distributed) assigned to one or more vDesktop's virtual NICs. This setting is defined at a desktop pool level; therefore, all vDesktops within a given desktop pool will be on the same portgroup.

In the jailbreak scenario, the IT staff at a detention center has implemented a VDI to allow inmates to perform various training exercises. While the vDesktops have been locked down to prevent connectivity to the Internet, the fact that all of the vDesktops are on the same portgroup could pose a threat. The jailbreak scenario is shown in the following figure:

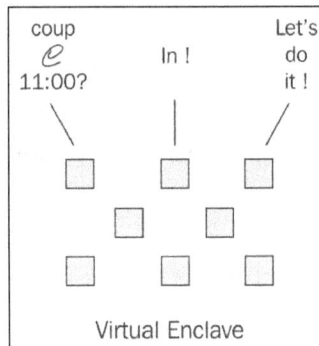

The biggest threat in the prison break scenario is that the various vDesktop users, while segregated from any other network connection (including connectivity to the Internet or to the production network of the detention center), will still have the ability to send data to one another. The threat is that multiple vDesktop users will leverage the fact that all of their vDesktop virtual machines are on the same portgroup and send messages to coordinate a revolt on the prison staff at a specific time.

For example, if 30 inmates are logged in to a VDI and start trading discrete messages to assault the prison staff at 11:00 a.m., that could pose a huge risk for the prison staff in terms of their own personal safety, the safety of the facilities, and the safety of the nearby community.

While there is no out-of-the-box solution to prevent this type of communication (arguably, the built-in Windows firewall can be of use in this scenario), Reflex Systems does offer the ability to segregate individual virtual machines from one another. In addition, VMware vShield could potentially be used to provide this virtual segmentation.

For environments with a high rate of volatility (expansion, contraction, View Composer refreshes, and so on), this solution — regardless of whether VMware, Reflex Systems, or another security solution is used — will require a significant amount of customization, scripting, and integration work.

USB redirection and filtering

The USB device is redirected from a physical device to the virtual desktop using **USB Request Block (URB)** network redirection. The USB device driver needs to be installed on the virtual desktop, but it does not need to be installed on the client machine. Recent enhancements in VMware View have improved device compatibility as well as expanded support for USB redirection on Windows, Mac, and Linux hosts.

In a growing number of organizations, USB hard drives are prohibited. This is because of the risk of data leakage from end users copying sensitive data to a USB hard drive and then misusing the device or using the USB hard drive's data maliciously. However, simply blocking all USB devices may disallow the following perfectly accepted USB devices:

- Pointing devices
- Audio headsets
- Transcription playback pedals
- Medical equipment, for example, a patient monitoring device
- Scientific equipment, for example, a metering device
- Photographic equipment, for example, a video recorder
- Audio equipment, for example, USB MIDI interfaces
- Authentication devices, for example, a card reader

Therefore, it's important to not simply block all devices, but build a white list of allowed USB devices. This is known as **USB filtering**.

The following figure is an illustration showing the three main levels available for USB filtering:

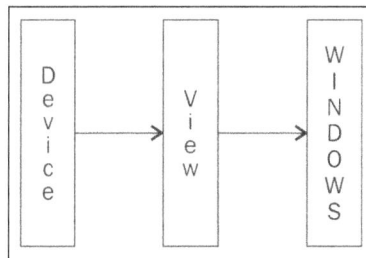

There are three integration points where USB filtering can be applied; they are as follows:

- End device
- View Connection Server
- Windows desktop operating system

In addition, USB filtering can be applied to:

- An entire classID to allow or disallow an entire class of devices (for example, a USB mass storage device)
- A **Vendor ID (VID)** and **Product ID (PID)** to allow or disallow a specific device (for example, a Kingston mass storage device)

USB filtering on the end device

One of the benefits of using PCoIP zero clients is the ability to create device profiles and apply them to all zero clients in an environment. In this manner, a single USB filtering device profile could be created and applied to all zero clients in an environment. By locking the devices down with a complex password, the device's profile will only be controlled by, for example, the **Teradici Management Console**. Therefore, any policy defining USB filtering will not be able to be overridden. By managing USB filtering at the end device, such as with the Teradici Management Console, permissions can be granted on a device ID or device class. This allows great flexibility in management (for example, USB thumb drives are disallowed unless they are made by IronKey).

The drawbacks of applying USB device filtering at the device level is that it strongly discourages **bring-your-own-device (BYOD)** programs. These programs encourage end users to use the device that they are most comfortable with. As the device will ultimately be connecting to an organization-owned vDesktop and all work will be performed on the vDesktop, it is of less or no concern where the end device is in such a scenario.

Using device profiles for USB filtering means that a profile must be built for each device, and each device must be managed.

In many organizations, the move to a VDI solution is to get out of the business of managing end devices and instead enabling the end user workforce to use their preferred method of computing.

USB filtering via View Connection Server

VMware View Connection Server also provides a mechanism for performing USB filtering.

The following screenshot shows the USB access policy setting in the **View Admin** console:

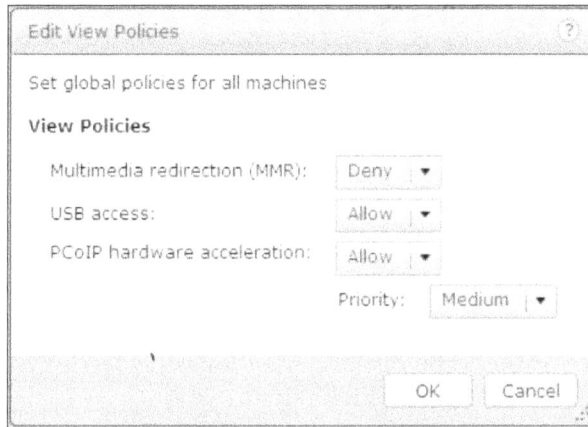

From within the **Policies | Global Policies** section of the View Admin console, **USB access** can be set to the all-encompassing, **Allow** or **Deny**. This does not allow fine-toothed management of only granting access to specific devices. Instead, this allows or disallows USB redirection for all devices.

Another method that is similar in the all or nothing approach is to not install the USB redirection component of the VMware View Agent from within the vDesktop template or parent VM. This is not recommended as it is limiting future capabilities within the environment.

USB filtering via the Windows operating system

An IronKey-encrypted USB drive has a device class of **Windows Portable Devices (WPD)**.

The following screenshot shows a USB device from within the guest operating system:

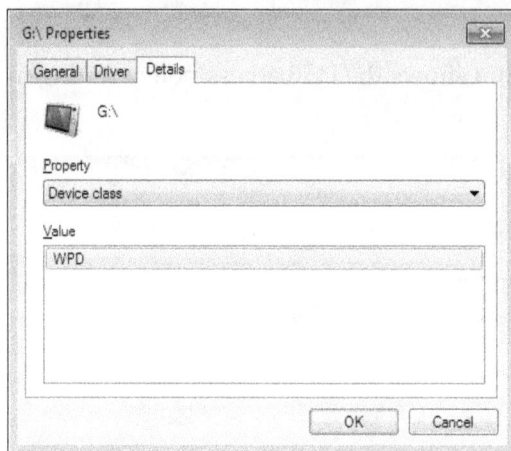

This information can be found by opening the **Properties** tab from within **Device Manager** with the applicable device highlighted.

The following screenshot specifically shows a USB device ID:

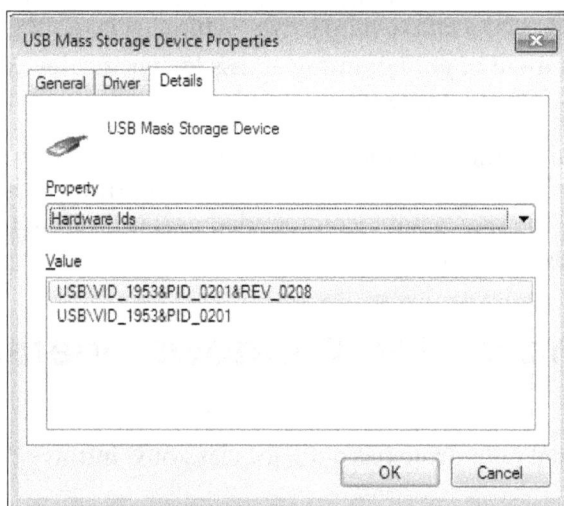

Under **Hardware Ids** of the given device (for example, IronKey thumb drive), the PID and **firmware revision (REV)** can be found. In the preceding example, VID is 1953, PID is 0201, and REV is 0208.

NirSoft makes a free product called **USBDeview** that is a handy utility to quickly find the PID, VID, serial number, and other information about a specific USB device as well. It also shows the information in a more user-friendly manner (`http://www.nirsoft.net/utils/usb_devices_view.html`).

The following screenshot shows the use of USBDeview to identify the ID of a USB product:

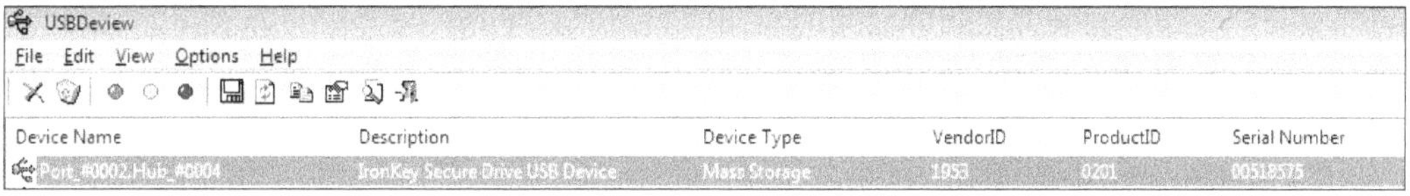

In the preceding example, the IronKey thumb drive has a **VendorID** of **1953** and a **ProductID** of **0201**.

The device class GUID is also needed to configure USB filtering. It can also be found under the **Properties** tab from within **Device Manager**.

The following screenshot shows the registry key for hardware filters:

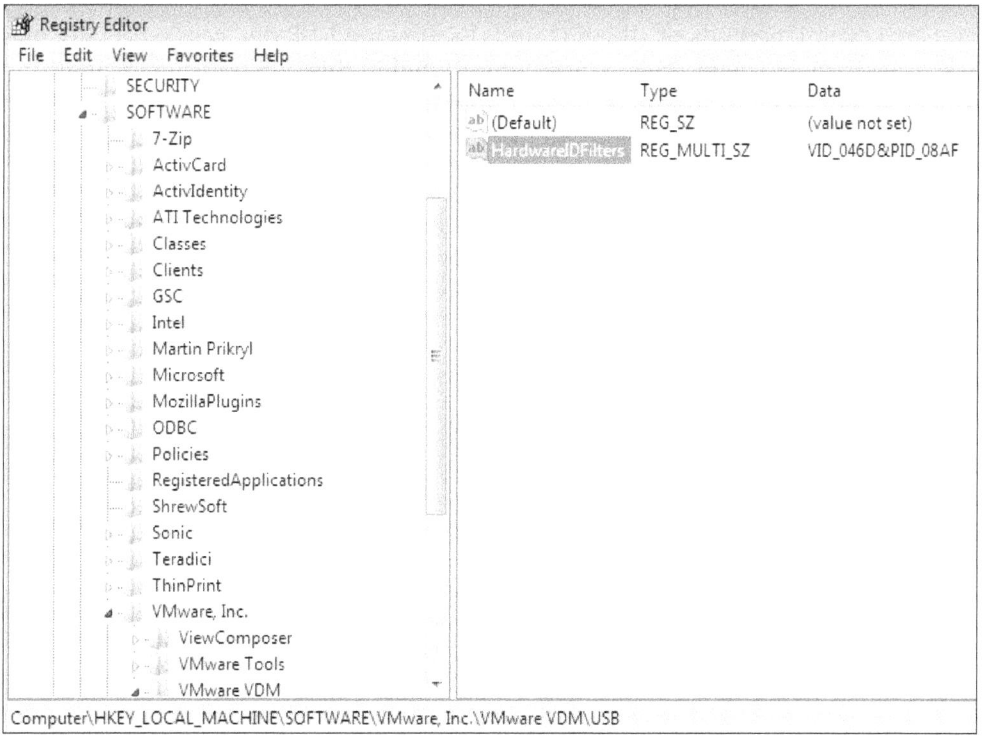

For example, to disallow all IronKey-encrypted thumb drives (VendorID 1958, ProductID 0201), **VID_1958&PID_0201** would be added to the **HardwareIDFilters** key at the location `Computer\HKEY_LOCAL_MACHINE\SOFTWARE\VMware, Inc.\ VMware VDM\USB\`.

The registry change takes effect immediately and does not require a reboot. Now, when an end user attempts to connect their IronKey-encrypted thumb drive, they will receive the error. The following screenshot gives an example of the error message a user may receive when attempting to use a USB device in an environment where that USB device is prohibited:

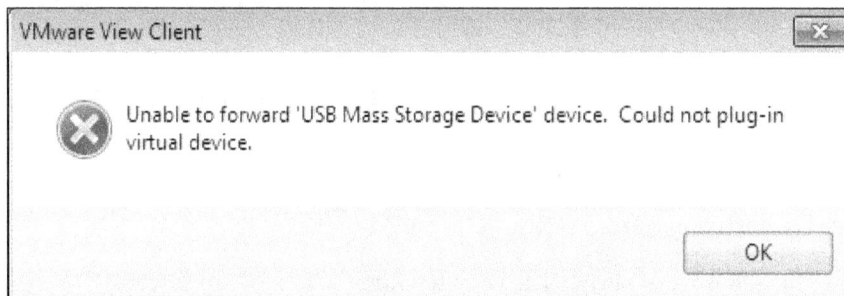

There are several methods of allowing and disallowing USB devices (especially mass storage devices). However, the techniques outlined in this section fundamentally apply to all devices and should be used as a best practice. The most secure way of performing USB filtering is to block all devices except those defined on the white list.

You can define USB policy settings for both View Agent and Horizon Client. After connecting, the Horizon Client will download the USB policy settings from View Agent and uses the settings in conjunction with the settings for the Horizon Client USB policy and decides which devices it allows to be used for redirection from the client computer.

The template file (`vdm_agent.adm`) for the View Agent Configuration contains policy settings that are related to the authentication and the environmental components of the View Agent, and includes USB redirection. These settings are applied at the computer level. The View Agent preferentially reads the settings from GPOs at the computer level, or from the registry found at `HKLM\Software\Policies\VMware, Inc.\VMware VDM\Agent\USB`

The official documentation for this can be found at `https://pubs.vmware.com/ horizon-view-60/index.jsp#com.vmware.horizon-view.desktops.doc/GUID- 433CDB2E-6A71-4A1A-9B05-02B65CC53205.html`.

Smart card authentication

Smart card authentication is a mechanism by which a plastic card, typically with gold-plated contact pads, is used to store certificates used by the end user to authenticate. Smart cards are used throughout many industries, including military, healthcare, education, retail, and the scientific community. The advantages of smart card authentication are as follows:

- It requires the end user to have the authentication mechanism
- It requires the end user to successfully provide the answer to a challenge (PIN)

Smart card authentication is a two-factor authorization mechanism that requires the end user to physically possess a smart card as well as enter in a PIN successfully. The PIN does not authenticate the end user to the domain; instead, the PIN authenticates the end user to the certificate on the smart card. The certificate on the smart card is then used to authenticate the end user to the domain. Smart card authentication is already a standard practice within hospitals, education facilities, the scientific community, and military organizations.

Smart card authentication requires the following:

- One or more certificates
- Middleware (for example, ActivClient from ActivIdentity)

> Middleware should be installed before the VMware View Agent to avoid any **Graphical Identification and Authentication** (**GINA**) chaining issues; the proper installation order is VMware Tools, then Smart Card Middleware, and then VMware View Agent.
>
> It may also be beneficial to set smart card removal behavior to lock the workstation for persistent solutions or log off for nonpersistent solutions.

- Smart card
- Smart card reader (for example, SCR331)

In addition, the following prerequisites must be met:

- The smart card option should be installed during the VMware View Connection Server installation process
- The VMware View Connection Server should be configured to allow smart card authentication

- The middleware (for example, ActivClient) should function properly and should be configured with the necessary certificates

- The `locked.properties` file on all of the VMware View Connection and Security Servers in the environment has been configured to use the master keystore holding one or more **Certificate Authority (CA)** certificates for the respective user certificates in use for the smart cards

The smart card configuration should be nearly identical for any organization (with only the certificates being the differentiator). It is important to note that while most smart cards may look the same, there are approximately a dozen or so smart card models on the market. The make and model of the smart card can typically be discovered via the smart card middleware in use, for example, ActivClient.

The following screenshot shows a given smart card in the **ActivClient** console:

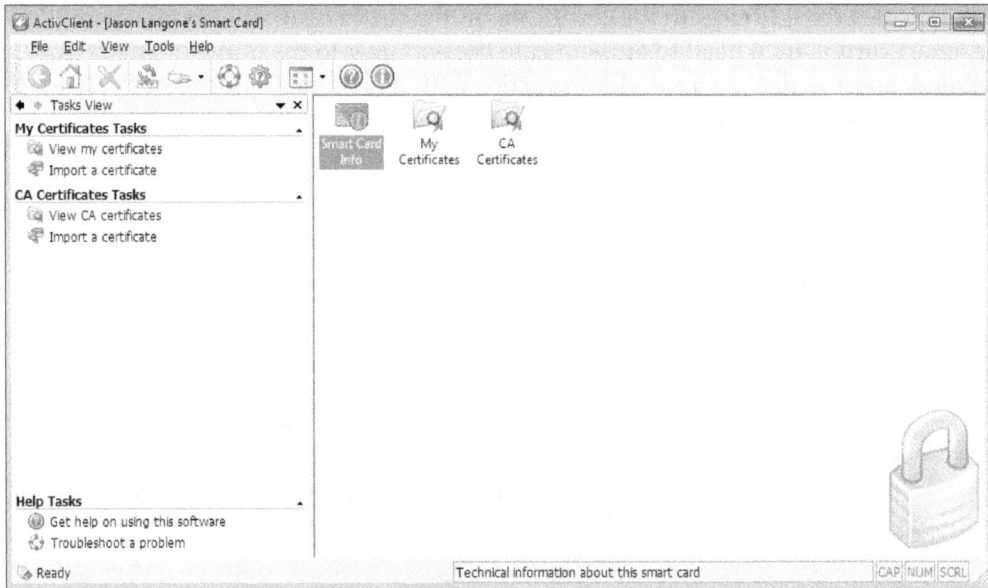

In the preceding screenshot, a card has been inserted into an approved card reader (for example, SCR331). There are three options on the home screen within ActivClient. Clicking on the **My Certificates** folder opens the user certificates stored on the smart card. Clicking on **CA Certificates** opens the CA certificates stored on the smart card and is used to validate the user certificates.

Opening the **Smart Card Info** object brings up the screen shown in the following screenshot, which shows smart card information in ActivClient:

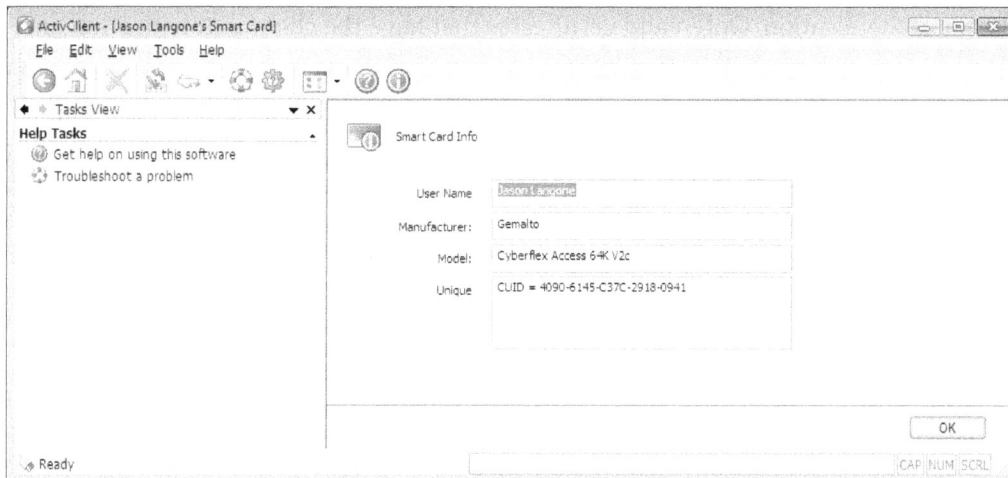

As shown in the preceding screenshot, the **Manufacturer** of the smart card in question is **Gemalto** and the **Model** is **Cyberflex Access 64K V2c**. In addition, the username (typically associated with an Active Directory user account of the same name) is also displayed in the **User Name** field.

The following screenshot shows the certificates on a given smart card:

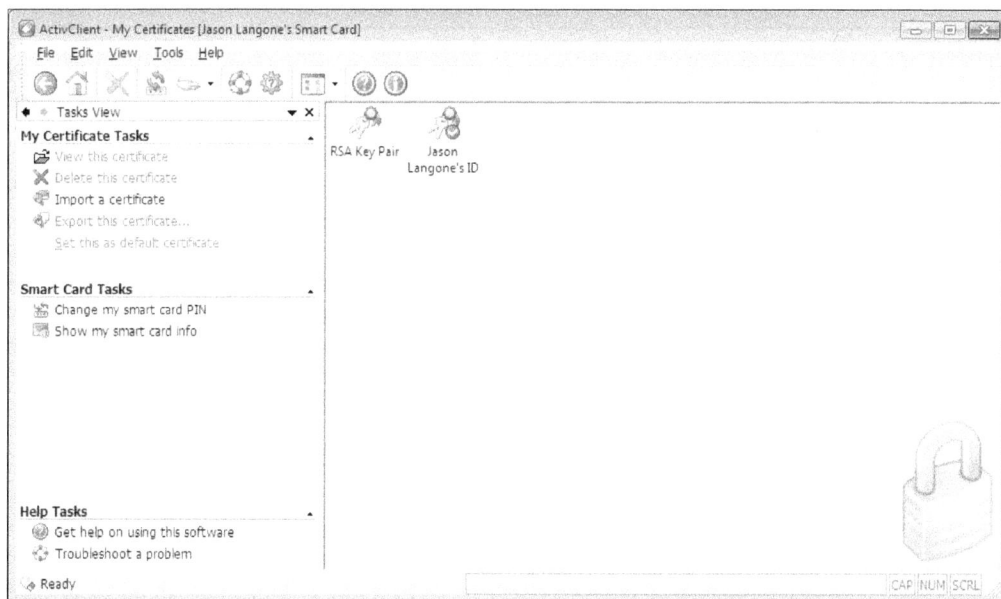

While only one user certificate is shown in the preceding screenshot, it is possible to have multiple user certificates stored on a smart card. VMware View will filter through the user certificates and prompt the end user to select which certificate to use for authentication. Only valid certificates that have the client authentication and smart card logon role will be displayed.

The following screenshot shows certificate details of a smart card via ActivClient:

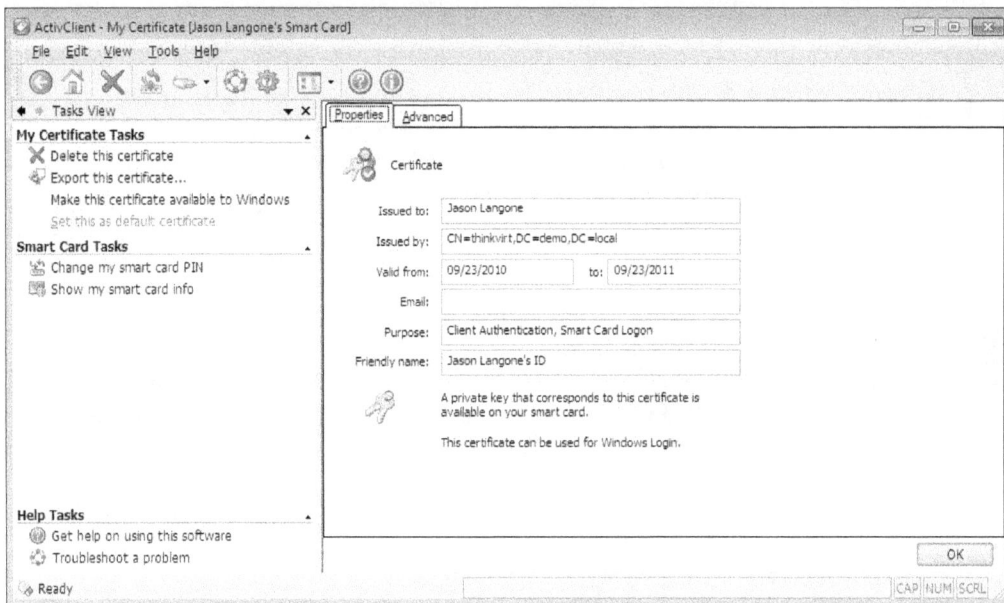

The preceding screenshot shows the **My Certificate** screen from within ActivClient. The principal name of the issuing CA for the user certificate (for example, `thinkvirt.demo.local`) is displayed. It is important that the name resolution to the issuing CA be fully functional. Malfunctioning DNS resolution can impact smart card authentication times.

Additional smart card information from VMware can be found in the *Smart Card Certificate Authentication with VMware View 4.5 and Above* whitepaper at `http://www.vmware.com/files/pdf/VMware-View-SmartCardAuthentication-WP-EN.pdf`.

Configuring smart card authentication for VMware View Connection Servers

Smart card authentication is supported by PCoIP zero clients, thin clients, and thick clients. It is important to verify that the exact card reader model, card model, and certificates in use are supported in the VMware View/Teradici PCoIP support matrix. These documents are available at `http://www.vmware.com/` and `http://www.teradici.com/` respectively.

In addition, smart cards are often used to provide a secure mechanism for **Single Sign-On**, which is the ability to log in to the VMware View environment once (and not for every time a session is connected or reconnected to a vDesktop).

To mandate the use of smart card authentication, go to the **Edit View Connection Server Settings** tab found under **View Configuration | Servers**.

The following screenshot shows advanced smart card configuration options:

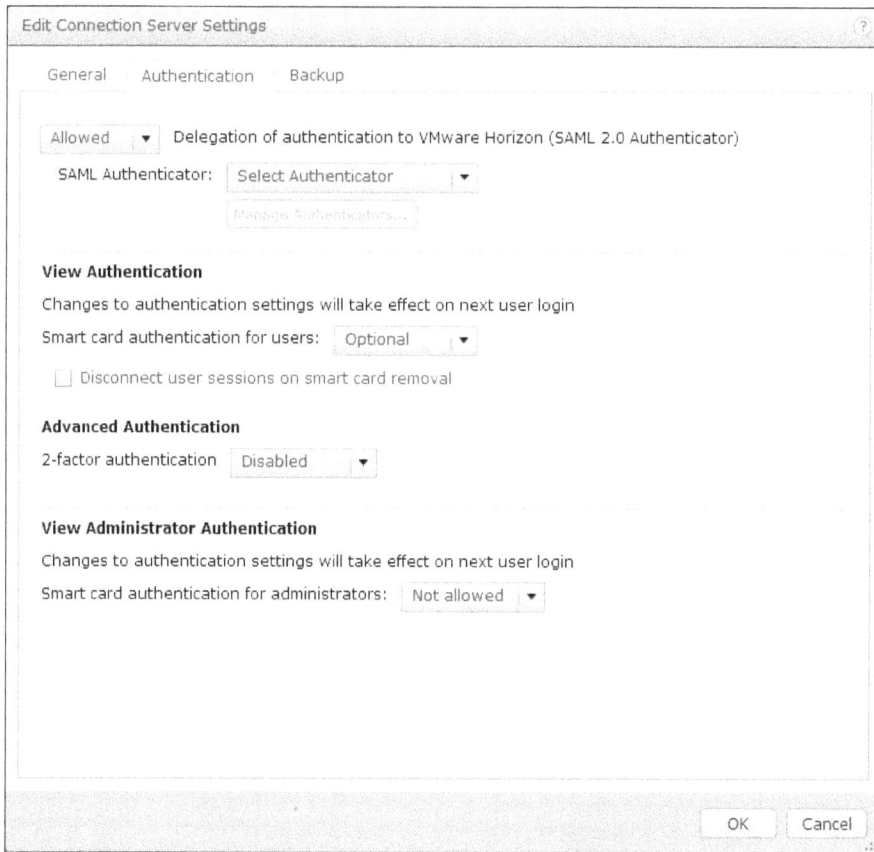

Smart card authentication for users can be set to **Not allowed, Optional,** or **Required**. In addition, sessions can be set to disconnect upon smart card removal by selecting the **Disconnect user sessions on smart card removal** checkbox.

In many secured environments, the required option will be configured to enforce that any incoming requests to access a vDesktop in the VDI are authenticated by the use of a user's smart card.

In addition to configuring smart card authentication in the VMware View Admin console, there is a main file of importance during configuration: `locked.properties`.

The `settings.properties` file, also located in the `\sslgateway\conf` subdirectory, contains configurations for the certificate used by the VMware View Admin console for HTTPS encryption; the value for which certificate to use is stored in the `keyfile` string. In addition, the `settings.properties` file contains the hashed password necessary to use the certificate; the value for the password is stored in the `keypass` string.

Preparing the environment for smart card authentication

To prepare the environment for smart card authentication, perform the following steps:

1. The first step is to verify a fully functioning DNS and NTP environment as certificate-based authentication is very sensitive to the time drift or difficult in resolving servers within the **public key infrastructure (PKI)**.

2. Next, the CA certificate must be downloaded. This can be done by opening a browser and pointing it to `http://<CA_SERVER>/certsrv`, where `<CA_SERVER>` is the **fully qualified domain name (FQDN)** or IP address of the CA server.

3. Select the **Download CA Certificate** link with **DER encoding** (default) selected. Save the certificate to the VMware View Connection Server under `\VMware View\Server\jre\bin`.

4. Launch the command prompt with administrative permission (for example, right-click on the **Command Prompt** icon and select **Run As Administrator**). Navigate to `\VMware View\Server\jre\bin`.

5. Next, type the following command to generate the keystore:

```
keytool -import -alias view4ca -file certnew.cer -keystore trust.
key
```

6. The `certnew.cer` file is the CA certificate that was downloaded in a previous step. The `trust.key` file is the generated keystore that will be used by the VMware View Connection Server to verify end user certificates stored on their smart card.

7. The `keytool` utility will then prompt for the CA certificate's password as well as to whether the certificate should or should not be trusted.

8. Once the keystore has been successfully generated, copy the file (for example, `trust.key`) to the `\VMware View\Server\sslgateway\conf` subdirectory.

9. Next, create a text file named `locked.properties` within the `\VMware View\Server\sslgateway\conf` subdirectory with Notepad (or a similar tool).

10. Enter the following text:

```
trustKeyFile=trust.key
trustStoreType=JKS
UseCertAuth=true
```

11. Restart the VMware View Connection Server service.

Configuring smart card authentication for VMware View Security Servers

For environments that leverage one or more VMware View Security Servers, it is important to configure the View Security Server to also utilize smart card authentication (as well as configuring the appropriate certificates). Otherwise, only internal users or users bypassing the VMware View Security Server will be able to leverage their smart card for authentication.

The steps are identical to those listed in the *Configuring smart card authentication for VMware View Connection Servers* section.

The following figure shows an illustration of the location of the `locked.properties` file:

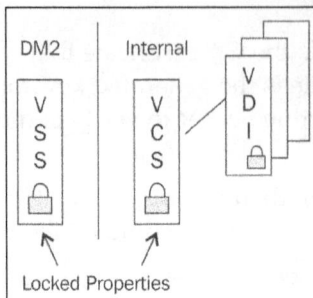

Locked Properties

Therefore, the easiest way to configure a VMware View Security Server (shown as **VSS** in the preceding figure) is as follows:

1. Copy the `trust.key` file (or other appropriate keystore file) to the `\VMware View\Server\sslgateway\conf` subdirectory.

2. Copy the `locked.properties` file to the `\VMware View\Server\sslgateway\conf` subdirectory.

3. Restart the VMware View Security Server service.

Notice the simplicity of the preceding steps if a VMware View environment is leveraging the same PKI and same keystore for the CA certificate, which is likely for almost all VMware View solutions using smart cards. Therefore, it is quite possible to script the copying of the files from one server to the other, as well as restarting the appropriate service (for example, VMware View Security Server service) when necessary.

RADIUS and two-factor authentication

As part of a VMware View solution, IT may be required to have a third-party authentication manager to provide a centralized authentication management across different systems. The IT may also need to provide a more secure user verification mechanism using two-factor authentication.

There is a document with a step-by-step guide for IT Administrators to integrate VMware View 6.0 with Microsoft Network Policy Server and a RSA Authentication Server in order to enhance the View's authentication functions. The guide is found at `http://www.vmware.com/files/pdf/techpaper/vmware-horizon-view-radius-two-factor-authentication-setup.pdf`.

Configuring the U.S. Department of Defense Common Access Card authentication

U.S. Department of Defense Common Access Card (DoD CAC) smart card authentication is a mechanism approved by **Homeland Security Presidential Directive 12 (HSPD-12)** and used by US military installations for authentication to IT assets. CACs also serve as a general identification card pursuant to the Geneva Conventions.

Personnel log in to their physical desktop by entering their CAC into a USB smart card reader, laptop smart card reader, a thin or zero client with an integrated card reader, or a keyboard with an integrated card reader. Once the card has been read, the end user is prompted to enter his or her PIN.

It is entirely possible to use CAC authentication inside the vDesktop without even configuring it as an acceptable authentication mechanism to get to the vDesktop. For example, if ActivClient is installed and configured properly within a vDesktop but smart card authentication has not been configured on the View Connection Server environment, then the smart card cannot be used to connect to the vDesktop. However, once connected to the vDesktop, the smart card can be successfully used to authenticate within the VDI (for example, an RDP connection). In normal smart card operation, authentication using a smart card will prompt the end user for his or her PIN. While this scenario is possible, it is far from the preferred solution, as connecting into the VDI is not done via smart card authentication. Configuring CAC authentication encompasses the techniques used in standard smart card authentication configuration and adds a few minor considerations.

Perform the following steps to configure CAC authentication:

1. On the VMware View Connection Server, navigate to the `\VMware View Server\Server\sslgateway\conf` subdirectory.

2. Create a subdirectory named `certexport`. Within `\certexport`, place all of the `.cer` files that are applicable. This directory is used to generate a current or future `master keystore`.

3. The next step of configuring the CAC authentication is to generate or obtain a `master keystore`, which contains all of the US DoD and intermediate CA certificates. The `master keystore` file should be placed in the `\sslgateway\ conf` subdirectory found within the `VMware View installation` directory on the View Connection Server. Instructions on how to generate a `master keystore` are outlined later in this chapter.

4. Copy the `truststore` files to the `\sslgateway\conf` subdirectory.

Name	Type
certexport	File folder
email ca 20.cer	Security Certificate
emailca20	File
error.fm	FM File
locked.properties	PROPERTIES File
log4j.cfg	CFG File
masterkeystore	File
truststore1	File
truststore2	File
truststore20	File
vdm.p12	Personal Informati...

The preceding screenshot shows the `\\sslgateway\conf` subdirectory of a working VMware View Connection Server configured for CAC authentication.

5. Now that all of the certificates are in the proper location, VMware View Connection Server must be configured to use the certificates.

6. Next, open the `locked.properties` file, which can also be found in the `\sslgateway\conf` subdirectory. If the file does not exist, it should be created using Notepad or a similar utility.

7. The contents of the `locked.properties` file should be similar to:

```
trustKeyFile=masterkeystore
trustStoreType=JKS
useCertAuth=true
```

The preceding code assumes that the `master keystore` file is actually named `masterkeystore`. The line `trustStoreType = JKS` defines that the trust store is a Java keystore generated with the **Java Runtime Environment (JRE)** `keytool.exe` or a similar utility. The line `useCertAuth = true` enabled the use of the certificate.

Once the settings have been applied, restart the VMware View Connection Server service or the VMware View Security Server service. At this point, it's also important to verify that the View Admin console is still functional, as a malformed `locked.properties` file can prevent the View Admin console from loading properly.

Certificate revocation configuration

A **Certificate Revocation List** (**CRL**) is used to prevent users whose end user certificate has been revoked (for example, the end user is an employee who has been terminated) from successfully authenticating to the environment. VMware View supports CRLs and **Online Certificate Status Protocol** (**OCSP**) to check the certificate revocation status of a given certificate. If both OCSP and CRL are configured on a VMware View Connection Server or VMware View Security Server, VMware View will attempt to use OCSP first and then fall back to the use of a CRL if OCSP fails. VMware View will not fall back to OCSP from the use of a CRL if the CRL check fails.

Configuring the use of CRL

The use of a CRL is configured by editing the `locked.properties` file and adding the following lines:

```
enableRevocationchecking=true
allowCertCRLs=true
crlLocation=<URL_OF_CRL>
```

The `enableRevocationchecking` and `allowCertCRLs` strings enable VMware View to perform certificate revocation checking. The `crlLocation` string is used to define the location of the CRL. An example of a value for `crlLocation` is `http://cert.demo.local/certEnroll/ocsp-ROOT_CA.crl`.

Configuring the use of OCSP

The use of an OCSP is configured by editing the `locked.properties` file and adding the following lines:

```
enableRevocationchecking=true
enableOCSP=true
allowCertCRLs=true
ocspSigningCert=<OCSP_Signing_Cert>
ocspURL=<URL_OCSP>
```

The `enableRevocationchecking` and `allowCertCRLs` strings enable VMware View to perform a certificate revocation check. The `enableOCSP` string enables OCSP. The `ocspSigningCert` string is used to define the certificate used by the OCSP authority and the `ocspURL` is used to define the location of the OCSP responder.

Configuring the use of both CRL and OCSP

To configure the use of both a CRL and OCSP, insert all of the preceding fields and their appropriate values into the locked.properties file.

> Please note that the allowCertCRLs=true string only needs to be listed once.

In addition, the following should be added to the locked.properties file:

```
ocspCRLFailover=true
```

The ocspCRLFailover string allows the VMware View Connection Server or VMware View Security Server to use a CRL if OCSP fails.

SSL protocols and ciphers

The cipher suites along with security protocols that Horizon View Client 2.2 uses to communicate with View servers are not configurable. If you have configured your Windows client systems to use a specific cipher though GPO, such as configuring SSL **Cipher Suite Order** group policy settings, the Horizon View Client 2.2 for Windows will not honor these GPO settings. If this is required, do not upgrade to this version of the Windows client.

In some cases, Horizon View Client 2.2 could allow connections using a weaker cipher suites and security protocols than those required by the connection server or security server. When you are planning the security settings in your Horizon View deployment, be sure to examine these settings so that you make an informed decision about the clients to use. There is more information at http://kb.vmware. com/selfservice/microsites/search.do?language=en_US&cmd=displayKC&ext ernalId=2062292.

Prohibiting the use of copy and paste functions

In some environments, administrators may want to prevent end users from copying and pasting between their vDesktop and their thick or thin client. The proper way to prevent the copy and paste functions is via the group policy of the vDesktops.

This is defined in the `PCOIP.ADM` template available on any View Connection Server in the `\extras` subdirectory. This setting can be found in `Computer Configuration\Admin Templates\PCoIP Session Variables\Not Overridable Admin Settings\Configure PCoIP Virtual Channels`.

Within this setting, there is an allowed and disallowed list. If a virtual channel is listed on both the allowed and disallowed list, it will be disallowed. In View 4.6 and later, the virtual channel responsible for the clipboard (`mksvchan`) no longer needs to be explicitly mentioned. Instead, the administrator can simply check the disable clipboard processing on the PCoIP host and enable the policy.

The following screenshot shows the settings of the clipboard process:

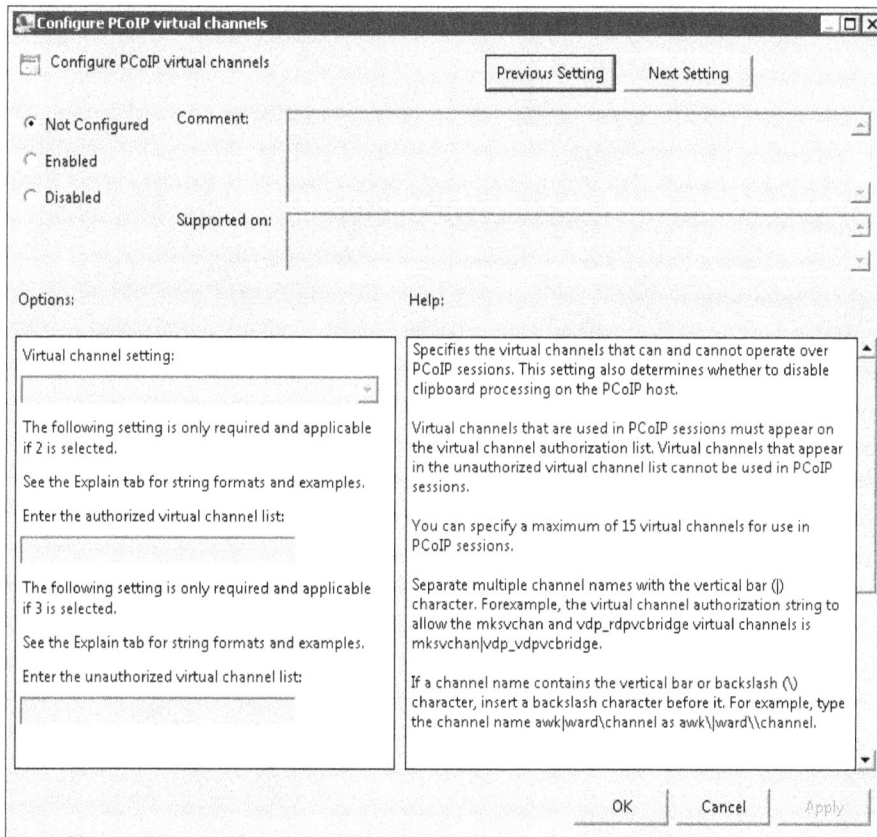

The **Disable clipboard processing on PCoIP host** setting is read at the time of connection or reconnection. Therefore, changing the setting from **Not Configured** to **Enabled**, for example, will go into effect on the next login and not the existing session.

View Connection Server tags

VMware View Connection Server uses tags to control access to specific desktop pools in an environment with multiple View Connection Servers. Any given VMware View Connection Server can have no tags, one tag, or many tags. Tags are defined under **View Configuration | Servers | Edit View Connection Server Settings** in the View Admin console.

The following screenshot shows the use of a Connection Server tag (**thinkvirt**, in this case):

In the preceding example, a specific VMware View Connection Server has been assigned the **thinkvirt** tag. To assign multiple tags to a VMware View Connection server, separate the tags by either semicolons or commas.

Then, from within the configuration of a desktop pool, select **Browse** for configuration tagging from the **Pool Settings** tab.

The following screenshot shows the use of a restriction tag:

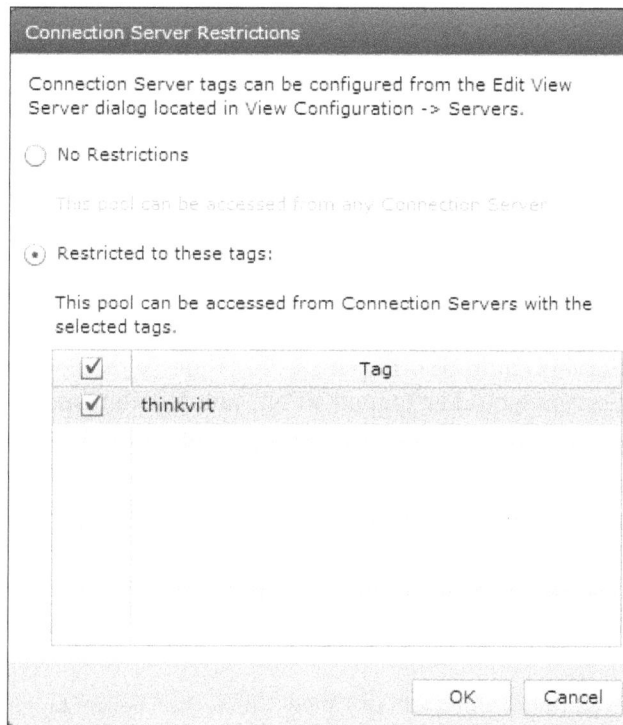

The preceding screenshot would show multiple tags if multiple tags were in use and would allow the administrator to select none, some, or all of the available tags.

> The **Tag** field will only be populated if at least one View Connection Server within the environment has a defined tag.

In the **Connection Server Restrictions** dialog box, there are two options:

- **No Restrictions**: This pool can be accessed from any VMware View Connection Server
- **Restricted to these tags**: This pool can be accessed from one or more VMware View Connection Servers with the defined tags

The following is a matrix of tag connection permissions:

Does the Connection Server have a defined tag?	Is the desktop pool configured to use tags?	Result
No	No	Able to connect
No	One or more	Unable to connect
One or more	No	Able to connect
One or more	One or more	Able to connect only if one or more tags match

One example of when this may be useful is if an organization has two separate inbound VPN environments. VPN_A is used by consultants and visitors. VPN_B is used by employees. If the organization wanted to restrict users of VPN_A to a desktop with limited capabilities and minimal applications installed, one or more separate View Connection Servers could be set up for VPN_A and VPN_B, respectively. The View Connection Servers would be tagged VPNA and VPNB respectively. Then, the limited desktop pool would only allow connections from VPNA, whereas the fully functional desktop pool would only allow connections from VPNB.

It's important to note that a VMware View solution can leverage more than one vCenter Server. Therefore, not only could tagging limit the pools an inbound user has access to, but the backend desktop pools could live on a completely separate virtual infrastructure.

> In addition, you could use View Connection Server tagging to identify which users were forced to use two-factor authentication and which were not.

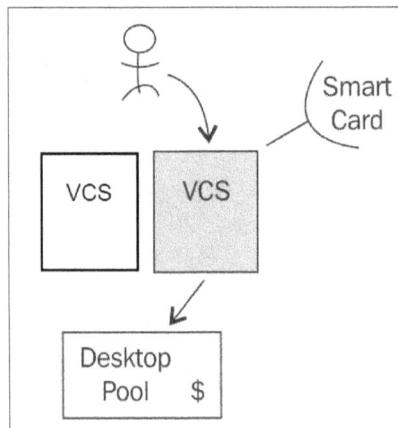

In the previous figure, the end user has more than one **View Connection Server** (**VCS** in the preceding figure) available to him or her. The gray VCS requires smart card authentication. For example, this VCS could be used by military staff or doctors who have been issued a **common access card** (**CAC**), whereby the white VCS could be used by civilians, interns, or temporary staff (who are not issued smart cards). Within the VDI, there exists a desktop pool that has several sensitive financial applications as part of its base image. By using VMware View Connection Server tagging, the financial desktop pool can be configured to only allow incoming connections from the gray VCS, thereby enforcing the use of smart card authentication for incoming users.

Forensics

Forensics, in terms of Information Technology, typically relates to the extraction of legal evidence from computer systems to support legal events. Forensics involves identifying, preserving, recovering, analyzing, and presenting collected data from a computer environment. Forensics is also a required component for many sensitive computing environments looking to leverage VDI solutions.

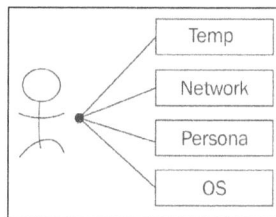

To understand how forensics is impacted by a VDI, it's first important to understand where user-authored or user-manipulated data may reside, as shown in the preceding figure.

The primary locations for user-authored or user-manipulated data are as follows:

- **Operating system**: For VMware View solutions that do not leverage View Composer or do not leverage redirection of the user's persona, user data will reside within the operating system partition.

- **Persona**: For VMware View solutions that leverage Microsoft roaming profiles, a persona management solution, for example, Liquidware Labs ProfileUnity TM, or VMware View's persistent user data drives, user data will reside within the persona partition. For Microsoft roaming profiles, AppSense or ProfileUnity, the user data will be stored on a network share. Therefore, ensuring that the network share that stores the user data is backed up according to the organization's policy is imperative as the location where forensics analysis will occur.

For solutions that use persistent user data drives, it is important to preserve these virtual disk files so that they can be attached to other virtual machines if the need to perform forensics arises. When user data resides in the persona layer, virtual machine volatility is of far less concern.

- **Network resources**: For network resources, such as file shares, web-based collaboration resources, the scope for preserving these data points is outside the scope of this book and relies more on understanding various platforms and how they provide auditing and data restoration capabilities.

- **Temporary location**: For solutions that leverage redirecting the user's profile, it's possible that configuration of the solution may miss user data due to misconfiguration and therefore would be discarded during a vDesktop or desktop pool View Composer task.

The biggest challenge for VDI, which requires forensics capabilities, is the use of nonpersistent desktop pools. Persistent desktop pools are automatically assigned once and therefore data, versioning, state, and so on are able to be maintained.

Summary

While a VDI solution is inherently secure in nature because the end user's data typically resides in a secure data center, it is still important to understand an organization's security posture, policies, and attack vectors and take appropriate measures where necessary. With end users connecting from any location, such as an unsecured Wi-Fi connection at a coffee shop, an Apple iPad over a 4G network, a corporate LAN, or a home cable ISP, it is important to protect corporate data and intellectual property. The use of smart card authentication—a solution rapidly gaining in popularity—is one strong approach for protecting the authentication entry point. Sound networking policies limiting traffic to defined ports, protocols, sources, and destinations is another key component of a secure VDI.

Finally, understanding basic fundamentals of data forensics to ensure compliance, if necessary, is an important skill to have within the VDI solution team. While, potentially, the majority of VDI solutions will not require in-depth forensic capabilities, understanding the data points to preserve, monitor, and collect are significant.

The next chapter focuses on the process of migrating from a physical desktop solution to a virtual desktop solution. There are many different approaches that can be taken, and the advantages and disadvantages of each will be covered.

10
Migrating User Personas

This chapter analyzes the strategies and techniques used to migrate a user population from a physical desktop environment to a virtual desktop solution. While many VDI solutions will be part of the new construction and not involve the migration of users, the majority of VDI solutions to be implemented will involve some components of user migration. This chapter covers the following topics:

- Separating personas from the operating environment
- The use of VMware View user data disks
- Operational considerations with user data

To help ensure success of the overall VDI endeavor, it is important to minimize the perceived impact of the transition to the end users. Part of this impact minimization is understanding how to properly migrate user-specific data, also known as the user's persona.

A user's persona consists of user preferences, application settings, themes, shortcuts, favorites, printers, and other unique configurations. In order to decouple a user's persona from a desktop, the persona must ultimately reside outside of the desktop operating system. Typically, user personas are stored on a classic network file share or a distributed filesystem share. By storing personas on a network share, a consistent end user experience can be delivered no matter which vDesktop resource a user connects to, as the persona is not bound to a specific vDesktop.

There are several solutions on the market that help with the migration of a user's persona, including everything from Microsoft's roaming profiles and folder redirection to AppSense, Liquidware Labs' ProfileUnity, VMware's own Persona Management, and VMware Horizon Mirage.

Migration of the user persona

In order to migrate a user's persona, it must first be decoupled from the desktop operating system. In a completely coupled scenario, the user's persona resides inside the operating environment of the physical desktop.

The following figure is an illustration that shows the characteristics of a physical desktop:

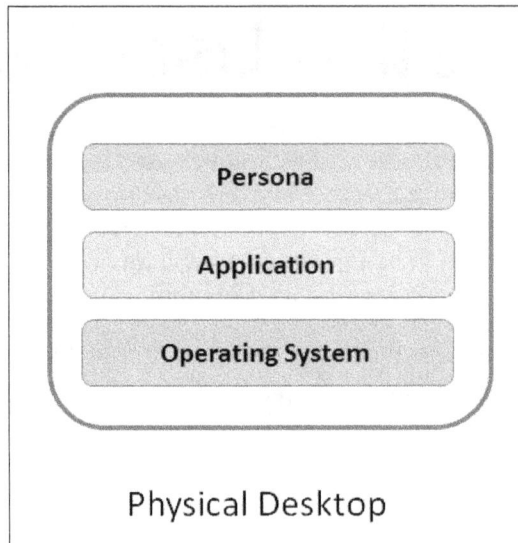

In the preceding figure, the operating system, applications, and user persona reside within the same environment. There is no application virtualization (for example, VMware ThinApp) or Persona Management solution (for example, ProfileUnity) in place. The first step toward successfully migrating the physical desktop in the preceding scenario to a fully functioning vDesktop is to separate the persona from the operating environment.

Separating a persona from the operating environment

By separating a user's persona from the underlying desktop, it can be freely migrated to another physical desktop, or ideally, to a virtual desktop. This is the same approach used in application virtualization where a given application is packaged via ThinApp for example, and is now untethered from the underlying operating system.

The following figure is an illustration that shows the decoupling of the user's persona from the physical desktop:

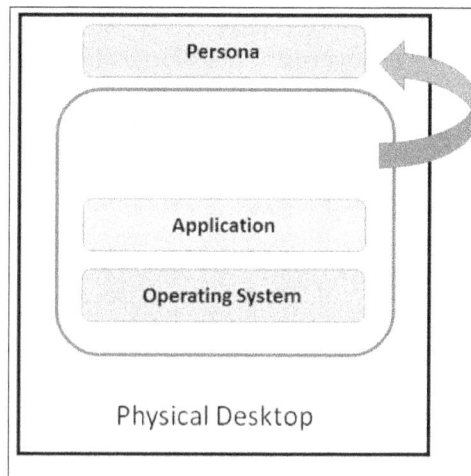

A few of the options to untether the persona from the operating environment of the physical desktop are as follows:

- Microsoft roaming profile plus folder redirection
- Liquidware Labs ProfileUnity
- AppSense
- VMware View Persona Management
- VMware Horizon Mirage

In this state, a physical desktop still contains installed applications, but customizations and other details that comprise the user's persona reside outside of the guest OS.

Folder redirection

Folder redirection works by redirecting the path of a folder (for example, \My Documents) to a new location, typically, a network share that is unknown to the user. An end user who has their \My Documents folder redirected to a network share will continue to open, save, and manipulate files in their \My Documents folder while the user is opening, saving, and manipulating files on a network share, as opposed to the local drive in the background.

The advantages of folder redirection are as follows:

- A user's data is accessible from any desktop resource, assuming that appropriate network connectivity exists

- The group policy can be leveraged to enforce disk quotas to minimize the space of a user's persona

- A user's data that has been redirected is likely to have a greater chance of recovery from a desktop failure, as production network shares are often backed up more frequently than desktops

With the native Microsoft solution, the `My Documents`, `Application Data`, `Desktop`, and `Start Menu` parent folders can be redirected. The subfolders of the aforementioned parent folders will also be redirected.

`My Documents` is a folder that a user will have read/write access to and is used as a place to save documents, pictures, media, and other data. `My Documents` is the default save-to location for many Microsoft applications.

The `Application Data` folder is used by applications to save customized user settings relevant to a given application. (Take special considerations when redirecting App Data as it can have negative performance issues.)

The `Desktop` folder is the folder that contains all of the items that reside on a user's desktop.

The `Start Menu` folder contains items found in a desktop's start menu list.

Profiles

In order to understand how roaming profiles work, it is important to understand what makes up a profile in a Windows environment. In Windows, a profile consists of the following:

- **Registry hive**: The registry hive, stored as `NTuser.dat`, stores the contents of `HKEY_CURRENT_USER`

- **Profile folder**: This is located in `C:\Users\User4`

Within the registry hive and profile folder are the configuration settings for things such as mapped printers, desktop shortcuts, drive mapping, unique processes, and logging.

In Windows, there are several types of profiles as follows:

- **Local profile**: This is the typical type of profile used and is created upon the first login of a user to a desktop.

- **Roaming profile**: This type of profile makes a local copy of the network-based master copy during login; when logged off, changes are copied back to the network-based master copy.

- **Mandatory profile**: This type of profile is used by administrators to specify settings for users; changes made by users are lost once the system is logged off.

- **Temporary user profiles**: A temporary profile is created each time an error condition prevents the user's normal profile from loading. Temporary profiles will be deleted at the end of the user session. This means that changes made by the user to desktop settings and files will be lost when the user logs off.

In many VDI solutions, especially those that are nonpersistent, a roaming profile or other profile management solution will be used. This is because roaming profiles allow any user to access any available vDesktop and still maintain their own unique personalization settings.

How a profile is built – the first login

To understand how a Windows profile is built, it is first important to understand the folder directory structure of C:\Users.

Under C:\Users, there are several folders as follows:

- Public: Anything stored in this folder is available to every user that logs into the computer. Contents of certain folders, such as Desktop, are merged with the user's profile.

- Default: Settings in this folder are used as a template for any new users who log in to the workstation, meaning that they do not already have a profile folder on the desktop.

- Username: Settings in this folder are unique to the specific user.

The first time a user logs in to a desktop, whether physical or virtual, he or she has his or her own unique profile folder created under C:\Users (for example, Windows 7 and 8). The contents of this folder are based on the contents in Default. In addition, any content in c:\Public is loaded as part of the profile.

How a profile is built – subsequent logins

Once a user has his or her own unique profile folder on a desktop, they no longer use the `Default` folder. This means that any settings or shortcuts that have been placed in `Default` after the user has already created a profile will not be reflected in the user's profile. However, shortcuts placed in the `c:\User\Public` folder will be reflected.

> If a user has administrative access to a machine and deletes a shortcut or file that originates from `Users`, that shortcut or file will be deleted for all the users on the machine. A shortcut or file placed in `c:\Users\Public` will immediately be displayed to any user logged in to the desktop.

Roaming profiles

Roaming profiles are profiles that are stored in a central repository and accessed on demand at the time of logging in to a desktop operating system.

The following figure is an illustration that shows a user's ability to log in to either of the desktops and still receive their profile settings:

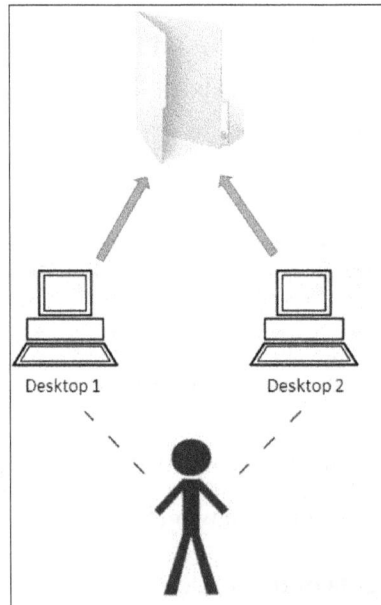

Using roaming profiles is a technique to store the user's profile folder on a network share, thereby decoupling the user profile from the actual desktop.

In an example scenario without roaming profiles, a user, Dwayne, walks up to a physical desktop, Desktop 1. Dwayne works on a document, changes his wallpaper, maps a printer, and then logs out. If Dwayne then walks over to a different physical desktop, Desktop 2, and logs in, he will not have any of the work, settings, or mappings he just made on Desktop 1. This is because Dwayne's profile physically resides on the local drive of Desktop 1.

In the same scenario, with roaming profiles enabled, Dwayne's documents, wallpapers, printer mappings, and other settings will be copied to a central network location upon logging off from Desktop 1. Therefore, when Dwayne logs in to Desktop 2, all of the settings, documents, and mappings will be downloaded from the central network location.

One of the drawbacks of roaming profiles is that it is possible to enter into a scenario where a user's profile is extremely large and the tasks of logging on and logging off are crippled as a profile is synced with the network share. For example, if a user has a 5 GB roaming profile and logs in to a machine for the first time, the entire 5 GB worth of data will be downloaded from the network location before the user is presented with a working desktop. Therefore, it's important to minimize the data that resides in the roaming profile to ensure a positive end user experience.

> Ensure that **Allow offline files** and/or **Allow offline caching** is disabled in the **Roaming File** configuration. If you are using a nonpersistent VDI solution and offline caching is allowed, it's possible that a user could log in to vDesktop and not download the current version of their own profile (because a cached copy exists).

Using roaming profiles with folder redirection for increased performance

As the majority of large files in a user's profile are likely to be in locations like as `Documents`, redirecting such a folder to a network location can ensure a user's profile is not overly bloated.

The following figure is an illustration that shows the segmentation of a user's persona with folder redirection and roaming profiles:

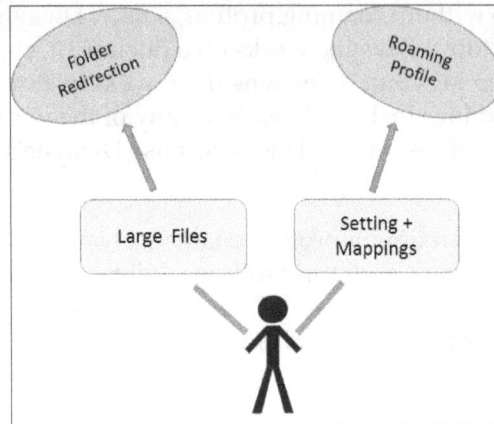

By combining folder redirection and roaming profiles, large files for example, documents stored typically in Documents can be redirected to a network location, while settings and configuration files can be synced via roaming profiles.

Other third-party solutions – Liquidware Labs ProfileUnity

While there are several profile management solutions on the market, Liquidware Labs ProfileUnity is a cost-competitive solution that maintains settings and configurations in the native Windows format versus storing them in a proprietary database.

In addition, ProfileUnity also provides additional benefits, such as the ability to do the following:

- Manage user profiles and folder redirection from one console
- Easily configure MAPI profiles for use with Microsoft Exchange Server
- Filter the execution of a script based on rules, machine class, OS, connection type, and so on
- Speed up logon times through the use of compression and profile corruption reduction technologies
- Present the same user profile when logging into virtual or physical desktops

In addition, for system administrators who are not overly comfortable with advanced group policy management, ProfileUnity has a fairly intuitive user interface for management.

View Persona Management

View Persona Management will allow you to migrate existing user profiles from a number of scenarios (legacy systems) to Horizon View desktops. After a profile migration is completed, the users log in to their View desktops and are presented with their personal settings and data that they used on their legacy systems.

To support these legacy system scenarios, View Persona Management provides a profile migration utility (migprofile.exe) and a standalone View Persona Management installer for the physical machines that the user is currently assigned to. You can then migrate from that physical computer to View desktops without upgrading the operating systems. The migration utility also allows you to move a user profile from an existing View deployment using operating systems that range from XP to Windows 7 or Windows 8 View desktops.

> For detailed information on how to set up and use the migration utility for a number of legacy scenarios, refer to the following publication at http://pubs.vmware.com/view-52/topic/com.vmware.ICbase/PDF/horizon-view-52-profile-migration.pdf.

Horizon Mirage

Mirage, which was purchased by VMware in 2012, is a unified image management solution for physical desktops, virtual desktops, and **Bring Your Own Devices** (**BYODs**) devices (endpoints). The dynamic layering and complete system recovery provides a quick and cost-effective way to deliver, manage, and protect updates to operating systems and applications across thousands of endpoints.

While this book is not about the features of Mirage, if you are using Mirage to manage your physical environment, you can move a user's persona from a physical endpoint to a View persistence desktop. This can be done one at a time or as a mass hardware migration option for many user machines. Placing the Mirage agent on the View desktop and using **Hardware Migration Wizard**, you can migrate the user persona. You will use the **Only Restore User Data and Settings** option to migrate users from Windows XP/Vista/Windows 7 machines to new Windows 7 or 8 virtual desktops. The OS of the virtual desktop must be the same as or newer than that of the physical endpoint. Only the user data and settings are restored to the replacement device. The existing OS and applications installed on the View desktop are retained.

> This is a very general overview of the process, and you should refer to the Mirage documentation that can be found at https://www.vmware.com/support/pubs/mirage_pubs.html.

Cutting over from a physical to a virtual desktop

Once the profile has been decoupled from the desktop, a user can log in to a physical desktop on Tuesday and a vDesktop on Wednesday, and maintain all the settings. A few things to consider are as follows:

- If upgrading operating systems is part of the migration, ensure that all of the settings from the older OS will be applied to the newer OS.
- If you're planning to provide the ability to go back and forth between an older and newer OS, special considerations might need to be made to ensure that settings will be applied. For example, wallpaper file types between Windows XP and Windows 7 are different.

Also, considering what type of desktop pool is implemented (persistent or nonpersistent) as well as what type of profile management solution is chosen (native Microsoft, Liquidware Labs ProfileUnity, and so on), the first login may take a significant amount of time.

Using VMware View user data disks

VMware View provides the ability to store a user's profile in a user data disk. The user data disk is tethered to a specific vDesktop in the VDI.

The following figure is an illustration that shows the user of a user data disk for profile management:

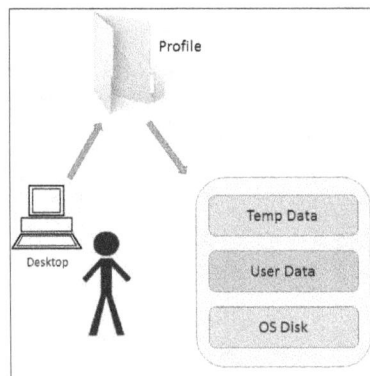

VMware View provides the ability to redirect a user's profile to a persistent user data disk. This disk is separate from the other disks that make up a user's vDesktop; however, a user's UDD can only be attached to one vDesktop at a time. Furthermore, UDDs can only be used with persistent desktop pools.

User profiles can be migrated to a UDD through the use of standard Microsoft tools or third-party solutions. Once a user profile has been completely and successfully migrated to UDD, it will no longer reside on the network share and its contents will only be accessible after you attach UDD (a .vmdk file) to a virtual machine.

Operational considerations with user data

In addition to technical considerations that need to be made in a VMware View solution, there are operational considerations to be made as well. One such consideration is the management of user data as it relates to human resource activities. Such activities include the hiring and termination of employees. For example, when an employee is terminated, the user data must be typically archived and stored for a defined period of time.

The following figure is an illustration that shows the management of user data disks in a VMware View environment:

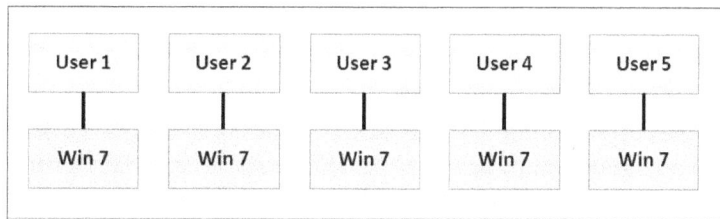

If user data disks are part of the solution, the user data disk must be detached from vDesktop when an employee is terminated and should likely be moved to a separate datastore dedicated to historical data. At some point, if the historical data is to be analyzed, the user data disk must first be attached to an existing virtual machine. This can become cumbersome for organizations with seasonal turnover, for example, groups that manage election campaigns.

The following figure is an illustration that shows the management of user profiles that reside in a central file share:

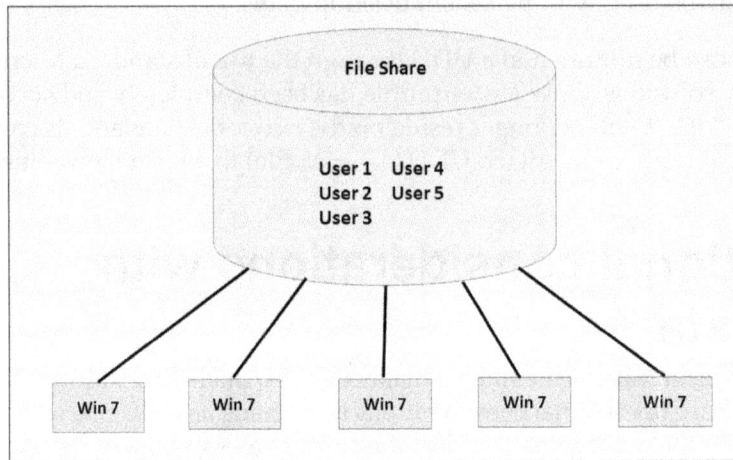

Using a central file share, all of the user data across an organization can be placed in a single location. Access to the file share is often controlled by a user's Active Directory account. Therefore, disabling a user's account (due to termination) also disables his or her access to the profile directory; however, the profile directory still resides on the file share until an administrator takes action (if necessary).

Summary

For brand new VDI environments (for example, a new classroom facility) that don't need to import user data, migrating user persona data is of no concern. However, for many organizations, the migration of user data from a physical desktop to a virtual desktop will be an important part of the implementation process. By decoupling the user's data from the desktop operating system, the user's settings can be maintained while the actual desktop is transitioned from physical to virtual. In addition, it is important to have an understanding of how the user profile solution may impact business processes, especially those related to human resources.

The next chapter will focus on backing up VDI as well as recovering it during an outage. While redundant design was covered earlier in this book, there are times when an unforeseen or unscheduled outage could cause a potential issue in VDI. Therefore, it is important to understand how to protect and recover from such outages.

11
Backing Up the VMware View Infrastructure

While a single point of failure should not exist in the VMware View environment, it is still important to ensure regular backups are taken for a quick recovery when failures occur. Also, if a setting becomes corrupted or is changed, a backup could be used to restore to a previous point in time. The backup of the VMware View environment should be performed on a regular basis in line with an organization's existing backup methodology. A VMware View environment contains both files and databases.

The main backup points of a VMware View environment are as follows:

- VMware View Connection Server — ADAM database
- VMware View Security Server
- VMware View Composer Database
- Remote Desktop Service host servers
- Remote Desktop Service host templates and virtual machines
- Virtual desktop templates and parent VMs
- Virtual desktops
    - Linked clones (stateless)
    - Full clones (stateful)
- ThinApp repository
- Persona Management
- VMware vCenter
- Restoring the VMware View environment
- Business Continuity and Disaster Recovery

With a backup of all of the preceding components, the VMware View Server infrastructure can be recovered during a time of failure.

To maximize the chances of success in a recovery environment, it is advised to take backups of the View ADAM database, View Composer, and vCenter database at the same time to avoid discrepancies. Backups can be scheduled and automated or can be manually executed; ideally, scheduled backups will be used to ensure that they are performed and completed regularly.

Proper design dictates that there should always be two or more View Connection Servers. As all View Connection Servers in the same replica pool contain the same configuration data, it is only necessary to back up one View Connection Server. This backup is typically configured for the first View Connection Server installed in standard mode in an environment.

VMware View Connection Server – ADAM Database backup

View Connection Server stores the View Connection Server configuration data in the View LDAP repository. View Composer stores the configuration data for linked clone desktops in the View Composer database.

When you use View Administrator to perform backups, the Connection Server backs up the View LDAP configuration data and the View Composer database. Both sets of backup files will be stored in the same location. The LDAP data is exported in **LDAP data interchange format (LDIF)**.

If you have multiple View Connection Server(s) in a replicated group, you only need to export data from one of the instances. All replicated instances contain the same configuration data. It is a *not* good practice to rely on replicated instances of View Connection Server as your backup mechanism. When the Connection Server synchronizes data across the instances of Connection Server, any data lost on one instance might be lost in all the members of the group. If the View Connection Server uses multiple vCenter Server instances and multiple View Composer services, then the View Connection Server will back up all the View Composer databases associated with the vCenter Server instances.

View Connection Server backups are configured from the VMware View Admin console. The backups dump the configuration files and the database information to a location on the View Connection Server. Then, the data must be backed up through normal mechanisms, like a backup agent and scheduled job. The procedure for a View Connection Server backup is as follows:

1. Schedule VMware View backup runs and exports to `C:\View_Backup\`.

2. Use your third-party backup solution on the View Connection Server and have it back up the `System State`, `Program Files`, and `C:\View_Backup\` folders that were created in step 1.

From within the View Admin console, there are three primary options that must be configured to back up the View Connection Server settings:

- **Automatic backup frequency**: This is the frequency at which backups are automatically taken. The recommendation is as follows:
  - ○ **Recommendation (every day)**: As most server backups are performed daily, if the automatic View Connection Server backup is taken before the full backup of the Windows server, it will be included in the nightly backup. This is adjusted as necessary.

- **Backup time**: This displays the time based on the automatic backup frequency. (Every day produces the 12 midnight time.)

- **Maximum number of backups**: This is the maximum number of backups that can be stored on the View Connection Server; once the maximum number has been reached, backups will be rotated out based on age, with the oldest backup being replaced by the newest backup. The recommendation is as follows:
  - ○ **Recommendation — 30 days**: This will ensure that approximately one month of backups are retained on the server. This is adjusted as necessary.

- **Folder location**: This is the location on the View Connection Server, where the backups will be stored. Ensure that the third-party backup solution is backing up this location.

The following screenshot shows the **Backup** tab:

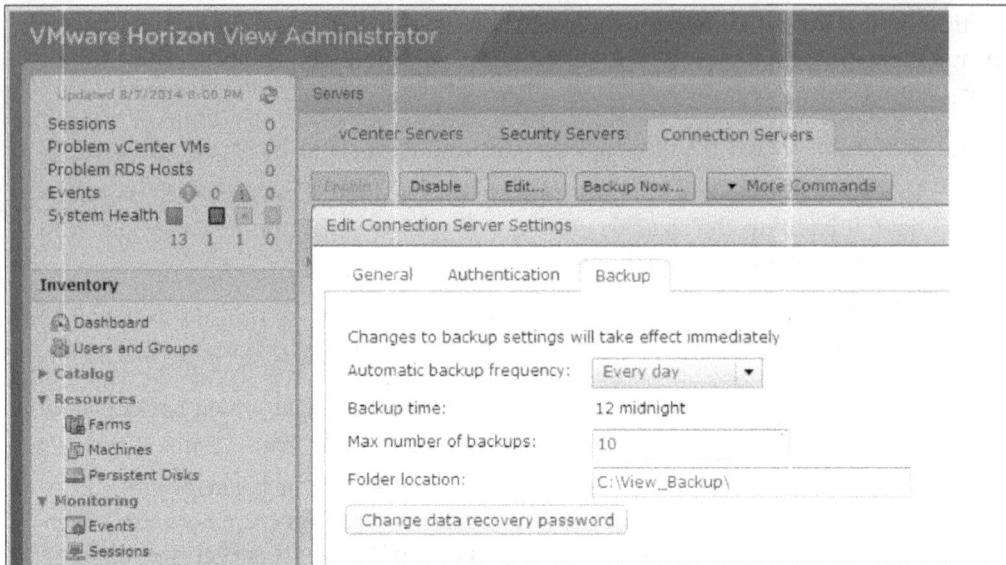

Performing a manual backup of the View database

Use the following steps to perform a manual backup of your View database:

1. Log in to the **View Administrator** console.
2. Expand the **Catalog** option under **Inventory** (on the left-hand side of the console).
3. Select the first pool and right-click on it.

4. Select **Disable Provisioning**, as shown in the following screenshot:

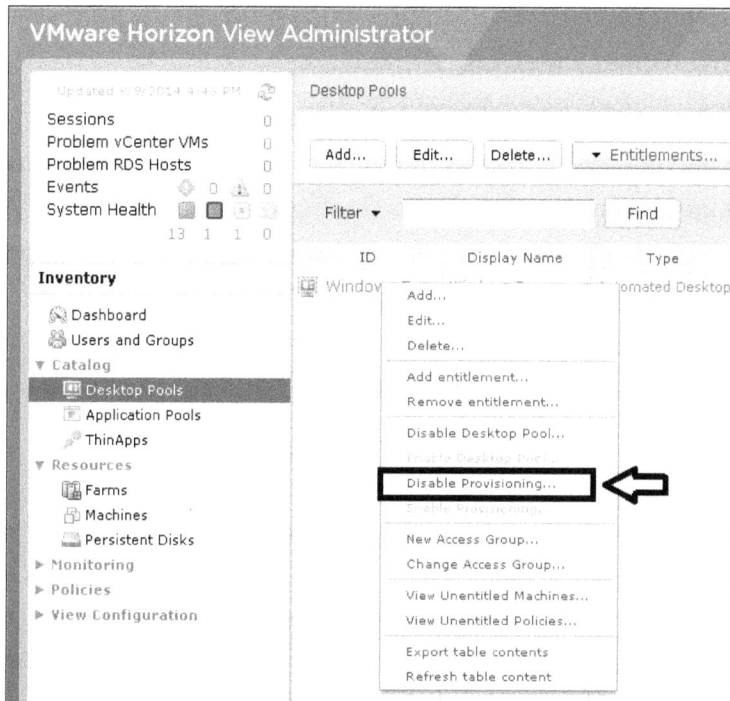

5. Continue to disable provisioning for each of the pools. This will assure that no new information will be added to the ADAM database.

After you disable provisioning for all the pools, there are two ways to perform the backup:

*   The View Administrator console
*   Running a command using the command prompt

The View Administrator console

Follow these steps to perform a backup:

1. Log in to the **View Administrator** console.

2. Expand **View Configuration** found under **Inventory**.

3. Select **Servers**, which displays all the servers found in your environment.

4. Select the **Connection Servers** tab.

5. Right-click on one of the Connection Servers and choose **Backup Now**, as shown in the following screenshot:

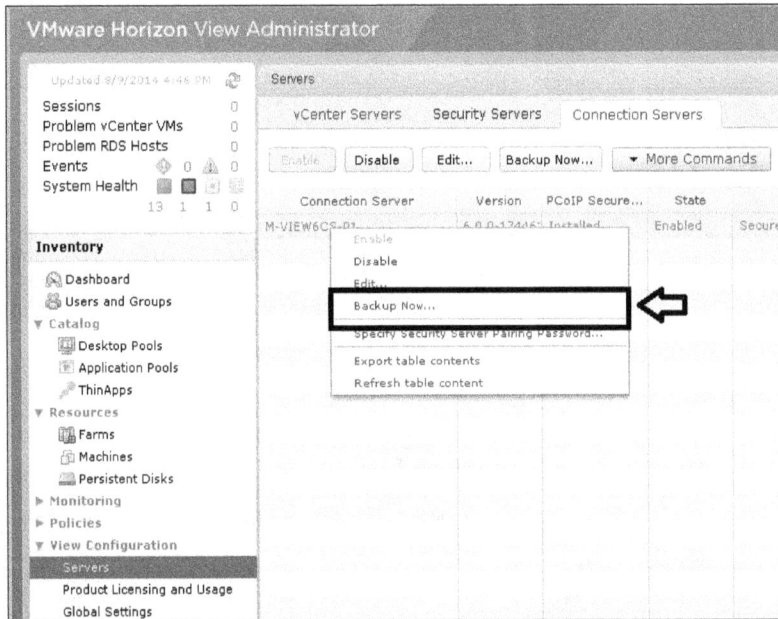

6. After the backup process is complete, enable provisioning to the pools.

Using the command prompt

You can export the ADAM database by executing a built-in export tool in the command prompt. Perform the following steps:

1. Connect directly to the View Connection Server with a remote desktop utility such as RDP.

2. Open a command prompt and use the cd command to navigate to `C:\Program Files\VMware\VMware View\Server\tools\bin\`.

3. Execute the `vdmexport.exe` command and use the `-f` option to specify a location and filename, as shown in the following screenshot (for this example, `C:\View_Backup` is the location and `vdmBackup.ldf` is the filename):

Once a backup has been either automatically run or manually executed, there will be two types of files saved in the backup location:

- **LDF files**: These are the LDIF exports from the VMware View Connection Server ADAM database and store the configuration settings of the VMware View environment
- **SVI files**: These are the backups of the VMware View Composer database

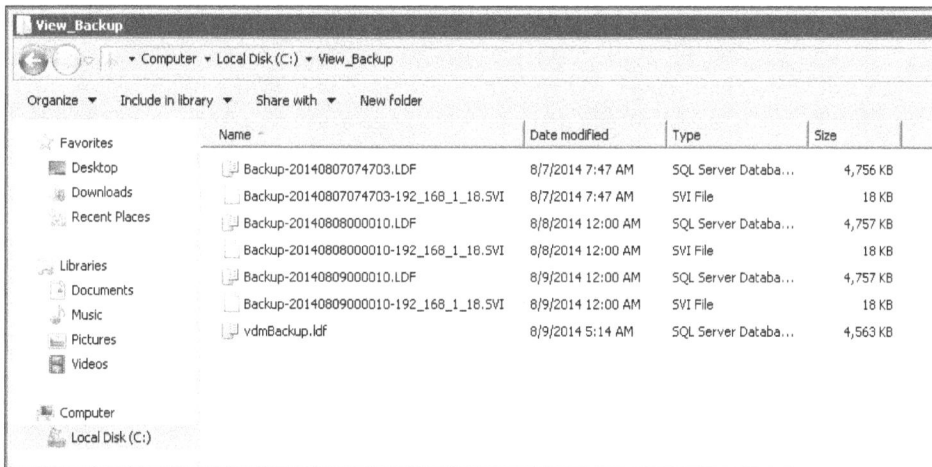

The backup process of the View Connection Server is fairly straightforward. While the process is easy, it should not be overlooked.

Security Server considerations

Surprisingly, there is no option to back up the VMware View Security Server via the VMware View Admin console. For View Connection Servers, backup is configured by selecting the server, selecting **Edit**, and then clicking on **Backup**. Highlighting the View Security Server provides no such functionality.

Instead, the security server should be backed up via normal third-party mechanisms. The installation directory is of primary concern, which is `C:\Program Files\VMware\VMware View\Server` by default.

The `.config` file is in the `...\sslgateway\conf` directory, and it includes the following settings:

- `pcoipClientIPAddress`: This is the public address used by the Security Server
- `pcoipClientUDPPort`: This is the port used for UDP traffic (the default is `4172`)

In addition, the `settings` file is located in this directory, which includes settings such as the following:

- `maxConnections`: This is the maximum number of concurrent connections the View Security Server can have at one time (the default is `2000`)
- `serverID`: This is the hostname used by the security server

In addition, custom certificates and logfiles are stored within the installation directory of the VMware View Security Server. Therefore, it is important to back up the data regularly if the logfile data is to be maintained (and is not being ingested into a larger enterprise logfile solution).

The View Composer database

The View Composer database used for linked clones is backed up using the following steps:

1. Log in to the **View Administrator** console.
2. Expand the **Catalog** option under **Inventory** (left-hand side of the console).
3. Select the first pool and right-click on it.
4. Select **Disable Provisioning**.
5. Connect directly to the server where the View Composer was installed, using a remote desktop utility such as RDP.

6. Stop the **View Composer** service, as shown in the following screenshot. This will prevent provisioning request that would change the composer database.

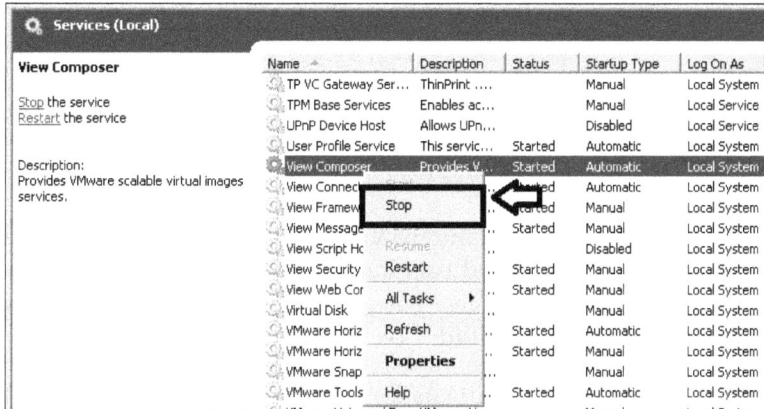

7. After the service is stopped, use the standard practice for backed up databases in the current environment. Restart the Composer service after the backup completes.

Remote Desktop Service host servers

VMware View 6 uses virtual machines to deliver hosted applications and desktops. In some cases, tuning and optimization, or other customer specific configurations to the environment or applications may be built on the **Remote Desktop Service (RDS)** host. Use the Windows Server Backup tool or the current backup software deployed in your environment.

RDS Server host templates and virtual machines

The virtual machine templates and virtual machines are an important part of the Horizon View infrastructure and need protection in the event that the system needs to be recovered.

Back up the RDS host templates when changes are made and the testing/validation is completed. The production RDS host machines should be backed up if they contains user data or any other elements that require protection at frequent intervals. Third-party backup solutions are used in this case.

Virtual desktop templates and parent VMs

Horizon View uses virtual machine templates to create the desktops in pools for full virtual machines and uses parent VMs to create the desktops in a linked clone desktop pool. These virtual machine templates and the parent VMs are another important part of the View infrastructure that needs protection. These backups are a crucial part of being able to quickly restore the desktop pools and the RDS hosts in the event of data loss.

While frequent changes occur for standard virtual machines, the virtual machine templates and parent VMs only need backing up after new changes have been made to the template and parent VM images. These backups should be readily available for rapid redeployment when required.

For environments that use full cloning as the provisioning technique for the vDesktops, the gold template should be backed up regularly. The gold template is the master vDesktop that all other vDesktops are cloned from. The VMware KB article, *Backing up and restoring virtual machine templates using VMware APIs*, covers the steps to both back up and restore a template. In short, most backup solutions will require that the gold template is converted from a template to a regular virtual machine and it can then be backed up. You can find more information at `http://kb.vmware.com/selfservice/microsites/search.do?language=en_US&cmd=displayKC&externalId=2009395`.

Backing up the parent VM can be tricky as it is a virtual machine, often with many different point-in-time snapshots. The most common technique is to collapse the virtual machine snapshot tree at a given point-in-time snapshot, and then back up or copy the newly created virtual machine to a second datastore. By storing the parent VM on a redundant storage solution, it is quite unlikely that the parent VM will be lost. What's more likely is that a point-in-time snapshot of the parent VM may be created while it's in a nonfunctional or less-than-ideal state.

Virtual desktops

There are three types of virtual desktops in a Horizon View environment, which are as follows:

- Linked clone desktops
- Stateful desktops
- Stateless desktops

Linked clone desktops

Virtual desktops that are created by View Composer using the linked clone technology present special challenges with backup and restoration. In many cases, a linked clone desktop will also be considered as a stateless desktop. The dynamic nature of a linked clone desktop and the underlying structure of the virtual machine itself means the linked clone desktops are *not* a good candidate for backup and restoration. However, the same qualities that impede the use of a standard backup solution provide an advantage for rapid reprovisioning of virtual desktops. When the underlying infrastructure for things such as the delivery of applications and user data, along with the parent VMs, are restored, then linked clone desktop pools can be recreated and made available within a short amount of time, and therefore lessening the impact of an outage or data loss.

Stateful desktops

In the stateful desktop pool scenario, all of the virtual desktops retain user data when the user logs back in to the virtual desktop. So, in this case, backing up the virtual machines with third-party tools like any other virtual machine in vSphere is considered the optimal method for protection and recovery.

Stateless desktops

With the stateless desktop architecture, the virtual desktops do not retain the desktop state when the user logs back in to the virtual desktop. The nature of the stateless desktops does not require and nor do they directly contain any data that requires a backup. All the user data in a stateless desktop is stored on a file share. The user data includes any files the user creates, changes, or copies within the virtual infrastructure, along with the user persona data. Therefore, because no user data is stored within the virtual desktop, there will be no need to back up the desktop. File shares should be included in the standard backup strategy and all user data and persona information will be included in the existing daily backups.

The ThinApp repository

The **ThinApp** repository is similar in nature to the user data on the stateless desktops in that it should reside on a redundant file share that is backed up regularly. If the ThinApp packages are configured to preserve each user's sandbox, the ThinApp repository should likely be backed up nightly.

Persona Management

With the View Persona Management feature, the user's remote profile is dynamically downloaded after the user logs in to a virtual desktop. The secure, centralized repository can be configured in which Horizon View will store user profiles. The standard practice is to back up network shares on which View Persona Management stores the profile repository.

View Persona Management will ensure that user profiles are backed up to the remote profile share, eliminating the need for additional tools to back up user data on the desktops. Therefore, backup software to protect the user profile on the View desktop is unnecessary.

VMware vCenter

Most established IT departments are using backup tools from the storage or backup vendor to protect the datastores where the VM's are stored. This will make the recovery of the base vSphere environment faster and easier. The central piece of vCenter is the vCenter database. If there is a total loss of database you will lose all your configuration information of vSphere, including the configuration specific to View (for examples, users, folders, and many more). Another important item to understand is that even if you rebuild your vCenter using the same folder and resource pool names, your View environment will not reconnect and use the new vCenter. The reason is that each object in vSphere has what is called a **Managed object Reference** (**MoRef**) and they are stored in the vSphere database. View uses the MoRef information to talk to vCenter. As View and vSphere rely on each other, making a backup of your View environment without backing up your vSphere environment doesn't make sense.

Restoring the VMware View environment

If your environment has multiple Connection Servers, the best thing to do would be delete all the servers but one, and then use the following steps to restore the ADAM database:

1. Connect directly to the server where the View Connection Server is located using a remote desktop utility such as RDP.

2. Stop the **View Connection** service, as shown in the following screenshot:

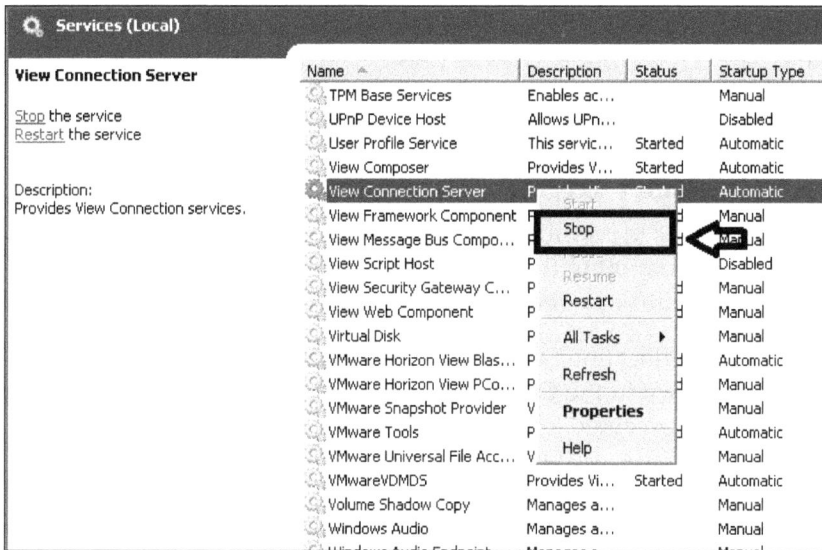

3. Locate the backup (or exported) ADAM database file that has the `.ldf` extension.

4. The first step of the import is to decrypt the file by opening a command prompt and use the `cd` command to navigate to `C:\Program Files\VMware\ VMware View\Server\tools\bin\`.

5. Use the following command:

```
vdmimport -f \View_Backup\vdmBackup.ldf -d >\View_Backup\
vmdDecrypt.ldf
```

6. You will be prompted to enter the password from the account you used to create the backup file.

7. Now use the `vdmimport -f [decrypted file name]` command (from the preceding example, the filename will be `vmdDecrypt.ldf`).

8. After the ADAM database is updated, you can restart the View Connection Server service.

9. Replace the delete Connection Servers by running the **Connection Server** installation and using the **Replica** option.

To reinstall the View Composer database, you can connect to the server where Composer is installed. Stop the **View Composer** service and use your standard procedure for restoring a database. After the restore, start the **View Composer** service.

While this provides the steps to restore the main components of the Connection server, the steps to perform a complete View Connection Server restore can be found in the VMware KB article, *Performing an end-to-end backup and restore for VMware View Manager*, at http://kb.vmware.com/selfservice/microsites/search.do?cmd=d isplayKC&docType=kc&externalId=1008046.

Reconciliation after recovery

One of the main factors to consider when performing a restore in a Horizon View infrastructure is the possibility that the Connection Server environment could be out of sync with the current View state and a reconciliation is required.

After restoring the Connection Server ADAM database, there may be missing desktops that are shown in the Connection Server Admin user interface if the following actions are executed after the backup but before a restore:

- The administrator deleted pools or desktops
- The desktop pool was recomposed, which resulted in the removal of the unassigned desktops

Missing desktops or pools can be manually removed from the Connection Server Admin UI.

Some of the automated desktops may become disassociated with their pools due to the creation of a pool between the time of the backup and the restore time. View administrators may be able to make them usable by cloning the linked clone desktop to a full clone desktop using vCenter Server. They would be created as an individual desktop in the Connection Server and then assign those desktops to a specific user.

Business Continuity and Disaster Recovery

It's important to ensure that the virtual desktops along with the application delivery infrastructure is included and prioritized as a Business Continuity and Disaster Recovery plan. Also, it's important to ensure that the recovery procedures are tested and validated on a regular cycle, as well as having the procedures and mechanisms in place that ensure critical data (images, software media, data backup, and so on) is always stored and ready in an alternate location. This will ensure an efficient and timely recovery.

It would be ideal to have a disaster recovery plan and business continuity plan that recovers the essential services to an alternate "standby" data center. This will allow the data to be backed up and available offsite to the alternate facility for an additional measure of protection. The alternate data center could have "hot" standby capacity for the virtual desktops and application delivery infrastructure. This site would then address 50 percent capacity in the event of a disaster and also 50 percent additional capacity in the event of a business continuity event that prevents users from accessing the main facility. The additional capacity will also provide a rollback option if there were failed updates to the main data center.

Operational procedures should ensure the desktop and server images are available to the alternate facility when changes are made to the main VMware View system. Desktop and application pools should also be updated in the alternate data center whenever maintenance procedures are executed and validated in the main data center.

Summary

As expected, it is important to back up the fundamental components of a VMware View solution. While a resilient design should mitigate most types of failure, there are still occasions when a backup may be needed to bring an environment back up to an operational level. This chapter covered the major components of View and provided some of the basic options for creating backups of those components. The Connection Server and Composer database along with vCenter were explained. There was a good overview of the options used to protect the different types of virtual desktops. The ThinApp repository and Persona Management was also explained. The chapter also covered the basic recovery options and where to find information on the complete View recovery procedures.

The next chapter will cover many of the new and exciting features found in Horizon View 6. It will cover new solutions that allow you to extend your View solution to multiple data centers and explains the all new application-and desktop-hosting options.

12
Exciting New Features in Horizon View 6

So far, we have covered the core features of Horizon View 6 and discussed the basic setup and typical settings to get you started on proving a VDI solution. There are several new features in View 6 that were not covered in the previous chapters. This chapter will provide information and, in some cases, basic setup help about those features.

This chapter will cover the following new features:

- Cloud Pod Architecture
- Application publishing
- Unified workspace
- Integration with virtual SAN technology
- Other features

Cloud Pod Architecture

This is an introduction to the brand new capability of VMware Horizon 6, **Cloud Pod Architecture**.

Horizon Cloud Pod Architecture's main features are not only high availability, but the ability to scale-out virtual desktops that are provided by View 6. Now, the virtual desktops can be deployed across multiple data centers or sites and then managed globally through a single administration console. Cloud Pod Architecture will create the foundation for deploying virtual desktops from different locations (including global locations), along with the benefit of centralizing the operations and management of that View infrastructure.

Cloud Pod Architecture will allow end users access to their vDesktops from anywhere in the world and by using the nearest data center location it will ensure the best end user experience. Now everyone, from the end users to vDesktop administrators, will benefit from this new architecture. The new capability will allow vDesktop administrators to:

- Balance the workloads across multiple sites
- Manage vDesktops spread out across the multiple locations from a single location
- Provide the virtual desktop with a disaster recovery solution
- Incrementally scale any View deployments that are currently deployed

As an example, consider Cloud Pod Architecture installed with four cloud pods and each cloud pod is placed in a different data center. The underlying Horizon View infrastructure design will consist of the essential View computing components, which includes the VDI infrastructure along with the virtual desktops. This allows users to connect to a virtual desktop from any of the deployed cloud pods regardless of where they are. This also allows the desktop administrators to manage the entire virtual desktop environment from a single entitlement layer. The solution helps achieve benefits such as effective resource utilization, disaster recovery, and support for a solution that incorporates a roaming desktop/home solution. This also gives users the mobility they want, but it simplifies the management for all the data centers for the vDesktop administrators.

Another key feature of the Cloud Pod Architecture is the ability to provide high availability and scaled-out virtual desktops in Horizon View 6. Virtual desktops that are provided by View can be deployed using a block and pod architecture. Review the *View Building Blocks* and *View Pods* sections found in the *View Architecture Planning Guide* and the *Administering View Cloud Pod Architecture* manual found at `https://www.vmware.com/support/pubs/view_pubs.html`.

Prior to this View 6 release, a single View pod could have up to five View blocks and scale up to 10,000 desktops, which were all deployed in a single data center. If the need was to go beyond 10,000 desktops, then multiple View pods would need to be deployed. The issue with this solution is each one of the View pods would need to be managed separately and each independent entity has a set of user entitlements.

With the new Cloud Pod Architecture in Horizon 6, the multiple View pods can be combined in the same or different data centers and this allows for an entitled desktop from any location.

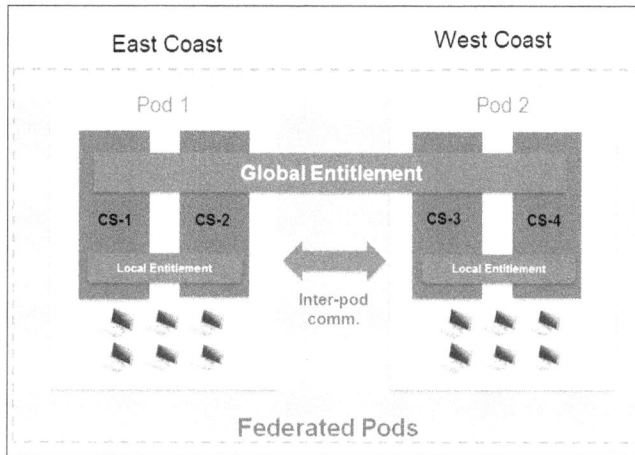

The preceding figure shows the two View pods (**Pod 1** and **Pod 2**). Pod 1 is located in a datacenter on the east coast and Pod 2 is located in a datacenter on the west coast. Each pod has two connection servers that are named **CS-1** and **CS-2** in Pod 1, and **CS-3** and **CS-4** in Pod 2. Pod 1 and Pod 2 each maintain their entitlements for the users and provide the association of a user to a virtual desktop in each of their respective pods.

With the new architecture provided by Horizon View 6, the following new elements are provided:

- The first is the global entitlement layer that spans the multiple pods. This is shown as the single component spanning Pod 1 and Pod 2 in the preceding figure
- The second item to observe is an interpod communication layer, shown with bidirectional arrows between the pods

This new configuration also provides three major benefits:

- It supports an active-active deployment; in the case of multiple datacenters, the components are managed efficiently. The end users are entitled to desktops in one or, if necessary, multiple data centers.
- Multiple pods are consolidated within a single datacenter. The multiple desktop pods in the same datacenter can also be consolidated and managed centrally through the global entitlement layer.
- Disaster recovery is possible. The global entitlement layer can assign a user a desktop in both Pod 1 and Pod 2. In the event that Pod 1 becomes unavailable, the user would have access to a desktop in the second pod. Note that this is feasible only if desktops in Pod 1 and Pod 2 are being synchronized using a data replication solution.

View pods are also used to connect users to desktops in different data centers. Connecting the desktop to a user who logs in from anywhere would involve the following steps:

1. The user inputs the IP address or URL associated with their View environment, which would provide the address of a Connection Server (or a load balancer), and then enters their credentials.

2. The Connection Server verifies both the local and the global entitlements for the approved user.

3. The Connection Server then collects the current desktop state information using the interpod protocol and presents to the user a list of entitled desktops.

4. The user then selects the desired desktop.

5. If the desktop is remote, the Connection Server uses using the interpod protocol to launch the remote desktop.

6. The remote desktop is connected to the user directly or through a local tunnel.

Three use cases for this desktop access solution are:

- **A global roaming desktop**: When the end user needs to connect to a desktop only for the purpose of using their Windows-based applications

- **A global home desktop**: This is the typical case and it is where the same persistent desktop is given to the end user

- **Local scale desktop**: In this use case, there are multiple pods at each site and each offer a standard nonpersistent desktop pool

Global entitlement

Global entitlement controls the mapping of users to desktops in the Cloud Pod Architecture. This entitlement layer consists of the parameters shown in the following screenshot:

```
Name:      My Global Pool
Members:  user1, user2, group1
Desktops:Pod1:Pool1
          Pod2:Pool2
          Pod2:Pool3
Scope:     All
FromHome:True
```

The following is the review of the parameters of the global entitlement:

- **Name**: This is the name of the global entitlement.
- **Members**: These are the users and/or the groups that share the global entitlement.
- **Desktops**: These are the desktops the members of the global entitlement are entitled to.
- **Scope**: This controls the scope of the search after placing a new desktop session. This allows the administrator to control the cross-datacenter traffic.
- **FromHome (True/False)**: This controls where the search for the desktop starts. When set to false, it would start from the current pod and when it's true, the search would start from the home site of the user.

The scope parameter can be any one of the following:

- **Local**: This looks only in the local pod for the available desktops
- **Site**: This looks in all pods in the local site (same data center)
- **All**: This looks across all the pods for an available desktop to service the user request

Scale limits and maximums

The Cloud Pod Architecture was developed to scale View desktop deployments to hundreds of data centers along with tens of thousands of desktops. The first release of this solution has focused on the following scale-out parameters:

- Number of pods: 4
- Number of sites: 2
- Number of desktops: 20,000

Architectural assumptions

The following are the architectural assumptions needed to deliver the solution:

- Deployment can have both persistent and nonpersistent desktops
- All pods are accessible to each other across the corporate network
- A third-party load balancer provides the single-URL capability
- Replication of desktops and/or end user data is achieved by a third-party data replication solution
- The WAN links between datacenters have good latency features

Overview for the setup of Cloud Pod Architecture

The setup of Cloud Pod Architecture broadly consists of the following steps:

1. Add the first Connection Server and View desktop pools.
2. Add the second Connection Server and View desktop pools from a different location or data center. This Connection Server does not need to be identical in configuration to the first Connection Server.
3. Set up both the sites.
4. Initialize the first site *only*.
5. All other sites are joined to the first site.
6. Set up the pods and add the pods to sites.
7. Set up the global pools and add the Connection Servers to the global pools.
8. Entitle users to the global pools.

Here are few important points to note for the preceding procedure:

- Configurations are done using the command line from the Connection Servers
- Use the `LMVUTIL.CMD` file located in the `C:\Program Files\VMware\VMware View\Server\tools\bin\` folder
- Command-line switches are case sensitive

Setting up Cloud Pod Architecture

There needs to be two Connection Servers with desktop pools to set up the architecture. In this section, we will break down the steps needed for the setup.

Step 1 – The first pod and Connection Server

The first step is to initialize the View Connection Server in the primary pod. This will make the primary pod a master.

On Horizon View Connection Server 1, run the `lmvutil --authAs [username] --authDomain [domainname] --authPassword "*" --initialize` command.

Here are a few points to note for the preceding command:

- This command turns on the ability to run federated pods

- This command must be executed once on the primary pod

- This command can be executed on any of the Connection Servers in the primary pod

- This command will automatically configure LDAP across the Connection Servers

- This command must not be executed on any other connection server in the primary or secondary pods

- The global LDAP listener uses port 22389

The following screenshot shows the output:

Step 2 – Joining the second pod to the first pod

You need to join subsequent pods to the first pod so that they can synchronize. This is done from a secondary site connection server command line from the same folder as the primary connection server.

Execute the `lmvutil --authAs [username] --authDomain [AD.domain] --authPassword "*" --join --joinServer [primary_connection_server] --userName domain\username --password [password]` command on the second View Connection Server.

Here are a few points to note for the preceding command:

- The first set of credentials authenticate to the primary connection server for synchronization and the second set authenticates the local (secondary) connection server to execute the command

- This is one of the only commands that must be executed from a secondary connection server

The following screenshot shows the output:

```
Command Prompt                                                                    _ □ X
C:\Program Files\VMware\VMware View\Server\tools\bin>lmvutil --authAs chuck --authDomain kingbr
ook.net --authPassword "*" --join --joinServer 192.168.1.18 --userName kingbrook\chuck --passwo
rd ABC123_
Enter password for kingbrook.net\chuck (authPassword):
Please wait until the requested task is completed. This may take several minutes.
Task is RUNNING (0%), waiting for completion...
Task is RUNNING (0%), waiting for completion...
Task is RUNNING (0%), waiting for completion...
Task is RUNNING (0%), waiting for completion...
Task is RUNNING (0%), waiting for completion...
Task is RUNNING (0%), waiting for completion...
Task is RUNNING (40%), waiting for completion...
Task is RUNNING (40%), waiting for completion...
Task is RUNNING (40%), waiting for completion...
Task is RUNNING (40%), waiting for completion...
Task is RUNNING (40%), waiting for completion...
Task is RUNNING (40%), waiting for completion...
Task is RUNNING (40%), waiting for completion...
Task is RUNNING (40%), waiting for completion...
Task is RUNNING (50%), waiting for completion...
Task is RUNNING (80%), waiting for completion...
Task is RUNNING (90%), waiting for completion...
Task is RUNNING (90%), waiting for completion...
Task is RUNNING (90%), waiting for completion...
Task is RUNNING (95%), waiting for completion...
Task is RUNNING (95%), waiting for completion...
Task is completed with result: SUCCESS

C:\Program Files\VMware\VMware View\Server\tools\bin>_
```

Step 3 – Validating the initial pod and Connection Server settings

You can validate the initial pod settings on the primary Connection Server to ensure the `join` command you completed in the previous step from the secondary Connection Server worked properly.

Execute the `lmvutil --authAs [username] --authDomain [domain] --authPassword "*" --listPods` command on the first Connection Server.

Here are a few points to note for the preceding command:

- This displays a list of the pods that the primary site is aware of
- The information is in the primary site at this point

The following screenshot shows the output:

```
Command Prompt                                                                    _ □ X
C:\Program Files\VMware\VMware View\Server\tools\bin>lmvutil --authAs chuck --authDomain kingbr
ook.net --authPassword "*" --listPods
Enter password for kingbrook.net\chuck (authPassword):
Pod: Cluster-M-VIEW6CS-01 [local]
    Description: null
    Owning site: Default First Site
Pod: Cluster-M-VIEW6CS-02 [remote]
    Description: null
    Owning site: Default First Site

C:\Program Files\VMware\VMware View\Server\tools\bin>_
```

Step 4 – Creating the first site

The next step is to organize the environment into multiple sites. You create the first site from the first Connection Server.

Execute the `lmvutil --authAs [username] --authDomain [domain] --authPassword "*" --createSite --siteName [sitename]` command on the primary Connection Server.

Here are a few points to note for the preceding command:

- The site is just a logical grouping of pods
- There is no response to the command

The following screenshot shows the output:

Step 5 – Creating the second site

You then create the second site, also from the first Connection Server by executing the `lmvutil --authAs [username] --authDomain [domain] --authPassword "*" --createSite --siteName [secondsitename]` command.

The following is a comment for the preceding command:

- No response is displayed to the command

The following screenshot shows the output:

Step 6 – Validating both sites

Run the `lmvutil --authAs [username] --authDomain [domain]`
`--authPassword "*" --listSites` command on the first View Connection Server
to verify that both sites have been created and everything was typed correctly. It is
important to make sure both sites have been created properly.

Here are a few points to note for the preceding command:

- The Connection Servers are displayed in the **Default First Site** field
- No Connection Servers are displayed in either of the defined sites

The following screenshot shows the output:

```
Command Prompt

C:\Program Files\VMware\VMware View\Server\tools\bin>lmvutil --authAs chuck --authDomain kingbr
ook.net --authPassword "*" --listSites
Enter password for kingbrook.net\chuck (authPassword):
Site: Default First Site
   Description: null
   POD Member: Cluster-M-VIEW6CS-01
   POD Member: Cluster-M-VIEW6CS-02
Site: KB-Site-1
   Description: null
Site: KB-Site-2
   Description: null

C:\Program Files\VMware\VMware View\Server\tools\bin>
```

Step 7 – Adding the first pod to the first site

Now move the first pod into the first site you created by executing the `lmvutil`
`--authAs [username] --authDomain [domain]   --authPassword "*"`
`--assignPodToSite -podName [podname] –siteName [target site name]`
command on the first Connection Server.

Here are a few points to note for the preceding command:

- The default name of the pod is `Cluster-[first connection sever you`
  `created the pod from]`
- No response is displayed to the command

The following screenshot shows the output:

```
Command Prompt

C:\Program Files\VMware\VMware View\Server\tools\bin>lmvutil --authAs chuck --authDomain kingbr
ook.net --authPassword "*" --assignPodToSite --podName cluster-m-view6cs-01 --siteName KB-Site-
1
Enter password for kingbrook.net\chuck (authPassword):
C:\Program Files\VMware\VMware View\Server\tools\bin>
```

Step 8 – Adding the second pod to the second site

Execute the `lmvutil --authAs [username] --authDomain [domain] --authPassword "*" --assignPodToSite -podName [second podname] -siteName [second site name]` command on the first Connection Server to move the second pod to the second site.

Here are a few points to note for the preceding command:

- The default name of the pod is `Cluster-[second connection sever you created the pod from]`
- No response is displayed to the command

The following screenshot shows the output:

```
C:\Program Files\VMware\VMware View\Server\tools\bin>lmvutil --authAs chuck --authDomain kingbr
ook.net --authPassword "*" --assignPodToSite --podName cluster-m-view6cs-02 --siteName KB-Site-
2
Enter password for kingbrook.net\chuck (authPassword):

C:\Program Files\VMware\VMware View\Server\tools\bin>
```

Step 9 – Validating pods in the sites

Validated pods have been successfully moved to their respective sites by executing the `lmvutil --authAs [username] --authDomain [domain] --authPassword "*" --listSites` command on the first Connection Server.

Here are a few points to note for the preceding command:

- The first Connection Server should display on the first site
- The second (and additional) Connection Servers should show in their respective sites

The following screenshot shows the output:

```
C:\Program Files\VMware\VMware View\Server\tools\bin>lmvutil --authAs chuck --authDomain kingbr
ook.net --authPassword "*" --listSites
Enter password for kingbrook.net\chuck (authPassword):
Site: Default First Site
   Description: null
Site: KB-Site-1
   Description: null
   POD Member: Cluster-M-VIEW6CS-01
Site: KB-Site-2
   Description: null
   POD Member: Cluster-M-VIEW6CS-02

C:\Program Files\VMware\VMware View\Server\tools\bin>
```

Step 10 – Creating a global pool for the local desktop pools

Create the global entitlement (global pool) for the local desktop pool. This will be the global pool that associates all local desktop pools.

Execute the `lmvutil --authAs [username] --authDomain [domain] --authPassword "*" --createGlobalEntitlement --entitlementName [Parent Pool Name] --scope [scope] ANY --isFloating` or `--isDedicated` command on the first Connection Server.

Here are a few points to note for the preceding command:

- Scope parameters can be `ANY` or `[specific site] LOCAL`
- The pool type can be (one or the other):
  - Floating: `-isFloating`
  - Dedicated: `-isDedicated`
- `GlobalEntitlement` creates the global pool that contains local pools from each site
- No response is displayed to the command

The following screenshot shows the output:

```
Command Prompt                                                           _□X
C:\Program Files\VMware\VMware View\Server\tools\bin>lmvutil --authAs chuck --authDomain kingbr
ook.net --authPassword "*" --createGlobalEntitlement --entitlementName Windows-7 --scope ANY --
isFloating
Enter password for kingbrook.net\chuck (authPassword):

C:\Program Files\VMware\VMware View\Server\tools\bin>_
```

Step 11 – Repeating step 10 for additional global desktop entitlements

Repeat the previous command for any global desktop pool entitlements. For example, you could have Windows 8 desktop pools you wish to assign global entitlements to.

Step 12 – Validating the global pools

To validate that the global pools were properly created, execute the `lmvutil --authAs [username] --authDomain [domain]  --authPassword "*" --listGlobalEntitlement` command on the first Connection Server.

Here are a few points to note for the preceding command:

- `GlobalEntitlement` will show the `SCOPE` value set to `ANY`, `LOCAL`, or the specific site defined
- Each global entitlement will display the `DEDICATED` value set to `TRUE` or `FALSE` depending on whether you defined the entitlement as `Dedicated` or `Floating`

The following screenshot shows the output:

Step 13 – Associating Local Connection Server desktop pools with global pools

The next step is to associate the local desktop pools (also referred to as child pools) on the first View Connection Server with `GlobalEntitlement` or parent pool defined in step 10.

On the first View Connection Server, run the `lmvutil --authAs [username] --authDomain [domain]  --authPassword "*" --listGlobalEntitlement --addPoolAssociation --entitlementName [Global Entitlement] --poolId [Child Pool]` command.

Here are a few points to note for the preceding command:

- The `poolId` is the Connection Server desktop pool defined with the View Administrator
- The View desktop pool IDs *do not* need to be of the same name across the Connection Servers for the global entitlements to work

- The function of this command is to associate the global pool ID with Connection Server pool ID

- The command must be executed from the Connection Server with the pool ID in question

- No response is displayed to the command

The following screenshot shows the output:

```
Command Prompt                                                                    [-][□][X]
C:\Program Files\VMware\VMware View\Server\tools\bin>lmvutil --authAs chuck --authDomain kingbr
ook.net --authPassword "*" --addPoolAssociation --entitlementName Windows-7 --poolId Windows-7
Enter password for kingbrook.net\chuck (authPassword):

C:\Program Files\VMware\VMware View\Server\tools\bin>_
```

Step 14 – Repeating step 13 for additional global desktop entitlements that were created in step 11

Repeat the previous command for all global desktop pool entitlements created in step 11.

Step 15 – Repeating step 13 for each secondary site created in step 5

Now, you must associate the mirrored local desktop pool with the local desktop pool (as defined by the View Administrator) that was associated in step 13 on the first Connection Server for the secondary site. This is done once for each additional site on the secondary connection servers joined in step 5.

Execute the lmvutil --authAs [username] --authDomain [domain] --authPassword "*" --addPoolAssociation --entitlementName [Global Entitlement] --poolId [Pool ID] command on the secondary Connection Servers.

Here are a few points to note for the preceding command:

- The poolId is the Connection Server desktop pool defined with the View Administrator

- The View Desktop pool IDs *do not* need to be of the same name across the Connection Servers for the global entitlement to work

- The function of this command is to associate the global pool ID with Connection Server pool ID

- The command must be executed from the Connection Server with the pool ID in question
- No response is displayed to the command
- This is one of few commands executed from a secondary connection server

The following screenshot shows the output:

```
Microsoft Windows [Version 6.1.7600]
Copyright (c) 2009 Microsoft Corporation.   All rights reserved.

C:\Users\chuck.KINGBROOK>cd \Program Files\VMware\VMware View\Server\tools\bin

C:\Program Files\VMware\VMware View\Server\tools\bin>lmvutil --authAs chuck --authDomain kingbr
ook.net --authPassword "*" --addPoolAssociation --entitlementName Windows-7 --poolId Win7-LC
Enter password for kingbrook.net\chuck (authPassword):

C:\Program Files\VMware\VMware View\Server\tools\bin>
```

Step 16 – Repeating step 15 once for each secondary site created in step 5

Now, you must associate the additional mirror local desktop pools with the local desktop pools.

Step 17 – Verifying global pool membership using the first Connection Server

Validate the global entitlement settings by executing the lmvutil --authAs [username] --authDomain [domain] --authPassword "*" --listAssociatedPools --entitlementName [Global entitlement] command for each global pool membership on the first Connection Server.

The following screenshot shows the output:

```
C:\Program Files\VMware\VMware View\Server\tools\bin>lmvutil --authAs chuck --authDomain kingbr
ook.net --authPassword "*" --listAssociatedPools --entitlementName Windows-7
Enter password for kingbrook.net\chuck (authPassword):
Found 1 remote associated pools.
Configured in the following pods:
    Pod  : Cluster-M-VIEW6CS-02
Local associated pool found:
    Id   : Windows-7
    Name : Windows-7
    Type : AUTOMATED

C:\Program Files\VMware\VMware View\Server\tools\bin>_
```

Here are a few points to note for the preceding command:

- The results only show remote associated pools.

- This information will shows up in the View Admin console. Click on the **System Health** window and expand the newly created **Remote Pods**, as shown in the following screenshot:

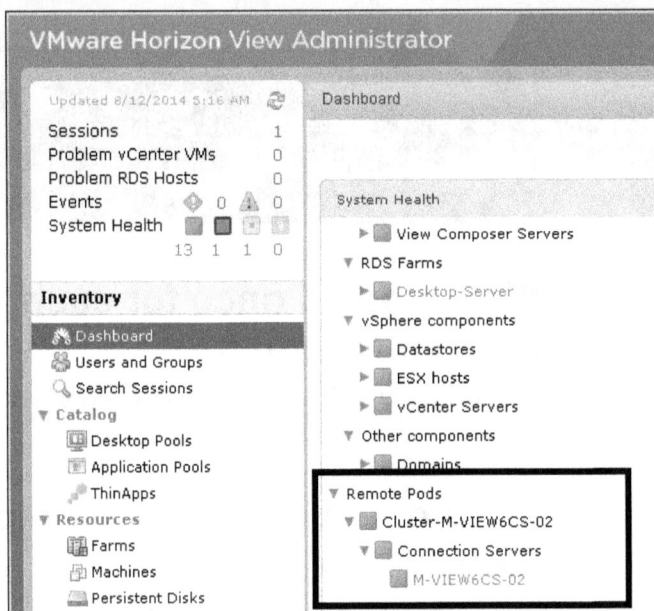

Step 18 – Repeating step 17 for the additional global pool defined in step 11

Execute the previous command for each global desktop pool entitlements created in step 11.

Step 19 – Entitling users/groups to the global pools

The final step of configuring global namespace is to entitle users. You can use an AD group or AD user. You repeat this for each group or user you want to entitle to the global pool.

Execute the `lmvutil --authAs [username] --authDomain [domain] --authPassword "*" --addGroupEntitlement --groupName "domain\group name" --entitlementName [global entitlement]` command on the first Connection Server.

Here are a few points to note for the preceding command:

- Entitlements are by AD user or group
- For user entitlement, use `-- addUserEntitlement` with `-userName` and the value `"DOMAIN\User Name"`
- For group entitlement, use `--addGroupEntitlement` with `-groupName` and a value `"DOMAIN\Group Name"`
- The values `DOMAIN\User Name` and `DOMAIN\Group Name` must be in quotes when a space exists in the value
- No response is displayed to the commands

The following screenshot shows the output:

Step 20 – Validating your Cloud Pod Architecture configurations

To validate your work, using the View Client, authenticate to the global name space or the Connection Servers directly. You should see all global and local entitled desktops, as shown in the following screenshot:

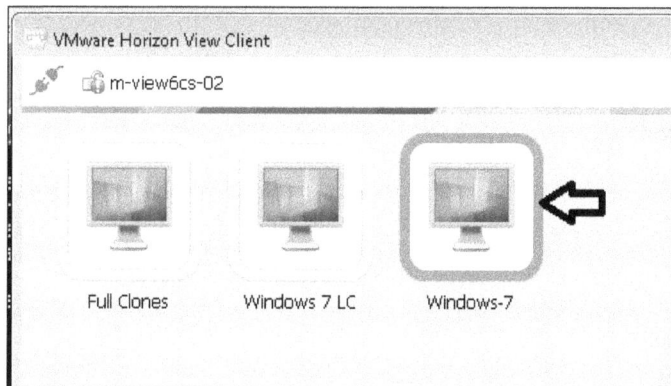

In conclusion, the Horizon Cloud Pod Architecture advances user mobility by providing desktops from any data center across any geographic location.

Application publishing

Application (Apps) publishing using RDS hosted apps allows Horizon Client access to applications along with full desktops running on Windows Remote Desktop Services hosts.

Let's take a moment and explain what this means and how it's different than a straight VDI solution. VDI delivers the entire desktop to a particular user. The desktop is an entire virtual machine with the OS and the applications. RDS uses the capabilities of Microsoft RDS (previously known as Terminal Services) and allows multiple users the ability to connect to a single OS but still allow individual desktop instances with the applications. With RDS, while you can present the full desktop, you can also just present an application without the rest of the desktop around it, as shown in the following screenshot:

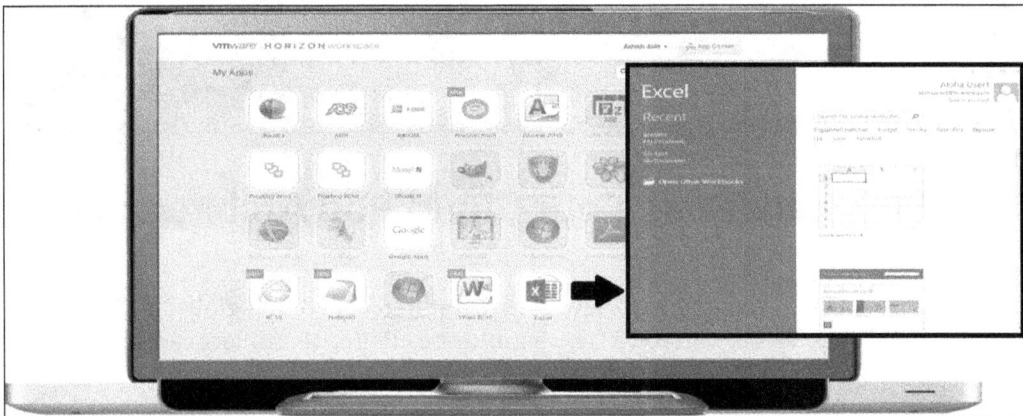

This reduces the need for multiple OS instances and also provides for better utilization of the resources. This is just as important is the reduced need for Microsoft licenses.

View 6 allows seamless access to Windows applications and desktops (see the preceding screenshot) from many types of clients, as long as they can run the Horizon View Client (Windows, Mac, IOS, Android, Linux, and Mac OS X).

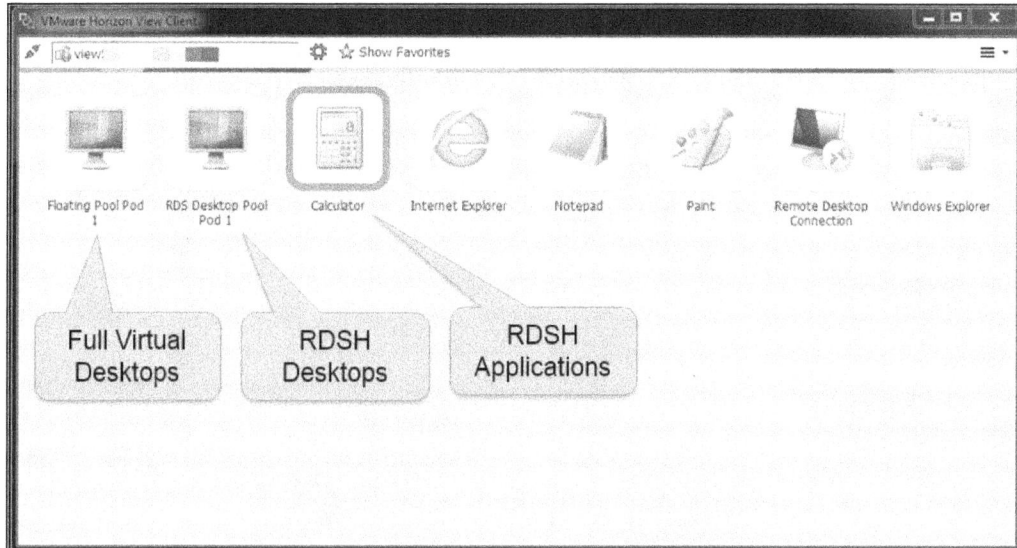

Applications are installed on Microsoft Remote Desktop Servers in the same matter as they are with Citrix XenApp. The connection uses the same PCoIP protocol that is being used to deliver a View desktop. The Horizon Client will be used to display both full virtual and RDSH desktops and the RDSH applications, as shown in the preceding screenshot. VMware uses the **Blast protocol** to allow access to desktops only, with only a HTML5 browser. This means the Horizon Client is not required.

A unified workspace

Building on the preceding solution, View 6 also has enhancements to the application catalog, known as a unified workspace. This will allow you to present not only your VDI desktops and RDSH desktops/apps, but also your **Software as a Service (SaaS)** applications, Citrix XenApp published applications, local ThinApps, Office 365, and more within a single workspace, as shown in the following screenshot:

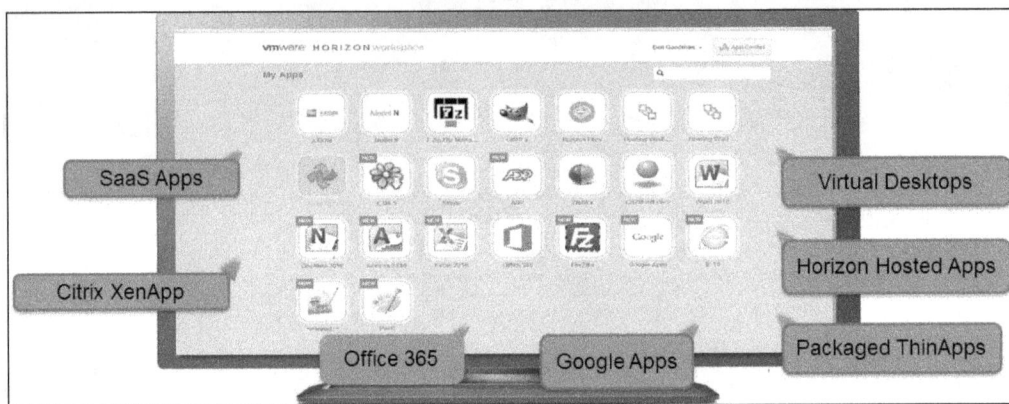

In 2012 at VMworld, VMware announced Citrix XenApp integration into Horizon Workspace and now has delivered that solution. Log on to Horizon Workspace Portal once and it will connect to the Citrix XenApp infrastructure and present published desktops and applications that you have the entitlement for.

Integrating XenApp with the Workspace Portal is relatively easy. You would deploy the Workspace Portal for Horizon 6 and then implement the Citrix Integration Broker. Next, configure the Workspace Portal to connect to the integration broker and sync the XenApp applications. When the synchronization has completed, the XenApp published applications that users are entitled to access are added to their Workspace Portal in Horizon. Finally, decommission the Citrix Web Interface. You can then launch it directly from View. This solution uses the local copy of Citrix Receiver (must be installed) to display the application. Once you are using Horizon as your application catalog, it *will* display both Citrix XenApp along with the VMware RDS applications. This provides a migration path from one to the other. You can upgrade View to enable app publishing (covered in the previous section) and pull in the same RDS hosts that are running XenApp, and then choose whether the apps are delivered through XenApp or Horizon View.

Now, the delivery of VMware ThinApps to Windows endpoints, which could include nondomain member devices using HTTP, is much easier. Microsoft Office 365 integration has been added to the Horizon Suite and this allows you to sign in once to View and then allows access to Office 365, SharePoint, and Outlook 365 Web Applications and is web-sited with a single authentication.

The new multi-forest Active Directory support has also been added. This allows for the support of directories from a single forest to multiple forests with multiple domains, which will simplify large enterprise deployments. The integration is done with a domain joined connector that is a virtual appliance.

Horizon View 6 integration with Virtual SAN

Before explaining how View works with **Virtual SAN** (VSAN), let's look at a quick overview of VSAN.

VSAN is one of the highlights of vSphere 5.5 and helps enhance VMware's future vision of their **Software-Defined Data Center** (**SDDC**) solution. VSAN is a software-based storage solution that is integrated into the ESXi hypervisor. It uses the host's local disk drives (you need both SSD and HDD) to aggregate them to appear as a cluster wide storage pool shared across all hosts. The following figure shows the VSAN solution:

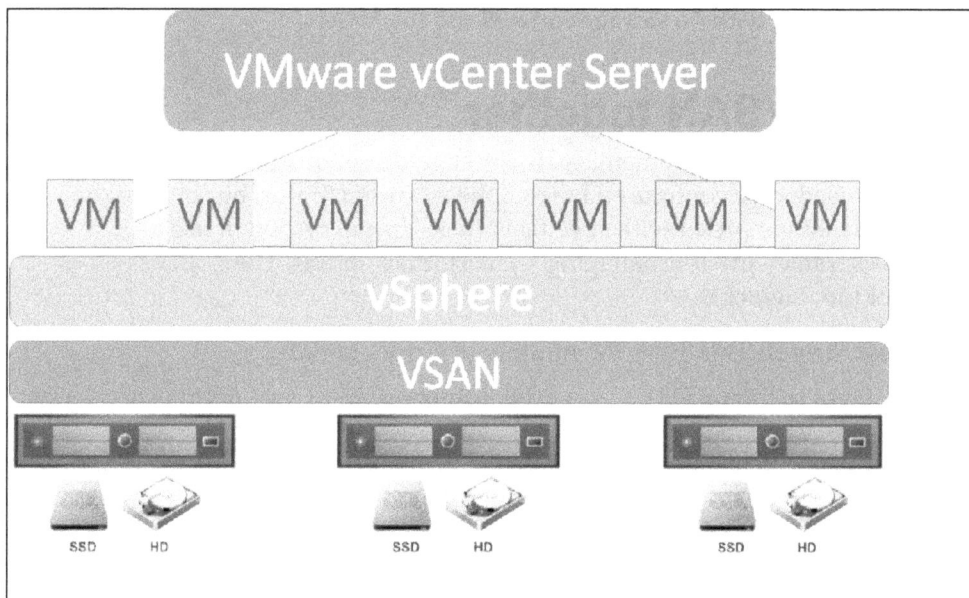

This creates a highly available and scaled-out clustered storage solution for hosting your VMs. Overall, it brings CPU, memory, and storage together which is the idea of converged infrastructure. It is a disruptive solution that is being developed and sold by other companies, such as Simplivity and Nutanix.

VSAN is integrated with vCenter and is managed through the vSphere Web Client. It works seamlessly with vSphere features such as HA, DRS, and vMotion. VSAN provides an easy setup and requires less effort to configure and manage than most traditional SAN solutions. Despite the ease of setup, it provides an enterprise performance scaling and features. Thin provisioning is available and VM snapshots, cloning, backup, and replication are supported using vSphere Replication and Site Recovery Manager.

VSAN requirements

You need a minimum of three vSphere 5.5 ESXi hosts containing local storage in order to create a VSAN solution. You can scale out to 16 hosts providing storage to the VSAN with the maximum cluster size of 32 hosts being able to use the VSAN storage.

You need at least one local hard drive (HDD) and one solid state hard drive (SSD) in each host. The SSDs are used as a read cache and write buffer while the HDDs are used for persistent storage. Not all hosts in the cluster are required to have local storage; some hosts can act as compute only nodes but you do need at least three with local storages to create a VSAN. Also, there is no requirement to have the same drive sizes. The VSAN requires each of the three hosts used to have at least 1x SSD and 1x HDD. Hosts with no storage can still use the VSAN.

View and VSAN together

Normally, in a VSAN deployment, each object gets a set of storage policies. The policies need to be configured by a vSphere administrator, but in Horizon View the policies are preset with specific values. Virtual SAN will use a policy-based framework for managing View storage objects. The policy is made up of four elements:

- **Disk stripes**: This gives the number of stripes of data
- **Failures to tolerate**: This gives the number of ESXi host failures to tolerate
- **Object spaces reservations**: Storage provisioning thick (100) or thin provisioning (0)
- **Cache reservation**: This reads cache reservation by percentage

View integrates with Virtual SAN 5.5 by automating the setup of storage policies based on the desktop pool type chosen when the pool is being created.

- **Linked clone disk profile**: A linked clone is a chain of delta disks used to track the differences between the original and the clone. Its features are as follows:
    - ° Disk stripes: 1
    - ° Failures to tolerate: 1
    - ° Object space reservation: 100
    - ° Flash read cache reservation: 0 percent

- **Replica disk profile**: A linked clone replica is created for every new desktop pool in the datastore and is based on the snapshot in use at any given desktop pool. When View storage tiering is enabled, a single replica per pool will be created. Its features are as follows:
    - ° Disk stripes: 1
    - ° Failures to tolerate: 1
    - ° Object space reservation: 0
    - ° Flash read cache reservation: 10 percent

    The profiles are different between persistent and floating pools when combined with linked clones. For floating pools, the failures to tolerate is set to 0.

    During provisioning, the replica disk object is created and does not grow afterwards. There is no need for object space reservation.

- **Persistent disk profile**: This is the renamed old user data disk and it is still possible to store the persistent disk within the Guest OS disk or in a separate disk. Its features are as follows:
    - ° Disk stripes: 1
    - ° Failures to tolerate: 1
    - ° Object space reservation: 100
    - ° Flash read cache reservation: 0 percent

How VSAN helps Horizon View

One of the major benefits of VSAN with Horizon View is the ability to create persistent virtual desktops without the need for a traditional shared array infrastructure, but continue to provide fault tolerance and top-notch performance. VSAN provides a great balance of performance and capacity. It also allows administrators to size the solution in accordance with the current workload, but change or adapt it over time.

Nonpersistent or floating virtual desktops can be deployed within VSAN and will also benefit from the highly available and resilient solution. VSAN has support for both linked and full clone deployment models. It also supports persistent and floating pool user entitlements.

If you are planning to use persona or roaming profile management solution with your nonpersistent virtual desktops, you can utilize VSAN or your traditional SAN. Administrators now have the flexibility and may choose different storage architectures for different use cases on the same View deployment.

Overall, VSAN reduces CAPEX for View deployments by leveraging the inexpensive server disks as shared storage along with avoiding the expense of specialized hardware. VSAN reduces OPEX by simplifying, and in many cases eliminating, the normal operations associated with storage configuration and provisioning activities. Yet, this powerful solution allows administrators to scale View deployments on demand by adding hosts when needed or adding disks (hot add) to existing server nodes.

Other new features

The preceding sections described some of the major features in the VMware Horizon View 6 release. There are many other features that may be just as important to you. Some of those features are:

- View Connection Server, security server, and View Composer are now supported on Windows Server 2012 R2 operating systems.
- Ability to send View logs to a Syslog server such as **VMware vCenter Log Insight**.
- Usage of the **View Agent Direct-Connection Plugin** to connect to RDS remote applications and desktops.
- Enhanced smart card authentication for View Administrator.

- Real-Time Audio-Video installs a new kernel-mode webcam driver on the View desktops and provides better compatibility with browser-based video applications and other third-party conferencing software.

- Space reclamation on virtual machines is supported for Windows 8/8.1 linked clones in a vSphere 5.5 or later environment.

- Windows 8.1 now can be used with View Persona Management. It is also supported on Windows Server 2008 R2 SP1 desktops that are based on physical or virtual machines.

- The **Blast Secure Gateway** (**BSG**) will now support up to 800 connections to remote desktops from clients that are using HTML Access. This new connection limit applies to a BSG on one View Connection Server instance or security server.

For a complete list of what's new, always have a look at the VMware site for the desired product. For Horizon View 6, refer to `http://www.vmware.com/products/horizon-view/`.

Summary

The VMware Horizon View 6 release provides many improvements in features and performance to the current solution as you would expect from a product release. But, with the View 6 release, VMware has added many new features covered in this chapter such as:

- Cloud Pod Architecture
- Application publishing
- Unified workspace
- Integration with the Virtual SAN technology

These new and welcome features allow you to extend the control of the View environment over a broader geographical distance along with application enhancements to provide a robust end-user experience. The Virtual SAN solution provides a better way to manage your storage and possibly reduce the total cost of your VDI solution.

This book has attempted to present the information on View 6 that was available at the time of writing. VMware continues to evolve the Horizon Suite, including View through R&D along with feedback from customers and partners. Always refer to the VMware website to get the most up-to-date information on any of the VMware productions you are using or testing.

Additional Tools

Every VDI architect has their own preferred set of tools. This toolset may include I/O stress test tools such as Iometer (available at `http://www.iometer.org/`), the VMware Fling (the OS Optimization Tool found at `https://labs.vmware.com/flings/vmware-os-optimization-tool`), or certain Visio stencils.

This appendix provides a few recommendations for tools that can be used to help in the design process and configuration of the VDI solution.

VMware View Planner

The View Planner, formerly known as **Reference Architecture Workload Code (RAWC)**, is a desktop workload tool that allows you to generate a realistic and adjustable workload with various applications on the virtual desktop. The results that are gathered are for items such as CPU usage, memory utilization, storage, and network. Then, the information can be analyzed to determine the readiness of a given environment to run the virtual desktops.

The View Planner can be found at `http://www.vmware.com/products/view-planner`.

There is a VMware Communities website for RAWC (`https://communities.vmware.com/community/vmtn/rawc`) that has additional information and reference architectures that have been created with RAWC.

Workspace Assessment

The **Workspace Assessment** tool by Quest, now a part of Dell, is a tool used to understand whether or not a VDI solution is a good fit for your users. You can use this before investing your time and the company's budget.

The 5-day trial gives you evaluation of unlimited users with no restrictions on functionality, but very limited time. The Workspace Assessment tool identifies which of your users are the best fit for hosted VDI, Terminal Server / RD Session Host, or application virtualization. Also, you get reports on your current network and user and application usage. It can help you determine the desktop, network, data center, and storage needs to help build a successful plan to migrate and also manage your users with virtual desktops and applications. You can find the information on this tool at `http://www.quest.com/landing/?ID=5515`.

The VDI calculator

This popular tool by Andre Leibovici can help you with performing calculations concerning the sizing of your VDI environment. It provides nearly 60 different inputs to come up with a result set. It's a comprehensive VDI tool that asks for details such as the number of VMs, the VM type, and other sizing information. You would also input the number of pools, parent VMs, and snapshots along with host information such as sockets per host, cores per socket, and VMs per core. Continue by inputting display protocol information, IOPS information, storage array capabilities, and more. For more detailed information on this valuable tool, visit the website for the online manual (`http://myvirtualcloud.net/?p=1927`).

While no design requires the use of these tools, the more you know about the current physical environment the better chance you have at providing a successful VDI solution.

VMware Hands-on Labs

VMware **Hands-on Labs** (HOL) is a great way to learn about new products or increase your skills with which you have limited experience. HOL is found at `https://communities.vmware.com/community/vmtn/resources/how`.

Create an account, choose **Mobility**, and select the course you want.

VMware TV

This website has plenty of informational videos on VMware products.
After going to the site, you can search for videos related to View 6.
The site is found at `https://www.youtube.com/user/vmwaretv`.

Websites and social media

The Internet contains a wealth of information related to VMware View, thanks to a very active community on websites, Twitter, and the VMware communities.

The following websites provide fantastic content around the VDI technology:

- `http://www.vdi.com/`

- `http://www.brianmadden.com/`

- `http://www.techrepublic.com/`

- `http://communities.vmware.com/index.jspa`

In addition, using social media is a great way for organizations to understand what others are doing in the VDI space (use the `#VDI` hashtag to filter based on the VDI-related topics). The following people are recommended on Twitter:

- `@andreleibovici`

- `@langonej`

- `@joshuatownsend`

- `@chrisdhalstead`

- `@simonbramfitt`

- `@brianmadden`

- `@vmwarehorizon`

- `@vladan`

- `@vdiinfo`

- `@vmwjourney`

- `@thinapp_pso`

- `@ronoglesby`

- `@vmwareview`

- `@jagaudreau`

In addition, VDI-related conferences, for example, BriForum, should provide a wealth of information around the current trends in VDI.

Index

DoD CAC authentication,
    configuring 253, 254
environment, preparing for 250, 251
prerequisites 245
RADIUS 252
requisites 245
SSL protocols 256
two-factor authentication 252
snapshots 25, 26, 180-183
soft PCoIP 110
Software as a Service (SaaS) 310
Software-Defined Data Center (SDDC) 311
solid state drive (SSD) 177, 203
solution design, formulas 153
solution design, physical server
    requirements 138, 139
solution design, pod 139
solution design, pools
  about 151
  View Connection Servers 151, 152
solution example, VMware View
  about 137
  solution design, physical server
      requirements 138, 139
  solution design, pod 139
solution, thick clients
  modification 90, 91
solution, thin clients
  modification 90, 91
SQL Express installation
  using, for View Composer 25
SSDs 214
SSL protocols 256
stateful desktops 285
stateless desktops 285
static binding
  about 130
  advantage 130
  disadvantage 130
stock keeping unit (SKU) 11
storage
  about 54, 55
  isolation, at data store level 55, 56
storage area network (SAN) 164, 203
storage inputs
  descriptions 40, 41

questions 40
values 40
storage I/O profile 203-205
storage overcommit 197, 198
storage overcommit level
  about 198
  aggressive 199
  conservative 199
  moderate 199
  none 199
  options 199, 200
  unbound 199
storage overhead per datastore
  features 218
  requisites 218
storage protocols 200
success criteria
  descriptions 43
  questions 43
  values 43
SVI files 281

T

tag connection permissions
  matrix 260
Target vDesktops 63
temp data disk
  about 28
  options 29
template 27
Template (full clones)
  type of failures 175
Temporary Internet files 194
temporary location 262
temporary user profiles 267
Teradici APEX offload card
  about 113-115
  APEX driver, for ESXi 114
  APEX driver, for Windows vDesktop 114
  components 114
  design considerations 117, 118
  offload process 115, 116
  offload tiers, defining 117
Teradici Management Console 240
Teradici PCoIP APEX offload
    decision tree 116

[PACKT] enterprise
PUBLISHING   professional expertise distilled

Thank you for buying
VMware Horizon 6 Desktop Virtualization Solutions

About Packt Publishing

Packt, pronounced 'packed', published its first book "Mastering phpMyAdmin for Effective MySQL Management" in April 2004 and subsequently continued to specialize in publishing highly focused books on specific technologies and solutions.

Our books and publications share the experiences of your fellow IT professionals in adapting and customizing today's systems, applications, and frameworks. Our solution based books give you the knowledge and power to customize the software and technologies you're using to get the job done. Packt books are more specific and less general than the IT books you have seen in the past. Our unique business model allows us to bring you more focused information, giving you more of what you need to know, and less of what you don't.

Packt is a modern, yet unique publishing company, which focuses on producing quality, cutting-edge books for communities of developers, administrators, and newbies alike. For more information, please visit our website: www.packtpub.com.

About Packt Enterprise

In 2010, Packt launched two new brands, Packt Enterprise and Packt Open Source, in order to continue its focus on specialization. This book is part of the Packt Enterprise brand, home to books published on enterprise software – software created by major vendors, including (but not limited to) IBM, Microsoft and Oracle, often for use in other corporations. Its titles will offer information relevant to a range of users of this software, including administrators, developers, architects, and end users.

Writing for Packt

We welcome all inquiries from people who are interested in authoring. Book proposals should be sent to author@packtpub.com. If your book idea is still at an early stage and you would like to discuss it first before writing a formal book proposal, contact us; one of our commissioning editors will get in touch with you.

We're not just looking for published authors; if you have strong technical skills but no writing experience, our experienced editors can help you develop a writing career, or simply get some additional reward for your expertise.

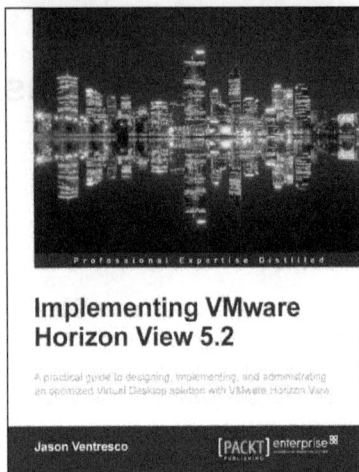

Implementing VMware Horizon View 5.2

ISBN: 978-1-84968-796-6   Paperback: 390 pages

A practical guide to designing, implementing, and administrating an optimized Virtual Desktop solution with VMware Horizon View

1. Detailed description of the deployment and administration of the VMware Horizon View suite.

2. Learn how to determine the resources your virtual desktops will require.

3. Design your desktop solution to avoid potential problems, and ensure minimal loss of time in the later stages.

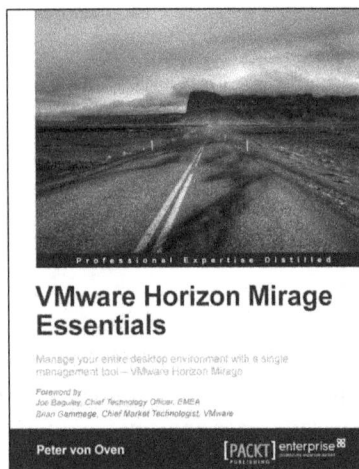

VMware Horizon Mirage Essentials

ISBN: 978-1-78217-235-2   Paperback: 166 pages

Manage your entire desktop environment with a single management tool – VMware Horizon Mirage

1. Deliver a centralized Windows image management solution for physical, virtual, and BYOD.

2. Migrate seamlessly to new versions of operating systems with minimal user downtime.

3. Easy-to-follow, step-by-step guide on how to deploy and work with the technology.

Please check **www.PacktPub.com** for information on our titles

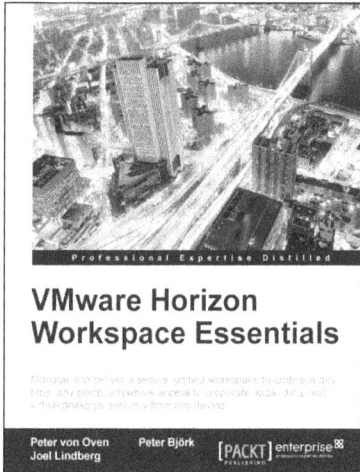

VMware Horizon Workspace Essentials

ISBN: 978-1-78217-237-6   Paperback: 158 pages

Manage and deliver a secure, unified workspace to embrace any time, any place, anywhere access to corporate apps, data, and virtual desktops securely from any device

1. Design, install, and configure a Horizon Workspace infrastructure.

2. Deliver a user's workspace to mobile devices such as Android and iOS.

3. Easy to follow, step-by-step guide on how to deploy and work with Horizon Workspace.

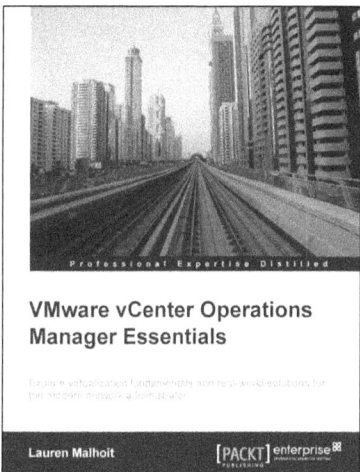

VMware vCenter Operations Manager Essentials

ISBN: 978-1-78217-696-1   Paperback: 246 pages

Explore virtualization fundamentals and real-world solutions for the modern network administrator

1. Written by VMware expert Lauren Malhoit, this book takes a look at vCenter Operations Manager from a practical point of view that every administrator can appreciate.

2. Understand, troubleshoot, and design your virtual environment in a better and more efficient way than you ever have before.

3. A step-by-step and learn-by-example guide to understanding the ins and outs of vCenter Operations Manager.

Please check **www.PacktPub.com** for information on our titles